BASTA

BASTA

My life
My truth

Marco van Basten
and Edwin Schoon

C CASSELL

Originally published as: Basta: Rauwe, eerlijke en openhartige
autobiografie van Marco van Basten by Lebowski Publishers,
Paul van Vlissingenstraat 18, 1096 BK Amsterdam. Copyright © Marco
van Basten, 2019; Copyright © Lebowski Publishers, Amsterdam 2019

First published in Great Britain in 2020 by Cassell, an imprint of
Octopus Publishing Group Ltd, Carmelite House,
50 Victoria Embankment, London EC4Y 0DZ
www.octopusbooks.co.uk
www.octopusbooksusa.com

An Hachette UK Company
www.hachette.co.uk

This edition published in 2022

Copyright © Octopus Publishing Group Ltd 2020, 2022
Text copyright © Marco van Basten 2020, 2022
Translated from the Dutch by Martin James in association with
First Edition Translations Ltd, Cambridge, UK.

ISBN 978-1-78840-354-2

A CIP catalogue record for this book is available from the
British Library.

Printed and bound in the UK.

10 9 8 7 6 5 4 3 2 1

Co-author: Edwin Schoon

Publishing Director: Trevor Davies
Creative Director: Jonathan Christie
Senior Editor: Leanne Bryan
Translator: First Edition Translations
Copyeditor: John English
Typesetter: Jeremy Tilston
Picture Research Manager: Giulia Hetherington
Production Controller: Serena Savini

This FSC® label means that materials used for the product
have been responsibly sourced

MIX
Paper from
responsible sources
FSC® C104740

CONTENTS

AUTHOR'S NOTE

No, I've never used crystal meth. Nor was I addicted to coke for years. I didn't lie round a swimming pool with naked women during a European Championship or a World Cup. And I wasn't addicted to gambling. I haven't even ever worn a wig. I'm afraid I must disappoint you.

A great deal has been written about me. A very great deal. Much of it is nonsense. I often didn't even read it. And mostly I didn't collaborate on it. I took no interest in it or threw it straight in a corner.

For years I didn't see myself as an interesting figure. More as a dead ordinary guy who could kick a ball pretty well, until he had to stop because of a rotten ankle. I felt the attention all that attracted was nothing more than excess baggage. Journalists, fans, spotlights, being placed in a footnote. Much ado about nothing, I thought. Irritating, if I'm honest.

This is because it distracted me from my goal: to be the best. And by that I really mean the best of all. In the world, that is. Everything had to stand aside for it and I went a long way towards it. You could almost call it a kind of blind craving. A primal instinct. Along, over or straight through, if necessary.

All the obstacles, all the barriers, I expertly cleared them out of the way. Opponents, referees, coaches, board members, yes, even fellow players. Usually within the rules, but sometimes also on, or over the edge. And this I became better and better at, ever more sophisticated. I'll never make football more romantic than it is. It's elite sport. And it's really hard, relentless. Eat or be eaten.

For the outside world, that is for people who didn't directly help me to achieve that sacred goal, it didn't necessarily make me a friendlier person. And you can't make an omelette without breaking eggs. I had learned that well before my tenth birthday, when we played football against the rough customers of Utrecht's Schimmelplein. If you had talent, they would kick you. Simple as that. Dish it out, evade, escape, score. That was the only answer.

And in football only one thing counts in the end: winning. In particular winning at the most important moments. And for that you need goals. And I don't mean tap-ins like the 6-0 against Sparta, nor the overhead kick against Den Bosch. No, I mean being decisive at moments that count. Winning finals. Or even better, deciding finals with your goals. This ambition was my fuel. The more difficult the situation, the greater the pressure, the more drive there was in me to come out of it, to escape, to score, to win.

I'd like to take you on my journey to the absolute top. As a shy, six-year-old boy from Utrecht, educated on the street and at UVV. Ten years later the great Ajax, substituting for the great Johan Cruyff on my debut. On to Milan with a European Cup Winners' Cup in the bag and being decisive for the Dutch team at Euro '88. Then of course that dreadful World Cup.

In December 1992 I stood on the summit of Olympus. I'd been voted the best footballer in the world and for the third time (just like Cruyff and Platini) the best in Europe. I had won three European Cups, scored winning goals in two finals, decided a major tournament and scored four times against IFK Gothenburg. No one had ever done that in the Champions League. You could say: it couldn't get any better than that. But my hunger for honours was not yet satisfied. Not by a long way.

The fall was hard. That same month I came tumbling down really hard. Just before Christmas I went under the knife with Dr Marti. That right ankle again. Four hours later my world would be changed for good, although I didn't know it at the time. I would never kick a ball decently again, never sprint again, never receive a ball perfectly again, never hear that wonderful rattling sound of a ball against the net again, never shout with joy like a child after a goal again.

For another three years I tried everything I could to get fit again. Absolutely everything. Far beyond the pain barrier. But it was over. In fact, in the end I was pleased if I could walk to the baker's without too much pain. It cost me a lot. And I've never really said much about it.

Everything I'd dreamed of was gone. First the struggle, which was not to be won, then the emptiness. I went into hiding for seven years. Radio silence. On the golf course, with friends, with my family. It takes you a while to internalize something like that.

Until recently I have always regarded myself as someone who learns from others. I remained determined, hungry, focused. I still hate losing, whatever game it is. That instinct remains dominant. Wanting to win. Achieving something great. Making the difference. That's what it's all about for me. Although that proved more difficult for me as a coach than as a player.

Only recently have I come to feel calmer. I've also never felt the need to look back. Until now. I realize that I've been through a lot. For the first time I have the idea that I myself have a story to tell, which may be worth the effort for others. Perhaps it's maturity, perhaps it's the calm, because I'm no longer active in football. I don't know. But I feel this is a good time to tell my story. From my perspective. My truth. The story that I've never told. In which I can also set things straight. I'll spare no one. Not least myself. The time is ripe.

Marco van Basten
Amsterdam, October 2019

PROLOGUE

I'm crawling across the tiles

1995

It's dark. And I'm crawling across the tiles. On my hands and knees. My bladder is full. To bursting. But as soon as I move too fast, my full bladder presses against my upper leg, and I nearly can't hold it. A urine-covered landing is the last thing I need. I must be patient, because it's at least two minutes to the bathroom. I know that now. To divert my attention from the pain, I always count the entire route. Whispering. I never reach the toilet before getting to 120. The doorsills are the most challenging part because my ankle has to go over them without touching them. Even the slightest touch makes me bite my lip to prevent a scream.

In the middle of the night the painkillers have more or less worn off, but I don't want to wake anyone up. They mustn't hear me because I don't want anyone to see me. Not even my loved ones. Or rather, especially not them. Over the last two months it's gone well, I'm glad to say, though I think Liesbeth sometimes pretends to be asleep to spare me the embarrassment. I can't explain it. Even with the painkillers the stabs of pain find a way through. It stops me thinking of anything else. For the last two weeks I've also been having trouble with my stomach because I've taken too many of these pills.

With every step I take I'm dying of the pain, ever since that stupid apparatus came off my ankle, eight months ago. It wouldn't get any worse whatever happens, the doctor had promised. I was a

1

professional footballer who could no longer play football and now I'm just an ordinary person who can no longer walk. I walk with a limp. I'm simply disabled.

It's like those rocky spikes in caves. Stalactites and stalagmites. Spikes of bone that stab into my leg from above and below, without protection, without cartilage. As soon as I lean on my foot, these spikes stab deep into my flesh. Standing is absolute hell. Even with painkillers.

Crawling to the toilet at night therefore is my only option. When I reach the bathroom doorsill, I put my left knee in the bathroom first and then rotate my whole body about its axis. Only then do I lift my right leg carefully over the sill. It usually goes all right, but this time I slip on a stray towel and my right foot touches the door frame. The pain cuts through to my core. I don't want to cry out, so I groan. I immediately break into a sweat.

I drop down onto my left side, to lie down for a moment. Just wait until the worst is over. I take a deep breath and very slowly try to exhale. Again. And again. I try to divert my thoughts from the stabs of pain in my ankle. Sometimes it helps if I think of God. I'm angry with him too. Furious in fact. What's this all about? Why must I go through all this nonsense? Is it a lesson in humility? Had I become too arrogant?

The pain had made me forget about my full bladder for a moment. Now I had to be quick, otherwise I was going to come a cropper. Just the job when your children want to come and clean their teeth in the morning. They're already having a rubbish time with their miserable father, who spends all day lounging on the settee.

I push myself up, cover the last four or five feet on my hands and knees and haul myself up onto the toilet. Emptying my bladder is a relief. I don't flush the toilet, because I don't want to wake anyone, and then I start the journey back to my bed.

I'm angry with myself too. You take a doctor at his word when he says that whatever happens it can't get any worse. It doesn't hurt to try. Now, it does hurt. It's been hurting for eight months now. And the question is for how much longer? Milan keep inviting me to come and watch matches, but I refuse point blank to appear there on crutches. A lame striker. I'd rather hide myself away in my own home. Like a wounded animal. Just let me sit in the dark.

I've tried everything: doctors, physios, acupuncturists and hypnotherapists, the list is endless. But no one could lessen the pain. Everyone wanted to help me. Everyone was of good will. Although I feel surgeons can be a little too important. Wanting to play God.

But none of it makes a ha'p'orth of difference now. None of it has helped a bit. It's far worse than it ever was.

Two years ago I was still a professional footballer. The best in the world, in fact. And now I'm crawling across the tiles, while dying of the pain, and the medicines are playing havoc with my stomach. I'm almost there. Back at my bed. When I've hauled myself into it, I hope to be able to sleep for a bit. If I'm lucky. It may take a while because I usually lie awake for a long time. So what. There's nothing I need to do tomorrow, except spend all day lounging on the settee. With a rotten ankle.

PART I

CHILDHOOD, AJAX AND EURO '88

1964–1988

JOOP AND JOPIE

That my grandfather was a Dutch weightlifting champion may bring a smile to your face, but it doesn't tell you much about me. And my father pilfering food from the Germans during the war by ripping holes in flour sacks on lorries, in the heart of Utrecht, may well have been courageous and bold, but it did nothing to add to my goal tally. Yet Joop, my father, was very important to me. He was football-mad. When I was little he worked as a coach, masseur and podiatrist at various amateur clubs, alongside his regular job with the local bus company. These odd jobs brought in a little extra cash for the family – for our summer holidays, which we used to spend at Lake Garda every year.

He had a son who was football-mad too, and 'Junior' – I had been a bit of an afterthought – turned out to be quite good at it. For him this was perfect. In his spare time he would focus all his attention on me. The rest of the family – my brother Stanley, who is six years older than me, my sister Carla, eight years my senior, and my mother Lenie – weren't so happy though.

My father started doing all things football with me very early on. He himself had been a dogged left-back at DOS who, with players like Tonny van der Linden and Hans Kraay Sr, became champions of the Western Netherlands Regional League. I never saw him play back then, and even towards the end of his career, at UVV, I have little recollection of him as a player.

Each week he would read the Dutch football magazine *Voetbal International* from cover to cover and on Sunday, after the TV programme *Studio Sport,* he would jot down his own team's line-up and do some sort of analysis on it. I would watch over his shoulder, fascinated by it all. Later on I started keeping records of all my own games in notebooks, just the bare facts. I did this for years, until well after I became a first-teamer at Ajax. Sometimes I would go with him on a Sunday if I didn't have a game myself. He would just stand on the touchline showing little or no passion or emotion. He was as laid-back as he was at home. Cool, calm and collected.

Consequently, his attention was fairly unequally divided between the children. He hardly ever went to watch Stanley, for example, who also played football. My brother and sister would complain and my mother was none too happy about it either. But for him football was all that mattered. And I had talent. He would take me wherever I needed to go.

One day we were running late for an important training session at the national football centre in Zeist. We were stuck in a huge traffic jam. There was no way he was going to let me be late; he was a stickler for punctuality. After about a quarter of an hour going nowhere, he suddenly said: 'I'm going to use the hard shoulder. If the police pull us over, I'll just say my ticker's playing up.' I was dumbfounded. He was such an upstanding individual. Grace before meals and church on Sundays. He was as nervous as could be as he drove onto that hard shoulder, because we didn't have the money to pay a fine. But he went for it anyway!

Another time, again it was a training session in Zeist, the rain had been pelting down all day, but we didn't think we needed to phone to check it was still on. That sandy soil in Zeist could take quite a lot, we thought. When we got there, through the heavy downpours, the car park was completely flooded and the playing area deserted. Rained off? We really were at a loss. We stood there like two drowned rats and people looked at us as if we were off our heads. This is what I really loved about him, that sense of commitment. When I finally made it as a footballer, it was the best thing ever for him; he really saw it as a reward.

At bedtime, he would always come and sit on the edge of my bed and we would talk through the events of the day. My match or my training session. Or about Ajax or Utrecht. It could have been anything, but actually it was only ever about football.

It wasn't that he was teaching me, though I think that's what he thought he was doing. It was more that we shared a passion. It was all about football, but without the chalkboard or paper, and not about tactics. When it came to my performances, he was perfectly clear: when they were good, they were very good, and when they were bad, they were very bad.

I wearied of this approach after a while. So I told him: 'If I did okay, then you can be a bit more critical, because I'm already feeling good. And if I didn't, then maybe you can be a bit more positive, because I'm already feeling down.'

He just wasn't all that tactful about it, as far as I was concerned. He didn't think it through. If I'd played badly, I was already in a bad mood, I was critical enough of myself. But in his eyes it was a real drama. I would get in the car for the journey home feeling rotten. And when I got out again, I was in a completely foul mood after another of his lectures. But it made little difference if I said anything. His attitude remained exactly the same until I was in the first team at Ajax.

One day we were playing DOS, at home, at UVV. I was nine. The visiting supporters were fairly boisterous. They came from a different neighbourhood, not the nicest of people, let's say. A little rougher.

The level of the amateur clubs in Utrecht was high in those days: Velox, DOS, Holland and Elinkwijk, but also Hercules and

Celeritudo. The talented players were part of the FC Utrecht and national youth set-ups, so we all knew each other. It was all about those derby matches, you had to win them. People knew I played for UVV and was pretty good.

The DOS parents went at it hammer and tongs. Total fanatics. 'Bring him down; go on, kick him!' Their players did actually kick me the whole time. This went on and on, but the referee did little about it. At one point I'd had enough. I walked off the pitch feeling really angry, close to tears, heading towards my father. But his response, in no uncertain terms, was: 'If you don't get straight back on that pitch, I'll kick you back onto it.' Eventually I did as he ordered. He added: 'Get stuck in, Marco. It's all part of the game, don't let yourself be intimidated.'

As a former player he knew the mores of the game, so I was okay with that. My mother never came to watch though. Well, she did once, at Easter, at Hercules, and it was a total disaster. She was really upset: 'Oh, what are they doing to Marco?!' It didn't bother me at all, nor my father of course. So at the end of the game we said to her: 'You'd better stay at home from now on, because this isn't going to help.'

In those early days I toughened up and got smarter in other ways too. At UVV we had a fair mix of good footballers and players who were more intent on roughing you up. Tough guys. You had to find ways to protect yourself from them, but it was an invaluable learning experience. Many of them came from the Schimmelplein, the other side of the Vleutenseweg. A rough neighbourhood compared with the Herderplein, where I always used to play my football.

We trained on clay then, but alongside the clay there were some grass korfball fields. When it had rained, we often went for a kickabout after training. There would be four or five of us on that korfball field, taking turns at dribbling, for as long as we could keep going, while the others tried to stop us with sliding tackles and plenty of kicking – it was no holds barred. That korfball field ended up an utter mess of course, because we would slide around all over it. But it did help us learn to sense what was happening behind us. When would danger pounce? It never ended up in a brawl though; we just tried to tackle each other really hard.

At the time I was just a perfectly ordinary schoolboy. I had a brother and a sister. I wasn't much good at school, but I wasn't bad either. We certainly weren't rich; we lived in a flat. But I never wanted for anything. I was just a boy who loved playing football.

One day I'll never forget. It was winter and it was frosty. All the matches had been called off. I often played football with Jopie, the boy next door, just outside on the Herderplein. He was a year older than me and had a little sister. He was a really good footballer and was already playing at UVV. At the time I was still at EDO.

That Saturday we were bored. It was cold. Jopie had an uncle who lived in Amsterdam, so we said: 'Let's go to Amsterdam.'

What did we know? We started walking towards Maarssen, alongside the A2 motorway. But of course we were going nowhere fast. After an hour we had got as far as the old Raak soft drinks factory, on the Lage Weide business park. By then we had realized that we weren't going to get to Amsterdam. So we had a change of plan: 'I know, let's go across these frozen ditches, to that lake. It might be fun to play on the ice there.'

Getting across the ditches was easy and then we reached the lake. A big, excavated lake, for industrial use. Jopie said: 'Come on, we can get onto the ice here.'

'Is it safe?' I asked. At the last minute I found a rope at the water's edge and said: 'Tell you what. Hold onto that rope, then if you fall, I'll still have hold of you.'

He went first. We were both holding tightly onto the rope. He was about eight or nine metres from the edge when, all of a sudden, he went right through the ice.

He was so startled, he let go of the rope and went straight down. Gone in a flash, into the depths.

He was wearing a woolly hat that day, a kind of Ard Schenk speedskating hat. Blue with a white stripe down the middle and two red stripes either side. That hat was still floating there on the water. I remember it quite clearly.

I didn't know what to do. I was only seven. I ran as fast as I could back to the Raak factory, a few hundred metres away. It was Saturday, so there were bound to be a few people around. I started shouting out as I got closer. The people there were worried and immediately called the police. But of course it was too late.

They kept me at the factory while the police and the divers went to the lake. They found Jopie, but he was already dead. So I didn't see him pulled out of the water, though I did understand he had probably drowned. Because you can't breathe under the ice.

At the time I didn't really have much idea of what being dead meant. My grandad had died when I was four. And I'd thought: okay, so when's he coming back? I had that a bit with Jopie as well to start with, that I do remember.

There was a huge fuss. And I had lost my friend. Not that I had to keep telling the story, because the police and my parents did that. But it was incessant. Everything around you made you realize it was a big thing: at school, where we lived, at the club.

We didn't talk about it at home. My father didn't think we should. It was shut away. But at school of course nothing else mattered – it was all anyone talked about.

It preyed on my mind for some time. I struggled to decide whether there was anything else I could have done. Should I have gone on the ice to get him? And should we have tied that rope around him instead of letting him hold it in his hands? These are the sorts of things you think about. I might have only been seven, but these thoughts stayed with me for quite a while. Could I have been more of a hero?

I did see his parents again. For them it was a tragedy. His father hit the bottle and I don't think he ever entirely got over it. He spent all his time propping up the bar at UVV. Losing Jopie was the end of the world for him. And his wife was completely devastated too.

I was very sad for a long time. I know that I had a small photo of him. I kept it for ages. I always had it with me or in my desk drawer. Sometimes I didn't know exactly where it was, but I still had it, that I was always sure of.

Later on, my father told me that after a few years he had taken the photo and torn it up. Because he thought enough was enough, all that focus on such a dreadful event. I can't be sure of that now, nor whether I was angry about it. But I do remember thinking: why do we have to get rid of it? Does it really matter? Is it doing anyone any harm?

Later, my brother and sister told me my father felt he had to keep me away from it. 'All that negativity with Jopie, it's not good for him.' They thought it rather silly of him, to make it such a taboo. As a father myself I'm much more open. I think you need to discuss things like that with each other.

About five years ago I met Jopie's sister again. She sent me a few photos of him.

The conversation was not in the least uncomfortable. It had of course been a complete accident.

THE BOOK IS CLOSED

As I grew older, I began to realize that my father spending so much time with me was causing problems for the family. Even I could see there was an imbalance. It caused a lot of friction at home. 'Junior' was getting too much attention and being spoiled and my father wasn't bothered about my brother and sister, who were six and eight years older. That's what they thought anyway. And my mother too. She found it difficult. There were sometimes heated discussions at the dinner table. My brother would shout at my father: 'I'm your son too, you know!' And my sister would say something like: 'I'm glad I'll be out of here soon.' My mother would become very emotional, but my father always remained chillingly calm. There was never any swearing and nobody threw anything – we were far too respectable for that – but in the end little changed. He just carried on precisely as before. He was the old-fashioned breadwinner, the man of the house.

When I was about 12 years old, my brother and sister both left home at about the same time. Stanley went off to Canada, Carla to Italy. A long way away. My parents and I moved to Johan Wagenaarkade. My father was often out, leaving me at home alone with my mother in the evenings and we would chat a lot.

It slowly became clear to me that my parents did not have a good marriage.

It had all begun with a spat about church. Before their wedding my father had got her to promise that she would go to his Catholic church, even though she was from a Protestant background. She did then officially convert, but in the end never actually set foot inside that church, and that didn't go down well with my father's family. But there was much more to it, I discovered. Their relationship was pretty much over by the time we got to Wagenaarkade.

My father spent all his time working to earn money and with me, while my mother would prepare the meals and look after the house. They lived in the same house, but without any real contact. It was exactly the same on holiday. They did hardly anything together and it got no better as I grew older. One day, when I asked her about it, my mother said: 'The book is closed, son.'

She and I would often spend those afternoons and evenings having intense conversations, sometimes until very late. We were similar in nature. Things could get very frank and emotional, but at the same time honest. The conversations were often delightful too. She would try to instil a bit of discipline in me. I was really spoiled and felt it was perfectly normal for everything to revolve around me. My father let me do anything I wanted, as long as I was playing good football, so I was difficult and disobedient. She would take me to task about it and that was good.

But I would stick my nose into her life too. I said what I thought of their relationship and that it was a pity she felt 'the book was closed'. 'Why don't you talk to him? Couldn't you try?' She listened to me, she understood what I was saying, but she couldn't see anything changing. My father was putting everything into what he cared most about: football and his footballing son.

Later on, my brother and sister told me that things had not been good between my parents for years before that. By the time I was 15 or 16 my parents had got to the stage of wondering what was going to happen once all the children had left home. My mother was worried,

I think. Maybe that's why it all went to pot in the end. Things really weren't looking too bright for her at all.

I never discussed any of this with my father though. He and I would only ever talk football.

IN FRONT OF THE MIRROR (1)

I recently came across a photo of myself as a youth team player at Ajax. And it reminded me: I was just 16 when I went to Ajax.

Ajax was a dream for any child. And one day that dream became reality. My very first match for Ajax, when that photo was taken, was for the A1 youth team. We played a club called Texas in The Hague. I remember exactly what I did as soon as I put that red and white shirt on: I stood in front of the changing room mirror, admiring myself. I took my time, shutting out everyone and everything around me. I turned around. There was a number 10 on the back. It was quite a moment for me. It felt fabulous, and I thought: 'Wow, I've made it.'

'ROLL, ROLL, ROLL A DRUM'

Mid-1980

I never really went to a stadium when I was little, because I always played football at UVV on Sundays. But when I was 13 or 14, I started going to watch FC Utrecht with a friend of mine, Ricky Testa la Muta. This meant we could play football ourselves on a Sunday morning and then go to Galgenwaard Stadium in the afternoon.

What an experience that was, as a youngster among the fans on the Bunnikside. Organized chaos, unusual characters everywhere you looked. A real eye-opener. These are the things I remember, and those well-known advertising jingles they played at every game. The roll-your-own tobacco ad 'Roll, roll, roll a Drum'. That one for Van Nelle – a real classic. Or the 'cool, clear Heineken' ad, tunes like that. For me it was all new, and I loved it. I was keen to find out what it was all about. Ricky and I were both footballers and both dreaming of a career in football, and this was a small part of it.

We were also part of the same motley crew that went to away games, to Go Ahead and FC Den Haag. That's special when you're 15. You feel tough when you go somewhere different in such a big group. You march down the street and everyone respects you. It makes you feel powerful. And the bigger the group, four hundred or even eight hundred strong, the more intense that feeling becomes. Many of those fans weren't intimidated by anything or anyone. Not that I ended up in any fights, but FC Den Haag away was really dangerous. You had to be careful. All sorts of minor incidents, police and disorder.

But those weekends suddenly became very different when I joined Ajax at the age of 16. FC Utrecht had made me an offer too, while Feyenoord and PSV Eindhoven had also tried to sign me.

This was at a time when growing pains had stopped me playing for nine months. Aad de Mos, head coach at Ajax, had wanted to know why I was no longer appearing in the scouting reports, so he had called Bert van Lingen in Zeist, who looked after the national youth teams. Bert had told him about my growing pains, but that I was on the way back and would be playing again soon. De Mos had then gone to the trouble of visiting us and talking to my father, to secure me, and also Edwin Godee, for Ajax.

In those early months at Ajax I was in the A1 youth team, while Edwin went straight into the seconds. Because we were only 16, our fathers would drop us off and pick us up during the week, but at the weekend my father wasn't available because he was an amateur coach. Edwin played all his matches with the seconds on a Saturday afternoon, while my A1 matches were always on a Sunday afternoon. That meant that early on Sunday morning I had to make my own way to Amsterdam by public transport: bus from home to Utrecht Central station, train to Amstel station and tram to De Meer.

In itself not particularly exciting on a Sunday morning, but in those days all the Eredivisie clubs were still playing on Sunday afternoon. And if FC Utrecht had an away game, their supporters would start to gather at Utrecht Central fairly early on Sunday morning. They went to those away games en masse. This was before the days of police escorts and all-in-one tickets. I really had to be on my guard, carrying my Ajax bag, because I didn't want to be seen by those travelling fans. Otherwise I'd be sure to have problems with them. They hated Ajax. Some of them even went around with dogs. They more or less took over the entire station. I remember that on days like these I had to keep my eyes open and make sure I wasn't recognized. Because by then people were beginning to know who I was, in Utrecht at least. A few times I found myself making a nervous dash across Utrecht Central.

I did actually once go to an FC Utrecht game wearing an Utrecht scarf even though I was at Ajax by then. In September 1981 they played Ernst Happel's great Hamburg side, in the UEFA Cup. The game was played at the Nieuw-Monikkenhuizen stadium in Arnhem, because the Veemarkthallen ground was too small. It became a battlefield. Supporters on the pitch laid siege to Happel's dugout. It was called 'the battle of Arnhem'. Ricky and I had good seats because his father had organized tickets for us. We were safely out of harm's way, well clear of the clashes.

We were particularly keen to see the game because Lars Bastrup was playing for Hamburg, the man to whom I owe my first nickname. For a while people called me 'Bastrup' because he was a striker too and our names were similar. Felix Magath, Manfred Kaltz and Jürgen Milewski were Hamburg's best known players. Magath was skipper and Happel was on the bench of course, until Utrecht supporters started pelting him with things. They even spat at him. FC Utrecht were no mean side though, with Hans van Breukelen, Aad Mansveld, Jan Wouters, Leo van Veen and Willy Carbo. But it was a disaster, with Hamburg going 4-0 up. They ended up winning 6-3, and the fans invaded the pitch. A real sight to see and a good old-fashioned European night.

And who else do you think was there, watching that same game, a row behind us? Aad de Mos. He looked at me in surprise. What's he doing here with that Utrecht scarf around his neck? You could almost see him thinking: what a weirdo, that Van Basten.

BUMFLUFF ON HIS FACE

Summer 1980

When Edwin Godee and I arrived at Ajax in the summer of 1980, we looked up to everyone and everything. We had to prove ourselves. I did reasonably well in the A1 team, scoring freely. That Sunday morning league was far too easy for us. We were still playing regional games then, against a host of amateur clubs. Every week we had a field day: 6-0, 8-1, 7-0. Scores like that were not uncommon and we coasted to the district title.

Gerald Vanenburg, who came from Elinkwijk like us, and was six months older than me, was already playing in the first team. Just like Frank Rijkaard. But I didn't see much of these players, because they trained during the day. The second team, in which Edwin played, trained at five o'clock. I trained with the second team from week one, so that our fathers could take turns dropping us off and picking us up, which fitted in better with their jobs. Assistant coach Hassie van Wijk was okay with it.

I thought it was great because I could measure myself against better and physically stronger players. The second team featured the likes of Sonny Silooy and John van 't Schip and there were many other players there who had already played in the first team, such as Jan Weggelaar and Martin Wiggemansen.

It was all a good deal tougher than in the A1 team. Edwin was physically fully developed fairly early on, and coped easily, but I wasn't fully grown yet. I was tall and skinny, a beanpole. The first time I went in the second-team changing room, the players must have wondered what I was doing there.

But I had to measure up to them physically and in the end it all turned out okay. I had competition from Rini van Roon, a big, strong lad who had been playing in the second team for a while and also had some first-team experience. After a few weeks I felt I had slightly better prospects, albeit in the longer term, despite the fact that he was already an experienced striker.

In November, when I was starting to feel I could cope with the level, I asked Hassie if I could have a go in the second team. 'Your time will come,' he said. Eventually he gave me a chance as second-team striker in February 1981, when Rini van Roon had appendicitis. I scored four times on my debut. It was a Saturday afternoon and we were playing at De Meer. The first-team players were meeting up in the stadium for their own match that evening. They saw my performance, and my reputation started to grow rapidly. 'That guy from Utrecht is one to hang on to, we must keep tabs on him.'

But I was more than happy just being able to train with the second team. There were some real hard men among them, such as the Dane Sten Ziegler, an experienced centre-back. He had made a number of first-team appearances, but was not getting much playing time with them, so he would sometimes play with us in friendly matches, to keep match fit.

Ziegler was once complaining about having to play with us again, because so many of us were young and inexperienced. He said: 'I've even played with one who doesn't even have any bumfluff on his face.'

I remember this took me aback and I thought: I think he means me.

LORD JESUS CRUYFF

1981

All at once there he was on the training pitch, one Tuesday afternoon. Johan Cruyff. He had asked Hassie van Wijk if he could join us, the second team, which was actually called the C team.

The great Johan Cruyff. He was something of a saint for me, my absolute hero. I had so much respect for the man. Unlimited, in fact. When we used to play football in the street, I was always Johan, and suddenly here I was, standing on the pitch with him. He was coming back from a groin injury and wanted to get fit again. Hassie of course was delighted that Johan Cruyff should ask this favour of him.

I remember that very first time like it was yesterday. At one point we played a game, two v. two. Him with Silooy against John van 't Schip and me. With two small goals. He kept talking about 'squeezing', we had to 'squeeze'. We didn't know the term at all, although we had some idea of what he meant: making the pitch smaller so you can defend the goal more easily. John and I had the giggles the whole evening. Squeezing? The ref won't let you do that, will he? Total nonsense.

But I had played games like that, two v. two, for hours on end behind my house, so he didn't need to explain anything to me. Any more than I needed to explain anything to him. He saw this at once. 'Hey, they're on the ball.' Van 't Schip was a smart player too; I was a little more frantic, a little more devious. That was how it had to be with Johan. They were really fun games and we loved them.

I was 17 then, Cruyff 34, but age was no barrier when we played football together. It was soon 'Johan this, Johan that'. He always retained that youthful enthusiasm and was just as passionate in those games as we were. And just as happy or disappointed if he won or lost.

He immediately lost himself in the game, laid out the strategy and actively coached us. As if we'd always done it that way. Physically it was barely noticeable that he was older. He was naturally so clever and skilful in games like that and so much quicker than anyone else technically and getting into position that his age just wasn't an issue.

It was a bizarre situation, though, perhaps even confusing. On the one hand I had enormous respect for the man, but at the same time I wanted to show him what I could do. Impudence won the day. Van 't Schip tried to play the ball between his legs. I didn't. I simply wanted to win. But now and again I did have to pinch myself, when it suddenly hit me: can this really be happening?

That evening took me back to the year before, when I was still in Utrecht with the amateurs. We had gone to see Gerald Vanenburg, who was playing in Ajax's second team, on a Saturday afternoon at De Meer. It was the first time I had seen that whole Ajax realm, including Rijkaard. After the match, as I was leaving the stadium on my own, all of a sudden there was Cruyff walking up the stairs. I had never seen him in real life before. We were going to walk past each other, it was unavoidable, and everything seemed to happen in slow motion.

I briefly thought about offering him my hand and saying: 'You don't know me, but remember my face. We'll be meeting again.' But I didn't. I didn't dare. The moment passed and we walked past each other in silence. He had no idea of course. I was 15 and playing at Elinkwijk that year, but it's a moment I'll never forget.

The great thing about Johan, playing with him that first time, was that I didn't really feel we were any different. All that counts in the world of football is how good you are, and Johan was particularly good. We weren't dopes, but we had to prove it and he knew that, and that for us it was just a matter of time and gaining experience. You felt it was genuine. One hundred per cent. There's a natural order of merit in the football world, depending on how good you are and what you can do with a ball. It's instinctive. How good you are ultimately determines the hierarchy in the changing room, not how old, how successful or how smart you are. A year later though I experienced his harsh side too. He could really lay into you.

One Saturday morning, I was taking part in first-team training. I hadn't got into the starting line-up yet, but regularly came on as a sub and ended up scoring nine goals in the first team that season. But that Saturday morning he was working with me. He had something to say about everything I did, every ball I played, every run I made. He spent the whole time lecturing me and putting me down.

I had no idea what he was thinking. I still don't. But presumably he saw something in me and decided to lay into me, to see how far he could go and to see whether or not I had what it takes to make it. And it had an effect. In the end I got fed up with his putdowns, I told him to 'get lost!' and walked off the pitch. Tears immediately welled up in my eyes, partly because I was startled by my own reaction. I'd had a go at Johan Cruyff, something of the Lord Jesus. God himself.

Hassie van Wijk chased straight after me. I hadn't even reached the edge of the training pitch when he caught up with me. 'Marco, don't let it get to you. Come on, back on the pitch. You've got to get through this. Johan means well, it's just coming out all wrong.' He too thought Johan was going over the top, ranting and raving at me like that.

I pulled myself together, went straight back out and gave it one hundred per cent. The strange thing was that Johan was now completely different towards me, that very same training session. Suddenly, everything I did was good. 'Well timed run to the near post,' he said out of the blue. 'That's good, making yourself available. Good dropping back.' Things like that.

Johan knew full well that he had gone too far. But he was just another kid from the streets trying his hand at amateur psychology. Fortunately, other players also told me not to read too much into this. Ironically, later he actually became my mentor and we ended up becoming very good friends.

VIDEO 2000

3 April 1982

The first time I was called up to the first-team squad we were due to play NEC. Coach Aad de Mos had phoned to say I was going to be needed that Saturday evening because there were so many injuries.

Seeing the standard from the bench in the first half, I felt I could hold my own. I was ready, and this was what I had always wanted. I came on as a sub straight after half-time, in place of Johan Cruyff. Which was unreal. Up front too, in a packed De Meer Stadium.

There was no rush of supporters from the stands going off for a bite to eat or a quick drink. Everyone stayed in their seats. I was aware of a bit of a buzz as I ran on the pitch, skinny as a rake. 'Who's that bag of bones coming on now?'

I played my natural game, already having plenty of matches under my belt with the A1 team and the seconds. I was eager and enjoyed being part of the action. All I wanted was for everyone to just give me the ball.

When Vanenburg crossed, I leapt high between two NEC defenders and nodded the ball back down into the bottom corner. Goal! On my debut! I was absolutely ecstatic and realized at once that I'd actually scored at De Meer, on my debut, on television. A dream come true.

After the match we went home. We'd missed *Studio Sport* and we didn't have a video recorder. So my father and I went to my friend Ruud van Boom's house. They had one of those Video 2000 systems and had recorded the match.

I couldn't wait to see what it was like, seeing myself in action, live on TV.

We sat there on the settee watching my debut and my first goal at the top level. For years we had watched the football on television on *Studio Sport*. And I realized that now everyone was watching me, which felt really weird.

Nothing much happened with the Ajax first team straight after that. De Mos asked if I wanted to be involved again against Sparta the following Tuesday and I said I'd have to think about it. That same week I was due to play for the Dutch youth team at an international tournament in Cannes for 16- to 17-year-olds. In the end I opted for the Dutch youth team. De Mos was less than impressed and didn't call me up again that season.

As it happened, we had a fantastic tournament that week in Cannes, a personal highlight for me being three goals against the Italian youth team. I exchanged my shirt for an Italian player's after that match and slept in it for years afterwards.

YOU'RE STANDING IN MY SUN

Summer 1983

'You're standing in my sun,' I said to John, emphasizing the 's' in 'sun' in that typical Amsterdam way, because we liked to mimic Johan's way of speaking as much as we could. I was irritated. And I was showing it. John and I were on holiday in Majorca, with a couple of friends, but we needed some time to get used to each other away from home.

Ever since we arrived, I had been keeping myself to myself. It wasn't that I had no interest in the holiday; on the contrary. It was wonderful, not having anything to do for a while. I had to get the past year out of my system. My first real season at Ajax was still fresh in my mind – 20 first-team matches altogether and nine goals. And I had my secondary education certificate in the bag. After a full-on 46 weeks I was physically and mentally drained. I was ready to lie on a towel in the sun. Not just for a little while, nor even a few hours. No, all day long. Sunbathing. Sweating out the stress of an entire season. So when 'Schip' went and stood in 'my' sun, it was really irritating.

'You've been lying in the sun for four hours already, man, what's up with you?' he said. 'What difference does a minute make?'

'And what about you with the jam!' I said. 'What was all that nonsense then?!'

He thought for a moment, and then he remembered. At the breakfast bar in the apartment, I had been quiet. Not really sociable after just a few hours' sleep and with a thick head after a night out. When he wanted me to pass him the jam, he just said 'jam!' as if it was an order. I looked at him as if he was a complete idiot, but after a few moments handed him the jam pot anyway. No further words had passed between us until that afternoon.

John dismissively kicked some sand over my feet. 'It's great fun being on holiday with you, Mr Grumpy.'

I felt the anger rising, but stayed in control. Then we both burst out laughing. I can take it from him, as he can from me. John went for a bit of a walk. There was lots to see on the beach, but I wasn't ready for that yet. I put the headphones of my Walkman back on. Wham! – 'Wake me up, before you go, go!' Before we left I had recorded three tapes of all sorts. Mainly Top 40. I was quite happy to shut myself away with that music.

That season I had only been allowed to train with the first team during the school holidays and at weekends, because I still had my education to complete. After academic level 4, general secondary level 4 was a piece of cake. My parents thought it was important, as I did myself. It would have been a mistake to let it go. By May I had finally done it and I was glad to get it over with.

After that summer I was finally able to engage fully with the first team. I couldn't wait, though it was a pity that Johan was going to Feyenoord. That was a bizarre turn of events, after all that wrangling with the chairman, Mr Harmsen. Anyway, once Lerby and Schrijvers had gone too, the youngsters were going to have to step up to the plate: Silooy, Schippie and Vaantje. Ronald Koeman joined us. I thought though that De Mos would rely more on the old hands: Ophof, Boeve and Schoenaker. Wim Kieft decided to cut his losses and went to Pisa.

Going to school that year and being a professional footballer at the same time sometimes led to some crazy situations. I was really keen to buy a car when I got my first contract and started driving lessons as soon as I turned 18, at the end of October. By December I had my licence.

There was a car showroom on the other side of the Herderplein. Every time I passed it on my way to school I would see this Porsche 911 Cabrio 3.0 Targa there. A light brown one, with a price tag of 27,000 guilders. I knew that if my contract was renewed after one season, I would be making 30,000 guilders. I was making more and more substitute appearances and things were going well, so every time I walked past that showroom, I thought: when I get my driving licence, I'm going to buy that car. Once everything was settled, I was ready to head straight to the Porsche dealer. But what I didn't know, because it was all new to me, was that a contribution to the players' pension fund had to be deducted from my pay first and then I had tax to pay as well. So in the end all I was left with was 35 per cent, which simply wasn't enough. I was really disappointed and in the end bought a beige and white Alfa Giulietta from my brother-in-law, Vanni, my sister's Italian husband, in Houten. Not a Porsche, it's true, but still a lovely car. It cost 9,000 guilders, so my first real contract meant I could afford that.

I was even allowed to keep the money I earned. I was still living with my parents and ate at home every evening, but didn't have to pay any board. Nor did my parents make much of a fuss about me suddenly earning so much money. Every morning I went to school as normal from my home in Johan Wagenaarkade, and from January I went in that Alfa.

The first time I remember parking next to the German teacher's dilapidated Saab just as the geography teacher was arriving on his bike. I particularly remember one lesson with that German teacher, Mrs Bosman-Ritsen. She was explaining the umlaut, and used Hansi Müller as an example. He was playing for VfB Stuttgart then and was another of our idols. She told us that sometimes his name appeared as

Hansi Mueller, because the 'ü' couldn't always be displayed on a screen in the stadium. She could do no wrong for us after that.

By now I was appearing regularly on *Studio Sport* and I was in the newspaper. Certainly, one or two things had changed, but I didn't suddenly start courting publicity. I wasn't much interested in fashion and popularity and I still went round with the same friends as before: Henri Relyveld, Ruud van Boom and André van Vliet. They were my mates.

I had a few fun evenings with John in Majorca. We would start doing Johan impressions, his voice, but also his way of smoking. We would sometimes fall about laughing. Johan had a very distinctive way of holding a cigarette and could keep talking while smoking. It took us a little practice, but we managed it pretty well.

On one of those evenings we had a good night out with members of a social club from the Amstelveen area, with too many Bacardi & Cokes. The night ended in bizarre fashion, at about five in the morning. Out of devilment one of the group decided to walk over a stationary car. He was spotted by a taxi driver, who immediately alerted his colleagues and the Guardia Civil. Within minutes there were eight taxis and three police cars on the scene, complete with flashing lights and sirens. We ran off in all directions, to stay out of reach of the police. Everyone managed to hide somewhere or get into an apartment, but John was wearing a pair of those flip-flop things, which slowed him down. He jumped over a wall to hide until they were gone. The whole thing quickly fizzled out, except that John had landed on a broken Coke bottle. But because of the alcohol or adrenaline he didn't notice straight away. It wasn't until we got back to the apartment that he saw the blood and prised out a piece of glass. At the first aid station in the morning they got another piece out.

I went with him after having only a few hours' sleep. I was dead tired. He went back to his room with some painkillers and a tetanus injection and later had to explain everything to Ajax. I went and enjoyed some more sunbathing on the beach. Same as every day. That evening we had also bumped into Linda de Mol. She had invited us to her birthday party the following day. It was her 19th.

While I was lying there on that beach, I was thinking about Mexico and the Under-20 World Cup, back in June. We had actually only just got back. Kees Rijvers was national coach. A lovely man. I was one of the youngest on the trip. I was still only 18, but played every game. I'd never seen anything like it – packed stadiums, a football-mad country and a completely different atmosphere.

It was a wonderful experience for us. Significant too. This was our chance to compete with the best players in the world. Four years earlier Argentina had become world champions with Maradona. That's what we wanted too, only we had hardly any international experience and this was in a completely different part of the world.

There was a whole group of us from Ajax: Schippie, Vanenburg, Godee, René Panhuis, Edwin Bakker, Sonny Silooy and me, and Robbie de Wit from Utrecht. It was expected to be the breakthrough tournament for Gerald Vanenburg, the rising star. But for us it became Mario Been's tournament, after he came on as a sub against Brazil. He had a fantastic game, going past five men and scoring. And that was in front of a crowd of 68,000 in Guadalajara. After that surprising 1-1 draw with favourites Brazil, the Mexican press immediately dubbed him the Dutch star player of the tournament. In the dressing room he relished the role. He was the man with bravura, with swagger. A real-life version of little Peter Bell, the fictional naughty boy from Rotterdam.

We went on to play two games in Monterrey, in the rainforest, where the humidity was more than 70 per cent. We beat the Soviet Union and drew with Nigeria, which earned us a quarter-final against Argentina. That was a strange game. Along with Brazil and Argentina, we were seen as one of the best teams in the tournament. The match was played in Léon, at an altitude of more than 2,000 metres, with a noon kick-off. This was a massive change for us, and it was also 42 degrees.

Despite the heat we played really well and I scored to put us one up, after a cross from John. At half-time we went in the dressing room, in the lower reaches of the stadium. It was a good deal cooler down there, 18 degrees or so. When we went back on the pitch, we were overwhelmed by that scorching heat. We could barely put one foot in front of the other. Slowly but surely we were worn down. Argentina didn't go 2-1 up until the 90th minute, a dubious goal at that. In the furore that followed, the massive travelling Argentinian support turned against us and started throwing coins. Vanenburg got one full in the mouth. In the end it all got out of hand and three of our players were shown red cards. A 2-1 defeat. Such a shame. Knocked out. But we felt positive because we had been able to compete with the best. The final saw Argentina play Brazil.

Following our elimination, we had a final evening in Mexico City before flying home. The whole trip had been an unbelievable adventure, but that last night we wanted to head into town with a bit of company. In the end Robbie de Wit and I went out on our own, because the rest didn't dare. We found some seedy dive in a dark alley where we got ourselves a couple of girls. I was finished first and really wanted to get out of there as quickly as possible, but was forced to wait a few minutes more, with Robbie's milky-white backside in my face.

Robbie's wobbly, milky-white backside. That's not an image you can get out of your head in a hurry.

On our return to the hotel we started dishing up all the gory details of our great triumph. We were sitting in a long corridor, all of us together. Naturally, everyone wanted to hear our story. I remember that Robbie was sitting with his back against a door and explaining everything in great detail. Just as he reached the end of his story, the door suddenly opened, and Robbie fell back. And who do you think was standing there? Kees Rijvers. We all jumped out of our skins. He had clearly heard everything and was seething inside. He kept himself together, you could see that, but he said that if you wanted to be a professional footballer, you had to behave like a professional.

Rijvers subsequently wrote a report on the tournament in *Voetbal International*. In it he said that De Wit 'had to show greater professionalism'. In that same piece he said that I was on course to be the Dutch team's future striker, which was great to read of course. Perhaps he had failed to appreciate my part in the adventure from behind that hotel door.

In Majorca we finally went to that party of Linda's. I can still feel my head banging, so I'll be brief. We made a real mess of that apartment. John was the most sensible of us, in that he wasn't allowed to drink because of the antibiotics for his foot. Although he didn't actually stick strictly to that.

But this meant he was able to fill me in on quite a lot of the details of the evening at breakfast the next day. At the end of the party we had all dived in the sea and for devilment had thrown our clothes in the air, where they got stuck on some telephone wires. So we ended up half-naked.

John was fairly clear about my role. He couldn't suppress a smirk as he related how there had been some massive paintings on the wall in the apartment when we arrived. The more I'd had to drink, the less steady I had apparently become and I had tried to grab hold of one of these paintings, bringing the whole whopping great thing crashing to the floor. That was enough to make John's evening.

All that going out had made it a taxing holiday, but now it was time for the serious work to start again. Luckily I had spent every day sunbathing, I was physically and mentally refreshed and recharged for a new season at Ajax. I was ready for it and keen to start well. Cruyff was now playing for our greatest rivals, and the game was already in my diary: 18 September, Olympic Stadium, Ajax v. Feyenoord. I wanted to challenge for a place in the starting line-up straight away. Up front, obviously. To score so many goals that they couldn't ignore me. We did of course have Jesper Olsen, another whiz kid. We had Schippie, Vanenburg, Rijkaard and Silooy, along with Schoenaker, Ophof and Boeve as the old guard. Ronald Koeman, another youngster. Hans Galjé, who would succeed Schrijvers. And one Johnny Bosman, coming up from the youth team, and a good header of the ball. We would have to wait and see.

HASSIE

1983–1984

In the autumn I caught glandular fever, at the beginning of November to be precise. I think it was the Austrian Felix Gasselich who gave it to me, because he sat next to me in the dressing room and he'd had it too. But maybe I was just more vulnerable because of the hard year before. I had spent the whole season switching between the first team, the second team and sometimes even the A1 team. I'd finished the season with the U-20 World Cup in Mexico and in between I'd also got my secondary education certificate.

I was really fed up because I had started the league campaign so well. For the first time I had a place in the first-team starting line-up, up front, and by the end of September I already had 12 goals under my belt. I had also made my debut in the national team and scored in my second and third internationals. That third one was the celebrated away game against Republic of Ireland where we were 2-0 down at half-time but ended up winning 3-2. I did that handstand of joy on the goal line when Ruud Gullit scored the winner.

It was actually good old Piet Schrijvers who had fired us up at half-time. 'If you want to win, you'll really have to go for it. No more mucking around.' We started playing with three strikers and, with Piet's attitude, it worked.

That week I had said to Schip on the bus on the way to an Ajax match: 'If I score on Wednesday, I'll become a millionaire.' Ha-ha. That says everything about how I was feeling at the time. I was still young, but things were suddenly starting to move very quickly. In September we had beaten Feyenoord, with Johan Cruyff, 8-2 in the Olympic Stadium, though that was a rather flattering scoreline. Feyenoord had been on top before half-time. I eventually scored three, but it was really Jesper Olsen's match. He was unstoppable that afternoon.

So when the doctor said I had to rest because of this glandular fever at the beginning of November, it was absolutely dreadful news. Eventually I missed all the matches in November and December and only started back training in January. The first time I was allowed to play again was in a friendly on Sunday 28 January, against the amateurs of HMSH in The Hague. I played the first half and went for a shower at half-time. About ten minutes into the second half the Ajax dugout collapsed, because some young home fans had climbed up to sit on it. De Mos got away with a bit of a scare, but board member Lou Bartels and Hassie van Wijk felt the full force of the collapse. Bartels ended up having to have two toes amputated, and Hassie five. Hassie also damaged a neck vertebra and that brought his coaching career to an end. He even ended up on disability benefit. That afternoon was a disaster.

Hassie had been my first coach at Ajax. He was the one who sent me back out onto the pitch after that bust-up with Johan. He was good-natured, when head coaches were usually hard. He provided the balance. As he did as assistant to De Mos.

It all happened before my very eyes. I was walking back to the pitch, heading for the dugout, hair wet from my shower. I was no more than 25 metres away when the thing collapsed. It was terrible. It was only later that I started wondering: what if I'd spent a little less time under the shower. A minute or two. Or if I'd got dressed quicker. Or if I hadn't answered that one question from that journalist. Then maybe I would've gone to sit in that dugout a little earlier. In between Hassie and Lou maybe.

FC VINKEVEEN

1984–1985

The year after Johan stopped playing was a strange one. He was part of the Feyenoord team that had become champions in May 1984, thumbing his nose at Ajax chairman Harmsen in the process. And he wasn't spending so much time in Amsterdam at that time; for the first time in years he was at home, sometimes in Barcelona, sometimes in Vinkeveen.

I had regular contact with him. As did John. In September John was experiencing some numbness, which had actually started on holiday. It turned out to be a herniated disc, and he went under the knife in Groningen. Johan was advising him at the time and travelled to Groningen with John's mother to ensure she could visit him. He took John a video recorder and some VHS tapes. Once there Johan got into conversation with the doctor and even wanted to be in on the operation himself, to make sure everything was done properly. John, who only learned of this afterwards, said in jest: 'It wouldn't surprise me if Johan had performed the operation himself.'

This is how involved he was at the time. It's the sort of attention you appreciate as a young player. That's what Johan did. Once John was up and about again, we would regularly call in on Johan in Vinkeveen. His wife Danny would often open the door and call out: 'Johan, it's the boys!'

Then we would have coffee and Johan would start talking about his experiences. In Spain, in America, always about football. We lapped it all up. After an hour or so we would, out of politeness, say: 'We really must be going.' But Johan would happily rabbit on for another half an hour at the gate. He was just so determined to get his vision, his ideas, across. You could see this in everything he did. He was completely obsessed with the game, always talking about his own specific match experiences that he had seen in our matches, because he followed everything. Really, Johan was a kind of endless source of pure love for football. And we thought it was wonderful. We had front-row seats.

We were also the first two footballers to be sponsored by Cruyff Sports, his sportswear brand. Jack van Gelder was taking care of things like this then. Twice a year John and I would go to that McGregor wholesaler's in Waalwijk and shop for free. It was brilliant. We would both fill up a whole shopping trolley. I remember Jack calling us at the end of the year: 'Lads, you've gone twice over budget.' But nothing else happened. And Johan never mentioned it either. All he talked about was football.

Sometimes we would be rather nervous standing at his door. I remember calling in on one occasion around the time of his birthday. We had no idea what to take with us, but we didn't want to turn up empty-handed either. We ended up buying an Azzaro fragrance, I remember that. He was really pleased with it, but after a minute or two he put it down and started talking about football again.

I have a vivid memory of the birthday of one of his daughters. At one point we were all playing football in his garden. He had a huge garden, with a bit of a meadow alongside. This was where we played a game with two of those small metal goals. Everyone joined in, Jordi with his little friends, Johan and me of course. One time we started heading the ball to each other and dashed off towards the other goal, without anyone being able to get the ball off us. We went past everyone by heading over them, a good 13 or 14 times. Then one of us scored. That was a lovely moment. Magical. You could see that childlike infatuation in him, that love of the ball and the game. It was something we shared. You never forget something like that.

He was a free agent, but he did follow the football and would come to watch us from time to time. And then the talk would take a different turn, because whichever way you looked at it, for us it was interesting to think that at some point Johan would become the Ajax coach.

Aad de Mos had been the Ajax coach for a few years. A top man, Johan himself had thought. It was under him that we'd defeated Johan and Feyenoord 8-2 in the Olympic Stadium. So De Mos was certainly no mug, but Johan was Johan. To us he seemed more exciting and more challenging. For our part there was certainly no preconceived plan, but things did start to move. As they tended to do with Johan. He had a lot of influence. He was very close to the newspaper *De Telegraaf* and in any event he had the ear of other people in the media. I experienced this later myself, when I became national coach. When Johan makes a case for something, all sorts of things start to happen.

That season, '84–'85, was not going at all badly in terms of results. We were even five points clear in April. The championship was within our grasp, but there had been rumblings in the group for several months. On our elimination from the UEFA Cup, in November against Bohemians Prague, De Mos had said in the newspaper: 'With Vanenburg and Rijkaard you can't win the war.' That didn't go down very well with the younger players. De Mos was always closer to the older players than to us. He was also perhaps starting to believe in himself a little too much, because two months later he said somewhere: 'Ajax are now following my lead.' Several people in the club weren't very happy about that.

The term 'FC Vinkeveen' first appeared in the newspaper that spring. It alluded to John and me, saying that we'd been spending a lot of time at Johan's every week, when we had perhaps only been there a few times at that stage. It was a time when Johan's name was beginning to do the rounds in connection with Ajax. De Mos claimed that John and I had deliberately gone around at training doing everything wrong, wasting time, creating conflict, and that we were being deliberately obstructive and arriving late. This was not the case at all though. But something clearly rankled with him – we were obviously irritating him.

On 23 April we played Utrecht away and De Mos put me and Schip on the bench. Out of the blue. It felt rather like a declaration of war. I was a regular in the starting line-up, that was self-evident. John may not have been, but he was still a permanent fixture in the group. De Mos told the press: 'Van Basten is off his game.' I wrote in my notebook beside that match against Utrecht: 'Aad de Mos has never been on his game.' We won 1-0 thanks to Rijkaard, so De Mos got away with it, but the fire was smouldering and *De Telegraaf* merrily carried on stoking it.

The next match was on Sunday 5 May, Haarlem v. Ajax. That week De Mos lay ill in bed. 'Spitz' Kohn, who took over for the week, put John and me in the starting line-up. You could see this at training on Saturday, the day before the match. We trained well, so it was logical. 'The best must play, obviously,' said Spitz Kohn.

On Saturday it was crystal-clear that John and I would be playing against Haarlem. But when this news reached De Mos, he travelled to Amsterdam on Sunday, even though he had a fever of 40°, and crossed out our names on the board. So John and I wouldn't be starting after all. He had a point to prove, whatever the cost. During the match he also sat on the bench.

We lost 1-0 that afternoon in Haarlem. On the bus back to Amsterdam you could cut the atmosphere with a knife. Everyone was upset. John and I, because we hadn't played, the rest of the players because they had lost and because the 'game' De Mos was playing was at the expense of the result, and De Mos himself because he had played for high stakes and lost. The buck after all stopped with him.

The next morning, Monday 6 May, was very strange. As always, we had a post-mortem in the press room at De Meer. De Mos took the floor and said: 'Things are clearly not going well. Maybe you can be more honest with each other without the coach around. So have a chat among yourselves about what went wrong and afterwards we'll come back in again.' He then left the press room with Spitz Kohn and went into the players' lounge to sit at the bar in the Tante Sien restaurant.

A discussion within the squad followed, which led to the conclusion: 'De Mos has to go, we can't go on like this.' We ended up having a vote and a very large majority said: 'Get rid of De Mos.' It all went super-fast, ten minutes or so all told. Dick Schoenaker was skipper then and he was given the job of telephoning the chairman at once.

It was an unusual situation, with De Mos and Spitz Kohn drinking coffee in the players' lounge, a few metres away, and waiting until we, the players, had finished talking. The bizarre thing was that there was only one telephone, and it was mounted on the wall in the kitchen at Tante Sien, behind the bar where De Mos and Kohn were sitting. So that was a bit tricky for Schoenaker.

Chairman Harmsen had a heating company in Diemen, just a stone's throw away. Schoenaker said something along the lines of: 'We need you here because we have a bit of a problem.' Ten minutes later Harmsen, a fairly surly man, walked in. Past De Mos, all the way to the press room, where we were. 'What's going on, lads?' and Schoenaker gave his explanation, with support from Rijkaard, me and the majority of the players' group.

Harmsen simply said: 'Well, he must go then, mustn't he.' He left the press room and asked De Mos to go to his office with him. He then promptly dismissed him. De Mos left immediately and I didn't speak to him again. The next day we had another match, so we had little time to dwell on it.

For De Mos himself it came as a complete surprise. We were top of the table, don't forget. But he did know that when Cruyff starts stirring, everything starts to move. Even though two years previously Harmsen had said: 'We'll never see Cruyff back here with us again.' That was after he and Johan had had their huge bust-up and Johan had gone to Feyenoord.

Three weeks later we became champions away at Roda JC. It was one big party, without De Mos, but with Spitz Kohn in the manager's seat.

Six weeks later Johan was presented as the new coach of Ajax, even though he didn't have his coaching badges yet so officially he was appointed as technical adviser. It therefore had all the appearances of a preconceived plan. John and I of course were keen to have him as coach, that was no secret, but at no time did we ever hatch a plan to unseat De Mos.

With Aad de Mos we had had a turbulent year, let's say a difficult season. It wasn't easy. It hadn't been a smooth ride, but a very bumpy one. Gradually, more and more of the players had begun to realize that this wasn't the way it should be.

So, Johan becoming coach was more or less inevitable. In the end the shadow of Johan was too much for De Mos. I'm not seeking to shirk my own responsibility in all this, we played our role in it too.

At that time De Mos was also in the early stages of his coaching career, and perhaps he had been slightly too keen to make his presence felt. In recent years I have come to know him as a level-headed man, one who has sensible things to say about football.

In 1988 he finally gained his revenge in Strasbourg, by beating Ajax in the European Cup Winners' Cup final, as coach of KV Mechelen. But by then I had long since gone to Milan.

'MARCO, MARCO...

YOUR MOTHER SHE'S A NUTTER'

16 October 1985

And then came that dreadful Wednesday night. I was playing for the Dutch national team against Belgium in Brussels, in the play-off for a place at the 1986 World Cup in Mexico. We lost 1-0. Kieft was sent off and I got a stupid yellow card, which meant I was suspended for the return leg in Rotterdam.

When I got back from Brussels at one thirty in the morning, my father picked me up and said: 'Your mother's had a heart attack.' Typical. Your mother. Not mum. But anyway. She had collapsed in her chair after walking the dogs at half-time. My father had called for help and she'd been rushed to hospital. He didn't think it made any sense to go there that night, but I did go first thing the next morning. She was reasonably bright and was going to be kept in for a while. My brother and sister were living in Canada and Italy respectively and couldn't come straight away. In those days a quick visit wasn't so easy.

But nine days later things took a dramatic turn for the worse when she had a stroke and ended up in a coma. Eventually, once she had regained consciousness, she had lost about 30 years of her memory, including her short-term memory. She barely knew who I was and no longer knew much at all. She never got back to being her old self after that.

Not long after my mother's stroke, when things were very bad, I was playing for Ajax against FC Utrecht. It was 1-1, I think, and I scored.

During that match FC Utrecht supporters were singing: 'Marco, Marco, your mother she's a nutter.'

I found this totally insensitive. It wasn't the classiest section of Utrecht supporters, it's true, but this was very low indeed. I think it's sad when you don't realize that this is the wrong way to put someone off. You expect there to be boundaries somewhere. I've often enough tried to intimidate opponents or said something negative myself to try to put someone off, but this really did go too far. At that point I felt I had to rise above it. This far and no further.

It was a tough lesson, but what do you learn from something like this? It gives you a thick skin and maybe you learn to shut yourself off. But this was a sad low point. In a strange way I'm glad that my mother was no longer able to hear it. But my father did, Utrecht through and through, and a former player at DOS, the forerunner of FC Utrecht. After that incident he never set foot in the Galgenwaard again.

By this time I had met Liesbeth and following my mother's illness, it wasn't long before I left my parents' home to move in with her in Amsterdam. I was 21.

'I'M NOT USUALLY LIKE THIS'

1985

We were in the Canary Islands. It was the first time we had gone in search of the sun on a winter break. John had taken his girlfriend Daniëlle with him and I had invited Liesbeth, even though we had only known each other for two months. It just felt right.

And who else should we find lying on the beach? Aad de Mos and Søren Lerby. Can you believe it? Six months on from De Mos's hasty departure from Ajax. It was certainly a little uncomfortable, apart from anything else because Søren was going out with Daniëlle's mother, the entertainer Willeke Alberti. But luckily no one made an issue of it.

Unlike the summer before, there was no sunbathing for me this time because I didn't have a whole season to get out of my system, though I did take the odd moment for myself. Liesbeth was fine about it, and didn't make a fuss. If I wanted to be alone for a while, she would go out with Daniëlle.

I had met Liesbeth sometime in October. I was out with Schippie one Sunday night, the night footballers go out. I'm not really much of a drinker, except in the summer holidays sometimes. In any event I stay away from beer, and tend more towards those sweet drinks: Bacardi & Coke, gin & tonic, Pisang Ambon, that sort of thing. Women's drinks really, I suppose, ha-ha. Anyway, I was never drunk, but that evening turned out rather differently.

I remember starting off in Le Berry, then moving on to La Bastille and at about two o'clock ending up in the Surprise Bar. We used to spend a lot of time on the Leidseplein in those days because it could get quite lively. At the start of the evening it was fairly convivial in Le Berry. Daniëlle was there – she hadn't been with John long – and some other friends. Liesbeth was there that evening too, with a girlfriend. She looked a bit alternative – dungarees, clodhoppers. Cool. John approached her first; he was a bit more daring than me. But he was already with Daniëlle, so naturally I took over. We hit it off straight away, though I've no idea now what we talked about.

On reaching the Surprise Bar we ordered some shots, Embryos or something they were called. I never really did shots, but for some reason I felt I had to join in this time. The drinks were a mixture of two or three different kinds of rum and they came one after another. At some point I was hammered. I remember saying to Liesbeth: 'I'm not usually like this, you know. I don't know what's the matter with me.' Somewhere between two and four o'clock I was out for the count.

One of my friends, Frank Kroon, took me home to his house in Amstelveen where he lived with his mother. First I threw up in the canal, then later on again at his home. But I knew nothing of this until the next morning. It was embarrassing. I had no idea how long I had spent talking to Liesbeth or how it had ended up.

The next morning was a disaster. I had training and I knew for sure that Johan, who was now the coach, would be wise to it straight away. Only it was my incredible good fortune that he was in New York that Monday because Amsterdam was bidding for the 1992 Olympic Games. He was there to do some lobbying. We trained indoors that day, because we had played a match the day before. It was a kind of cool-down training, with Cor van der Hart. I didn't really know what was going on, but I got through it okay.

John saw me arrive; he and Daniëlle hadn't left it late and he cottoned on immediately. I sat at the bar in the players' lounge, took a sip of milk and had to go straight to the toilet. John gave his considered opinion: 'Bassie's not going to be fit for anything today.' He kept looking at me and then burst out laughing. I felt really ill.

It was just a matter of getting through the day. After training I went straight home and said to my father: 'I'm going straight to bed. We had a flu jab at Ajax today and I'm not feeling too good.' I'm sure I had alcohol poisoning. On that Monday, Tuesday and Wednesday I slept from 4.30 in the afternoon until 8.30 the next morning. All I did was go to training and then back home to bed. I was wrecked.

I was still thinking about Liesbeth. Nothing had happened between us yet, but I did feel something was brewing. I kept wondering whether she would want to see me again. We didn't have mobile phones back then and I knew nothing about her, just her first name. So I decided to go back to Le Berry that next Sunday evening and luckily she was there too. I went straight up to her and said: 'This has never happened to me before.'

I explained myself to her and stayed on my best behaviour that evening. She laughed at my story. We were soon on good terms again. I had apparently uttered those sentences repeatedly the first evening: 'I'm not usually like this. I don't know what's the matter with me.' It actually became a bit of a thing for us. It was early October, I know that exactly because I was scoring lots of goals, a really ridiculous number of goals, at the time. I kept a record of it all in my notebook. They just kept coming: 20 in three months or so. Five against Heracles, six against Sparta. It felt like I was floating over the pitch. Everything

I tried came off. Six in one match, I had never known anyone do that in the Eredivisie before. Simply astonishing.

Liesbeth was the only one who didn't think it was anything special. She had no idea I was scoring so many because she didn't really follow football. 'Five goals? Is that good then?' She did later admit that this was when she had listened to the Sunday afternoon football commentary on the radio for the first time, and had sometimes heard my name mentioned.

A few weeks after we first met we were already becoming pretty close and I was going to meet her parents for the first time. When I rang the bell at her parents' home in Badhoevedorp that evening, her father opened the door. 'Come in,' he said. 'She's upstairs.'

I had seen a light on in her room as I drew up, so I said: 'Yes, I've just seen Esther.'

'Who?'

'Erm, Liesbeth, I mean.'

Weird. I have no idea why I said that. I don't know anyone called Esther. I was so embarrassed. Safe to say I must have made a less than perfect first impression.

Liesbeth meeting my parents didn't go entirely to plan either. My mother was very ill that month. Liesbeth only saw her in her hospital bed and not as she used to be. And my father was so busy with everything to do with my mother that he didn't really take Liesbeth in.

On that beach in the Canary Islands I thought a lot about my mother and the things she used to tell me when she was still okay. They had a completely different ring to them now. I was glad too that Liesbeth was there because the situation with my mother brought us closer together. That's why, strangely enough, it didn't in any way feel too soon for the two of us to be on holiday.

KLAUS FISCHER

The seventies

As a footballer I was pretty much an all-rounder because in my younger days I played all kinds of other sports too. You take something away from any sport you play. There was a wall on the Herderplein you could prop bikes up against. We used to play football tennis there all the time, with that wall as the net. In football tennis you learn to head the ball properly, to nod it downwards with great accuracy.

But at UVV, for example, I also used to play baseball in the summer and my friend Henri and I would play table tennis obsessively in his garage. Sometimes we would skip school and play the whole afternoon. We kept score on the walls. When we resumed the next day, I would check to see if Henri had secretly added a few points to his score. He did everything he could to win, just like me, although I was more the attacker and he the defender.

We mainly played in the winter. It wasn't uncommon for us to celebrate winning a game in the street, outside in the snow. Our sweaty bodies would be steaming. The neighbours must have thought we were utterly mad, stripped to the waist and running around in the cold like idiots. Every Friday evening I would go to a table tennis club in the Oog in Al area of Utrecht. I couldn't yet afford to become a member, but I was allowed to play there for nothing on proper match tables.

When I was 13 I was invited to play in a trial football match for District West 1, because I was doing well at UVV and in the Utrecht squad. This was what you dreamed of – the district squad, which could be the first step to something big. That 'West 1' match was to be on a Monday, but on the Friday evening before, I went to play table tennis as usual. That particular evening I tried to move one of the tables, but it slipped. I didn't want to break anything of course, because I was allowed to play there for free, so instinctively I tried to catch the table with my foot. It was amazingly heavy and landed right on my foot; my big toe turned blue and swelled up immediately. It just got worse and worse.

Then of course I had to cry off that trial match. What a disaster; I thought it was really terrible. I had missed a chance to play in the spotlight. That was the first time I'd missed a match with an injury and I hated that feeling even then.

I also used to play ice hockey with a friend, sometimes on the ice at the rink, but usually on roller skates, out on the square. The great thing about ice hockey is that it teaches you tricks. If for example you reach the puck later than your opponent, you can nudge his stick aside or lift it with your stick just as he goes to hit it. And that's allowed. Then he'll miss the puck and you can get it instead.

It's a trick I used in football too. When a long ball comes in towards the penalty area, the defender will sometimes be slightly ahead of you. If you stretch your leg out towards the ball but the defender gets there first, you know you're late. The trick then is to give the defender's leg a little nudge from the side when that leg is just off the ground and he will often miss the ball or fall over. I used to find it would sometimes make me fall over myself, so I could claim the defender had brought me down. It's something you can play around with because every situation is different. I certainly won the ball a few times in this way when I was actually late. And if the referee isn't exactly in line, as often happens with a long ball, he can't see exactly what's happened and he may award a free kick or a penalty.

In the long hot summer of 1975 we spent every day at the swimming pool. We came across boys on the springboards who were game for anything. You could get fairly high by bouncing on one of these boards, but if there was someone else on the board who put his weight on it at just the right moment, you could get extra high. We used to call it 'double bouncing'. We started doing more and more somersaults and trying to get higher and higher.

I loved it and was really fascinated by all that springboard stuff. I even spent three months going to diving lessons. We didn't just do it in the swimming pool, but in the gym too. We did all kinds of somersaults: forwards, backwards, sideways, you name it. It gives you a sense of space in the air. This is how you really learn to jump, dive and fall. More so even than football, with its regular and sliding tackles.

Every Saturday we would watch Bundesliga football on *Sportschau*, a German sports programme. At one time Klaus Fischer was the big name in German football. He did something new, something we had never seen before: it was an overhead kick. One of these goals, against the Swiss, was even voted Germany's goal of the century on German television.

We thought it was sensational. He scored by hanging in the air and kicking the ball backwards into the net. We had never seen anything like it before. And we wanted to do it too, so we started practising it, Klaus Fischer's overhead kick.

In the summers of '76, '77 and '78, after that Klaus Fischer wonder goal, I started making regular trips to the Maarsseveense Lakes with Ricky Testa la Muta and Edwin Godee, two of my football mates. There were lots of grassy areas there, around the lakes, but also sandy beaches that sloped very gradually into the water. We would spend long afternoons in the shallow water practising that kick of Fischer's. We would throw the ball in the air, fall backwards and try to kick the ball. It was more comfortable than falling on a patch of grass, because we landed in the water. We practised it a lot, week after week, all summer long.

OVERHEAD KICK

The match was starting to slip away from us. Den Bosch had pulled a goal back to make it 2-1. Then, in the 70th minute, Schippie passed the ball to Jan Wouters, who was usually an excellent crosser of a ball, but this time it was an ugly cross if I'm honest. The ball curled into the penalty area, with no great speed and well behind the man. I kept my eye on it and felt it would drop to head height just beyond the penalty spot. At this point I would be between the ball and the goal. My brain scanned the situation, recognized it and from that moment on my instincts took over.

I knew what I was going to do. I just didn't know what it would look like. It could go completely wrong. As the ball was going behind me, I had few options. I could maybe still have headed it, but that didn't seem like the best option to me. The ball was hanging in the air and I was stooping forward slightly, with my back to the goal defended by Van Grinsven, the Den Bosch keeper. In this sort of situation it's best to wait until the very last moment before taking off. The ball was about three metres away from me and I still had both feet on the ground. Then I put everything into taking off with my left leg. I knew I wouldn't get far if I didn't do that. I needed that momentum. As a result I reached my pivot point quicker and was able to hang backwards in the air. This was high-level gymnastics. My right leg was my usual take-off leg, but this time it was my left, which was more difficult, less natural.

It isn't just the skill of being brave enough to fall backwards. Everything has to be right. It's a precarious balance. You could put the ball in the net, but you could also break your neck. You don't see something like this on a football pitch very often because it requires such a high degree of coordination.

Ultimately, it's all about the whip. The whip with the other leg, not the take-off leg. This whip, the catapult effect, will only be powerful enough if you are hanging high enough in the air and are prepared to fall backwards and land somewhere you can't possibly see. It's something you have to have done repeatedly if you're not going to worry about where you're going to land.

The whip here was going to be with my right leg. It would allow me to hit the ball hard, to give it real momentum, but it also had to be precise. Otherwise it would end up being completely ridiculous.

So there I was, hanging nearly horizontally in the air, a good metre off the ground, I'd say. Just before the whip. It was a lovely sight. But at this point my left leg was of course higher than my right lower leg. My right knee was still bent, with my lower leg poised for the whip. It was like a whiplash. Whack. The ball, which had been gently falling, was now flying straight into the top corner. With much greater momentum. I was already falling and mainly concerned with not breaking my neck. I made sure I fell properly, onto an arm.

I hit the ground just as the ball flew into the top corner. For a moment the crowd didn't react. It had all happened so fast. It was no more than three seconds since the ball had left Wouters' foot. I thought: I reckon that's turned out all right.

That goal was beauty itself, because I had taken the ball so high. I had hung high in the air and the ball had gone in the top corner. So the execution was perfect. It even clipped the inside of the post on its way in, which I really liked. It's not something you see every day and people still talk about it, that overhead kick against Den Bosch.

STANDING NEXT TO DIEGO MARADONA

13 November 1986

Four days after the overhead kick I was making my first visit to the Lido, the famous night club in Paris. I was sitting in the front row next to Liesbeth and my father and I had bought a light-grey suit for the occasion. It was a little on the roomy side.

I don't really go in for all this glitz and glamour, but it was the presentation of the Ballon d'Or, the award for best footballer in Europe. This was Diego Maradona's night, the man who had more or less single-handedly turned Argentina into World Cup winners and who was breathing new life into Napoli as well. Who else should win the Ballon d'Or?

We had seen him crossing the Champs-Élysées on his way to the Lido surrounded by crowds of people. It was a circus. All the attention was on him, and there was nothing wrong with that. He was a phenomenon. All of a sudden there he was, just a few metres away from me. It was a very special moment.

But I wasn't there for Maradona. I was receiving an award too, the European Golden Boot for top scorer in Europe, for the 37 goals I had scored for Ajax.

For me just being in Paris was special. Apart from Liesbeth and my father, Ajax board members Lou Bartels and Ton Harmsen were there too.

We all went out to eat at some fancy restaurant. It was a completely new world for us.

Luckily, Ger Lagendijk from the players' union was with us too, because we were served smoked salmon and fried sole, which were completely new to my father and me. My father set about the sole with his knife and fork just as he would a piece of meat. He would have eaten it bones and all, but Ger quietly explained to him that there was a better way to eat fish like this, which was very thoughtful of him.

The show had barely begun when the presenter announced my name. It startled me, but I could stay where I was for the moment. A large screen appeared behind the stage. They were going to show some footage and I knew what of.

The room went dark and a grainy shot of the Ajax v. FC Den Bosch match at De Meer, four days earlier, suddenly appeared. There I was, horizontal in mid-air. The ball flew into the top corner. And then again, from a different angle. The applause was deafening.

A short while later Franz Beckenbauer presented me with the Golden Boot, but I didn't feel particularly comfortable with all the attention. Not long after, Maradona received his award and then we were standing on the stage together. He congratulated me on my overhead kick. I appreciated the compliment; it was Maradona after all.

ANKLE (1)

The De Meer Pact

1987

'What are we going to do about this, skip?' asked Johan, as he walked into his office and sat down behind his desk. He gestured to me to take a seat opposite. His words hung in the air for a moment, as if we both knew that there wasn't really a perfect solution to the situation we found ourselves in.

The office Johan and his assistants used was just a few square metres in size. If you entered the building on the left next to De Meer, it was the first door on the right. After that came the medical room, with the massage tables, then the showers and finally the dressing rooms.

It was really a rather small, austere space, looking out onto the two muddy practice pitches where the first team trained. On the wall were the latest team photo and a board with 11 red and white and 11 blue magnets. The red and white of course were always in a 4-3-3 formation. A pair of Johan's own brand of football boots stood by the heater.

It was the end of February, a bitterly cold Tuesday afternoon. The important European Cup Winners' Cup matches against Malmö were coming up. A tricky tie, especially with the wintry weather forecast for the first leg, away in Malmö the following week. Johan was finalizing his team to face the stubborn Swedes. The Cup Winners' Cup was suddenly a good deal more important now that the championship appeared out of reach again with PSV heading for the title. Just like the season before, Johan's first as coach, the team from Eindhoven was unassailable. That team, with Gullit, Van der Gijp, Thoresen, Lerby, Koolhof and Gerets, was simply winning everything again.

This hurt of course, especially if you were Johan Cruyff. In that previous season, '85–'86, we had been knocked out of the European Cup by Porto in the first round. A disappointing year, however loudly Johan protested that we were going through a 'learning process'. We had only won the Dutch Cup, beating the Roosendaal side RBC, which was cold comfort really. Though it did mean that we got to play in the Cup Winners' Cup.

And, after years of early European elimination, this was finally going well. Before the winter break we had beaten Bursaspor home and away and Olympiacos of Greece. Really convincingly too. The team was finally starting to play the way Johan envisaged. He had brought in Danny Blind and Jan Wouters to give the team better balance. The patterns of play were finally beginning to bed in, we were making each other better and the crowd was getting behind us.

On European nights De Meer would be full and the atmosphere electric. You could see Johan was starting to believe. He had made me captain the season before, even though I was still only 20. I wasn't really much of a talker, but he spurred me on, made me feel important, willing me to drag the team along in my wake. Attacking-wise it sometimes went a bit mad that year. We scored 122 times and I went on to become European top scorer with 37 goals. But in all the important matches, PSV, Feyenoord and in Europe, we fouled up. We had no desire to go through that again. Johan certainly didn't, nor did I, because it was my last year at Ajax. It was still a secret, but I had already signed a preliminary contract with AC Milan. With PSV having a big lead in the league again, the Cup Winners' Cup was crucial. The quarter-final was coming up fast: first leg in Sweden on 4 March and then at home at De Meer on 18 March.

So there we were, sitting in his office, and having to talk. It was unavoidable, we were both keenly aware of that. He was fed up with me having played so little since December. 'I know you're in constant pain,' he said, 'but we must go on, you have to play. I played in pain myself, it's all part of the game. And the doctors say it can't get any worse.'

Training had just finished and again I hadn't kept going right to the end. My tracksuit was covered in mud, it was soaking wet, the bottoms were sticking to my knees. I had given everything I had in me. But it wasn't enough for him. He wanted more.

The desire was huge, especially for him. Everyone had seen the previous season as a failure. So it was simple: Johan had to win something. And I was his captain, his best player, his top scorer. He needed me – he knew that and I knew that.

But he hadn't been able to count on me for weeks. Originally, I had felt pain in my left ankle and after the operation in December and the rehab, I had suddenly felt pain in the other one. I often had to pull out of training, like that afternoon, or was unable to play whole matches. Johan wasn't happy about it. So it was logical that he wanted to talk. I was no malingerer, I wanted nothing more than to play football, more than anything, but I had already played in pain so often. And now I was about to have a row about not playing, which went completely against the grain.

Johan slammed the door. No eavesdroppers. Outside the rain was beating down on the training pitch. You could have cut the atmosphere with a knife. It was a lively discussion and we both knew what it was all about. Head to head.

Johan broke the silence: 'Okay, Marco, what have you got to say?'

The misery had actually all begun on 7 December 1986, at the Oosterpark Stadium, against Groningen. They're always difficult matches, they never give you an inch.

That Sunday afternoon my brother Stanley was in the stadium to watch the game. This was special because he had been living in Canada for a long time. He knew I was now a well-known footballer in Holland, so he wanted to see me play. He sat next to my father in the stands at the Oosterpark, so I was especially keen to do my best that day. Having your older brother in the stands watching you play really means something.

The match didn't start too well for us. Midway through the first half I lost the ball near the halfway line and chased after it. Then I went in for a sliding tackle in our own half, by the touchline, on Edwin Olde Riekerink. I went in hard because I was annoyed about losing the ball. Straight away my right ankle hurt. Usually you just mutter 'ouch' and carry on, but the pain didn't go and I went off after half an hour. That didn't often happen to me because I was rarely injured.

When I watched the incident later on TV, I still couldn't understand it. Had I gone in too hard? I didn't think so. Had he gone in too hard? No, he hadn't. I hadn't really done anything stupid. At least not stupid enough to badly injure my ankle. Nor did I see that I had twisted my ankle or landed awkwardly. As far as I could see, it was just a tackle like any other in a match. I wasn't really any closer to knowing what exactly had happened that day than if I had been sitting there in the dugout with Johan.

What I do know is that I felt a lot of pain straight away. Too much pain to carry on playing anyway. That same evening I went to the hospital in Amsterdam with Dr De Groot for an X-ray. De Groot said to me: 'It's nothing serious, just give it time.'

I limped around for a few days but it didn't stop hurting; it wasn't going away. Coincidentally, I had surgery on my other ankle, the left one, on 15 December, a week after that Groningen–Ajax match. The operation on my left ankle was to be performed at the Prinsengracht Hospital by Swiss surgeon René Marti, the top ankle specialist in Europe, I was told. I had been having trouble with dancer's heel, a common injury among dancers. It had been causing me problems since the cup tie against RCH, in March 1986. We had played sluggishly in Heemstede that day. I had lacked sharpness myself. I had jumped and landed awkwardly on an RCH defender's foot. There was a reaction in my meniscus, but my left ankle was the main issue. I had problems with it for most of the rest of 1986. Whenever I took off from my left foot or landed on it I felt pain. The winter break seemed like a good time for surgery.

Spending a week in bed I paid little or no attention to my right ankle, but on leaving the hospital and having the left one in plaster, I had to put more weight on my right. And all of my weight when the plaster came off about three weeks later. After a while my left ankle was back to normal again, but I certainly asked too much of my right ankle at that time.

When the league campaign resumed my right ankle still hurt. I remember playing for the first team and coming on as sub against Excelsior. They taped up my ankle. They shaved it first and then put that white tape on top. It was like plaster. It's a mystery how I was ever able to play with it. I couldn't move it at all. I think I even managed to score with my right foot in that game, but don't ask me how.

Back in Johan's office there was a knock at the door. Physiotherapist Pim van Dort came in and quickly closed the door behind him, as if he knew that something was going on. Johan said he wasn't doing this for fun, he wanted to win something. He went on to say that Ajax had won nothing in Europe since the seventies. It was either the title or the Cup Winners' Cup. And as PSV were doing so well, he was going for the Cup Winners' Cup, he said. Therefore he needed me, but all he was hearing from me was that I was in pain. Right from the start of the season. First it was the left one. Surgery done. Now it was the right. Fine. He said: 'Listen, you've had surgery on your left ankle and now you're having trouble with your right one. We're a few months on and the doctor says it won't get any worse if you play on with it. So, what are we going to do?'

I had decided to wait until he finished speaking, but I knew what he was thinking. His father-in-law, Cor Coster, was my agent. So Johan knew that I had already signed a preliminary contract with AC Milan the summer before, despite it's not having been made public yet. And he knew that this would definitely be my last season at Ajax. So maybe he thought I was taking it easy, saving myself and not giving my all. But that was ridiculous. I always wanted to play. It's just that I was in a lot of pain.

The last six weeks, from the moment the plaster came off my left ankle, it had been a case of patching up my right ankle and making do. That afternoon included. My ankle had to be taped up before every training session. And after every training session the physio spent an hour and a half with me, massaging, rubbing in oil and bandaging. It was abundantly clear that my right ankle wasn't in the best of shape.

I was also taped up before every match. The joint could hardly move but the pain was undiminished, especially the next day. After every match that I did play I had to immerse my ankle in a bucket of ice. Whatever they tried, my ankle was still painful and swollen. And I really didn't know what was wrong with it.

On 14 December, the day before the surgery on my left ankle, Dr Marti hadn't looked at my right ankle because it was completely taped up. That much I remember. The next time I went to see Marti at AMC, the Academic Medical Center in Amsterdam, Johan went with me. He wanted to know whether it could do any harm if I played. I don't remember what Marti said word for word, but what it boiled down to was that basically it couldn't do any harm. It was just something I had to get through, it wasn't anything serious. That sort of thing. I think Marti may well have been a little in awe of the great Johan Cruyff.

In any event the pain was hampering me, at training and in matches. Every week we looked at what I could and could not do. For weeks I had had a specially adapted training programme and had already come to terms with the idea that this was the way I would have to manage for the rest of the season. There was nothing else for it.

Johan was silent for a moment, so I started to speak and explained that I was no malingerer and that I wasn't saving myself for Milan. A ludicrous idea. If he knew me at all, he would know that wasn't the sort of person I was. I wanted to play. Whatever the cost. But the pain I had had since Groningen was something I didn't understand and was difficult to explain. I hadn't wanted him to see me as a softie, so I had carried on training and playing despite the pain. I didn't want to give up and I believed that the ankle would heal once the season was over, during those seven weeks off.

Johan took a deep breath. I felt he wanted to bring the discussion to a close. 'We've been adapting the training sessions for you for weeks and giving you a separate programme. The physio is working on you full-time. We've been to the doctor and he thinks you can play. I don't know what you think, but we can't carry on like this. I'll make

66

a bargain with you. And then we'll say no more about it. You can skip league games if you feel you need to. Have your rest and recovery. But in return, and I want to be clear about this, you must then win that Cup Winners' Cup for us. And if you don't win it, I'll kill you.' He smiled and paused for a moment. 'Agreed?'

'Agreed,' I said. We nodded in agreement.

Shortly afterwards I entered an empty dressing room. Everyone else had showered and gone. I realized that what had just happened was a more or less absurd, childlike way of dealing with each other. A kind of basic level at which two footballers understand each other perfectly and come to an agreement, conclude a pact. I also realized, as I turned on the shower, that it's actually almost impossible to explain to people outside the game that sometimes this is how it works.

IN FRONT OF THE MIRROR (2)

13 May 1987

It was the day of the final, 13 May 1987. We were having our post-lunch lie-down and I was in my hotel room somewhere in the noisy heart of Athens, but I couldn't sleep. I was pacing up and down. At the tender age of 22 I was already captain of a European Cup Winners' Cup finalist and much was expected of me. After six years it would be one of my last matches for Ajax.

Somewhere in the back of my mind I knew I would soon be having seven weeks off and then Milan would beckon. Relocating with Liesbeth, to a new life, a new country and a new club.

But right now, more than anything, I was really nervous. I could feel it in every bone in my body, much more than the tension I normally felt before a key league game. This was my first final and I could be about to write history here.

Our opponents were relative unknowns, which did nothing to calm the nerves. Lokomotive Leipzig, a factory team from East Germany – hard workers, solid, defensive. An unpredictable counter-attacking side. In March we had comfortably beaten Malmö at home after a narrow defeat in Sweden. Despite missing a penalty, I had scored the decider in a 3-1 win. It had been a wonderful night at De Meer. At the end of the game the bucket of ice had been ready and waiting for my ankle because the pitch had been atrocious.

The first leg of the semi-final against Real Zaragoza had been more like synchronized swimming, following a cloudburst during the warm-up. Playing our normal game on that pitch had been impossible. The Spaniards had adapted to the conditions better in the early stages and had gone 1-0 up. Eventually we had changed our approach, constantly whipping the ball high in the air and going forward. The match had slowly swung our way and in the end we had won 3-2.

The return leg in Amsterdam, in front of a packed Olympic Stadium, was a flawless 3-0 win. We had played well and had been convincing, so Johan could feel satisfied – it was an advert for attacking football, his kind of football.

I looked out of the window. Athens was busy and everything in Greece seemed loud. I went back to lie on the bed – just two more hours until we set off for the stadium.

Over the past two years, but especially that season, Johan had slowly begun to forge the team into a successful side. Each player knew what he had to do to make the others better players. 'If you help each other, you'll get better together,' Johan would say. 'Get to know each other's strengths and weaknesses. Don't moan about them, but be smart and use them to your advantage. That's what'll make us stronger.' Things were indeed beginning to improve and now we were in the final. I had played every game and been a decisive influence, not just as captain, but also as driving force and goalscorer, despite my ankle. After that one conversation, Johan and I hadn't said another word about it. And now the time had come, 14 years on from Ajax's last European final, in which Johan himself had played.

All well and good, but we hadn't won anything yet. If we ran into the East German wall tonight, the party would be over. We were also missing a number of important players, and I wasn't happy about that. Blind and Spelbos were injured and John Bosman was suspended after his red card away to Zaragoza. Frank Verlaat was in the middle and youngsters like Robbie Witschge and Aron Winter suddenly found themselves having to play. Luckily, Frank Rijkaard and Jan Wouters would be with us. The question was whether Johan's routines were now so deeply ingrained that we would still be able to play our game despite bringing in the new players. In any event more would fall on my shoulders.

I felt restless, partly because I could feel some kind of primitive urge cutting right through all that tension. I went up to the big mirror next to the door and took a look at myself. After the game that night I didn't want to have to say to journalists: 'We've come a long way. We've played well. It wasn't our night.' No way. Of course, I was still young, but you never know what's round the corner. This could be my last chance.

I looked straight at myself and almost spoke out loud. This was my first final and I had to win it. If I didn't win the first one, it would become a bit of an albatross around my neck. Straight away I would be at a disadvantage if ever there were to be a second. Whatever happened, I had to win this time. I kept looking at myself until I was satisfied that this notion had forced its way into the very depths of my being. I told myself: forget the ankle; tonight's the night, Van Basten. No bull, eyes on the prize. You've got a job to do. And a game to win. That's how it has to be and nothing else.

It was a conversation with the mirror, a last-minute pep talk to myself. Win. Pure and simple. No excuses.

That night I scored the only goal, ducking down in front of my marker and reaching the ball just in front of the near post. Sonny Silooy's cross was actually a little too close to goal, forcing me to stretch as far as I could. The ball smacked off my head onto the ground and into the far corner. Boom. 1-0. And that's the way it stayed. I received the cup in a glow of delight. Pure relief. Winning my first final was a childlike pleasure, with Johan laughing his infectious laugh. That was how it should be.

'MARCO VAN BASTEN

IS IRREPLACEABLE'

31 May 1987

'Marco van Basten, Marco van Basten is great, he's the pride of Mokum, he's scoring every game.' The chant rang out loudly from the F-side that afternoon of 31 May 1987 when I played my very last match for Ajax. We had already won the Cup Winners' Cup and the Dutch Cup. The league was over, and all that remained was this fixture against PEC Zwolle at De Meer.

I was just 22 and on my way to AC Milan, but the Amsterdam fans were lavish in their praise of me that afternoon. I heard that chant again, especially for me, years later when I came up against Ajax as the coach of Heerenveen. Something like that sticks in your mind.

That afternoon the fences on the F-side were covered in banners saying Grazie Marco and Arrivederci Marco. We ended up beating Zwolle 5-2, with me scoring four goals, happily a send-off in style.

Cruyff took me off just before the end, after my fourth goal, to allow the crowd to show its appreciation. After the game the players carried me around on their shoulders and I was presented with flowers, which I threw into the crowd. In the end I took off my shirt and threw it over the fence on the F-side. It affected me more than I expected.

The game itself had ended in bizarre fashion. As Cruyff had already made two changes, the maximum number in those days, after I came off we finished the game with ten men. Stadium announcer Freek de Jonge had his own unique slant on it: 'Marco van Basten is irreplaceable.'

MILAN (1) – IN FRONT OF THE MIRROR (3)

Autumn 1987

I had just woken up. It was still cold outside and I could feel it through the window. It tended to cool down a lot at night in the Po Valley, to the north-east of Milan. I had absolutely no desire to get up, but breakfast with the rest of the team was in half an hour. Afterwards coach Arrigo Sacchi would go through some tactics with us again.

Maradona and Napoli trounced us in the league, but the race wasn't over yet. Every Monday *La Gazzetta dello Sport* would summarize the league simply by showing two cartoon figures in pursuit of one another. One was Maradona, the other Ruud Gullit. Ruud was our team's driving force and finisher. Everything he touched that year turned to gold. That picture in the paper encapsulated the whole season.

I was pleased Ruud was doing so well, catching the eye and attracting all the attention, as it meant I could focus on my recovery out of the limelight and little would be asked of me.

I slid out of bed and got to my feet. Berlusconi had got it absolutely right here. Everything at Milanello had been refurbished and it was now a top-notch facility. He had ordered the complete renovation of this training complex when he bought the club in 1985. The players wanted for nothing – good food, good sleep, good rest, good training. The latest medical facilities, a gym, pitches like billiard tables. It was simply football heaven, except that it didn't feel that way to me at all. In fact, the closer I got to that heaven, the more painful it was that I wasn't allowed to join in. Couldn't join in. The team was outstanding though, incredibly professional, collectively and individually. The right back, Tassotti, was wonderfully skilful and if you saw what he could do with those little practice balls, just not normal. Baresi was a superman – so quick, so perceptive, a leader. Maldini, at just 19, rarely needed to foul to stay in control. Class. And not forgetting Costacurta, who I would often come up against in training. There was no way past him. With a defence like that you were world class.

So it was incredibly frustrating that I wasn't able to show what I could really do. At training I would sometimes be at my best if I had a day when I wasn't in too much pain, but I never felt one hundred per cent. Since I had said there was no way I could play with my ankle as it was, Sacchi always chose Gullit and Virdis up front. He used to call it 'zonal pressing', but really it was just good defending. And Gullit would run himself silly up front.

I would discuss Sacchi's tactics with him, as I used to do with De Mos and Cruyff in Holland. He was always keen to talk, could never get enough of it in fact, but me telling the press after the first match that I thought we should play with three strikers turned everything on its head. They weren't used to that in Italy, questioning the coach's tactical plan. After that I spoke less and less to journalists. So much is written here and there are so many sports papers you can hardly keep up with them all. And they do make mountains out of molehills, so you're better off keeping your mouth shut.

In any event I hadn't had anything to say in the last few weeks, because I had been injured. I had little to say and there was nothing I wanted to say, mainly because I was afraid I would have to go under the knife again. I had made an appointment with Dr Marti because

I wanted him to have a proper look at my right ankle. It had been painful since January and wasn't getting any better. If I trained flat out, my ankle would be swollen again the next day and I couldn't do anything else. I wasn't getting anywhere.

I was lucky that my childhood friend Ricky Testa la Muta was around too. Close by, in fact. By chance I had heard from Ploon Konijnenburg that he was playing at Pro Patria, in Serie C, and we saw a lot of each other. In the early days I often hung around with Ruud, who sat next to me in the dressing room. But I couldn't keep up as he went on his merry way. Training camps, matches. He was becoming a big star, a huge personality. Since my ankle injury I had found myself rather isolated. The contrast between us couldn't have been starker, so it was great to have Ricky around. In the evenings we would chew the fat and regularly go out to eat with our other halves.

I had been introduced to the press in Milan in mid-July, alongside Ruud. It was really impressive, a different world, on a massive scale and with lots of razzmatazz. I was glad Ruud was the major acquisition; I felt rather uncomfortable that day, because I had no idea how my ankle was going to be.

Ajax's season had finished early and Serie A had started late, so I'd had seven weeks' holiday. Plenty of time for the ankle to get better then, I felt, but the nightmare soon returned. After three or four days' training it started playing up again. Damn thing, I thought, this is no good.

Milan's medical team had known about it, but they couldn't make it public. No one buys an injured striker, do they? So July and August had been miserable, because for weeks we had all had to keep up the pretence that everything was fine. It had been a strange situation because I had actually gone to Milan that summer injured. But exactly how bad it was I didn't yet know for certain.

Berlusconi fortunately did not panic, but by any stretch of the imagination it was no joke for him that one of his two acquisitions was unable to play. He did make it clear to me that he thought Milan should have known sooner. I said I had thought it would get better in the summer. He believed me.

Anyway, he seemed an all-right guy to me. The way he ran this club was inspiring. It wasn't the Dutch way. The big boss really was the boss and I like that. When he was due to visit Milanello, everyone was nervous for days in advance. Everything would be given a good clean and tidy up. The manager of the facility would dash around trying to get everything ready in time.

Berlusconi would nearly always arrive in his helicopter. He would land on the artificial grass pitch next to the dressing rooms. When he came in everyone would stand up and applaud. Ruud was totally unimpressed. He didn't like it, but I thought it was okay. Berlusconi would always make a speech, often about some business deal or other he had done. Or about how he had been negotiating this or that with some minister until four or five o'clock that morning and how he had wrapped up the deal. And about us having to do our utmost to achieve our goal: the championship, the Scudetto.

When he finished there would be more applause or he would ask Sacchi to say a few words and then add something himself. Berlusconi was someone who thought big. He wanted to become number one in Europe, that was his aim with AC Milan. He was a devotee and a big fan of Milan. His speeches always gave you a lift.

I also admired the business empire he had built up. You could see from all the facilities at Milanello that he had put everything into it. It was all top quality. He understood that if you wanted to achieve something it would cost a penny or two. I like that. Although Ruud would sometimes chuckle at the ostentation and show typical Dutch reluctance to stand whenever Berlusconi came in.

It all started with that glitzy period. I took part in pre-season and played in the early cup matches in August. For better or worse I fought the pain, but was unable to move freely. The first match in Serie A against Pisa I even scored a penalty. But it simply wasn't right, it wasn't getting any better. Increasingly, I was becoming a shadow of my former self. In the end I had really had enough of pretending all the time. I had been in pain since January and the pressure was simply getting too great. I couldn't muddle through any longer and I was completely fed up with it.

Milan had made it public three weeks before, saying I was having problems with my ankle and so wouldn't be playing for the time being, to work on my recovery. But there was no recovery, there was no getting better. Not with physiotherapy, not with rest, not with anything at all. The wretched feeling simply got worse.

I stood in front of the mirror. And suddenly it occurred to me that this was it, that this was the end. Despite my fighting spirit. My ankle would never get better, playing football in pain for months had messed things up. I would never again run around a football pitch without this pain. And I would never go on to become Milan's regular striker. That confidence I once had was no longer there. I could remember the look I had just before the Cup Winners' Cup final in Athens: fearless.

But that swagger, that bravado had gone now. The anxiety shot through my body. Could it really be? Could it be that this was it? Would there never again be a next match, would there never again be another goal? Would the Milan fans never see the real Marco van Basten? Would they never again cheer for my goals? I still had so much I wanted to show them, and to win.

Surely this couldn't be the end. That would have been so unfair. Once more I looked deep into my eyes. I refused to believe it, with every fibre of my being, but it was beyond me. I glanced at the clock and saw that I had just two minutes to put in an appearance at the breakfast table.

OPERATION MARTI

14 November 1987

'It's not looking good, young man.' Dr Marti looked serious. 'You've probably been playing with torn ankle ligaments for nearly a year. To put it simply, what I found in that joint was a complete mess.'

At the end of October Marti had felt we should operate as soon as possible, but Milan had stood by the view that I could recover through rest. The deadlock had been broken by the independent diagnosis of Antonio Villadot, a surgeon employed by FC Barcelona. His opinion had been clear: under the knife.

After the operation I lay in a daze in recovery. Marti stood at the foot of my bed, with an assistant alongside him. And even though I hadn't fully come round, I realized that this was dreadful news. He repeated most of what he had to say, so I could take it all in, but I just wasn't awake enough to respond properly. I knew from my previous appointments with him that he wasn't accustomed to being challenged and there was something about him that stopped you simply arguing with him.

What Marti had to say boiled down to the fact that my ankle had suffered serious damage. The lateral ankle ligaments had been torn some time ago, possibly even against Groningen, 11 months before. He explained that playing elite sport without the support of the ankle ligaments that hold the joint in place can be disastrous. A tear like this can pull off small fragments of bone where the ligaments attach to the bone. Incredibly painful, but that's not all. These fragments can find their way between the two bones that together form the joint, which makes matters even worse. Playing on can seriously damage the cartilage, and cartilage is the only protection you have between these two bones. And that's exactly what I had been doing for nearly a year – playing on.

There are two layers of cartilage to protect the joint. The bottom layer was badly damaged and while it had recovered a little, cartilage doesn't really ever come back as strong by itself. Marti had now screwed the ligaments to the joint. I had to take time to rehabilitate properly and stop at once if I felt any pain. Then I would be able to return to top level sport. But it was impossible to say for how long. He asked if what he had said was clear.

I briefly nodded my sleepy head and then let it fall back on the pillow. The news was painfully clear. And unthinkable.

ONCE A FINISHER...

You put up with a lot playing up front. I had once told my father I didn't want to play up front any more, but would rather play in midfield. I think I was about 12. I always played against older, bigger boys and was kicked to death. One day I'd had enough, but my father said: 'Midfielders, they're ten a penny, but good strikers are rare.' He wouldn't hear of it. So I took a deep breath and carried on playing up front.

In his first season as coach at Ajax, Cruyff put me at number 10 once, with Bosman as the lone striker, as an experiment. He saw me more in the role he himself had often played: the 'false nine', attacking, in the middle. He wanted me to play in a freer position, less dependent on the team, where I could dictate the play more, Platini style. Which I could indeed have done, but it would have meant a change of approach, requiring a different kind of fitness and a different kind of game. But I actually rather enjoyed being the finisher.

Bosman was also starting to score freely at the time and suddenly went ahead of me on the top scorers' list. This brought me up with a bump: wait a minute. What are we going to do about this? I wasn't happy about it at all. I was a bit too proud for that. I wanted to be decisive.

But Johan had grown up with players like Alfredo Di Stéfano, Real Madrid's Argentinian playmaker, in the late fifties and early sixties. He was a player who used to cover the entire pitch, which was the ideal for Johan. Five-time European Cup winner, scored in every final. That appealed to Johan's imagination. A complete footballer, in central midfield.

At Ajax, while Johan was coach, there was more freedom to drop back into midfield and play attractive football. Ultimately, it was more satisfying, being the number 10, being the playmaker. More stylish. But there came a time when I put it to one side. It was a case of yes, I believe it, and actually it was early enough in my career to come back to it again later on.

Once I began to play in Italy I concentrated more and more on finishing. My focus was on scoring, finishing pure and simple. Because there it's sacred. Being decisive. I could understand that and that's what I was good at.

I was a better goalscorer than Johan Cruyff, but he was much more of an all-round footballer. I also practised a lot as a finisher. I would encounter situations in front of goal so often that I actually became more skilful in how to handle them.

In Italy the top scorer in Serie A is called the *Capo Cannonieri* – king of the strikers. I like that. It's the way I feel too, I'm a finisher.

HOLLAND (1)

'And on the eighth day God created Marco'

Euro '88

ONE-TO-ONE WITH JOHAN

He came in hard, shoulder to shoulder. I leaned into him with my left shoulder while keeping the ball away from him under my right foot. He feinted as if to pass me on my left, but when I responded, I was suddenly pushing at thin air. He had turned lightning quick to my right and was trying to flick the ball away from under my foot, but my foot held firm. Despite his clever move he was unable to get the ball off me. He began to laugh and said: 'You're starting to look good again.'

It was a dull afternoon at Amsterdam's Olympiaplein ground, mid-February 1988. I was rehabilitating after the major ankle operation by Dr Marti in November. It had been three months now and physiotherapist Reinier van Dantzig had given me the go-ahead to start doing something with the ball again. Finally. I had just come over from Milan and he gave me the good news following his examination. I had grown impatient, and Milan too, but the lesson of last year had been hard and clear. Don't play if you're in pain, recover properly first.

Now Reinier was saying that I could even try some one-to-one duels. I needed no second bidding and immediately phoned Vinkeveen from his office. Johan, who had been sacked by Ajax a month before, jumped straight in his car. He had time on his hands of course. Barely an hour later we were kicking a ball about on the wet pitch at Swift's ground. It was dull, but we did have some fun. We started with a bit of tapping back and forth, but we steadily got more intense. Soon we were going hammer and tongs at one-to-one duels. Wonderful. Finally kicking a ball again, with hardly anyone looking on. That was one of the great things about Johan, he would do things like that. He had never lost that boyish enthusiasm and I could see he was enjoying it too.

Reinier stood watching and saw that my ankle was holding up okay, although we would have to see what the next day would bring. Anyway, it gave me hope of a return at Milan. Maybe a few sub appearances this year, although I was really aiming for next season. It was in any event a lost first year at Milan.

My ankle had withstood the first test, that was the main thing. 'No more rushing things.' Dr Marti had been clear about that. But having a kickabout in the rain with Johan on a Tuesday afternoon in Amsterdam was enough to make me happy. I could play again. Not for a moment did I give any thought to the European Championship that day.

AWAKE IN A STRANGE WORLD
Strange as it may seem, during the night of 19 to 20 May 1988 I was lying on a mattress on top of a desk in an office space in a Milan hospital. It had been a crazy evening: I had briefly suffered short-term memory loss, following a hefty smack on my cheekbone from the Real Madrid keeper. It had happened in a friendly match against the Spanish champions. This was a game Milan had arranged after winning the championship, to see how we might get on at European level. In the weeks before, I had finally got some game time under my belt and I had made my first appearance as a sub against Empoli on 10 April.

I was on the bench for those last five games. The team was doing well, so there was no reason to change anything, but I was still able to come on as a sub a few times. This included the decider away to

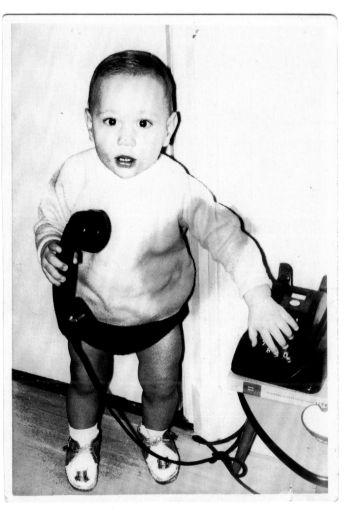

Marco as a baby.

Marco (centre) with sister Carla and brother Stanley.

Marco (front row, second from left) at EDO Utrecht, his first team, 1970.

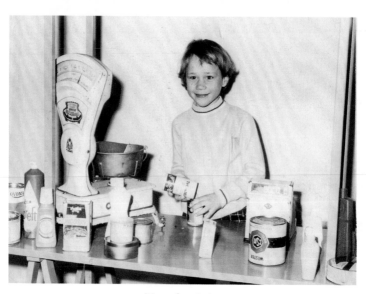

Marco, late sixties.

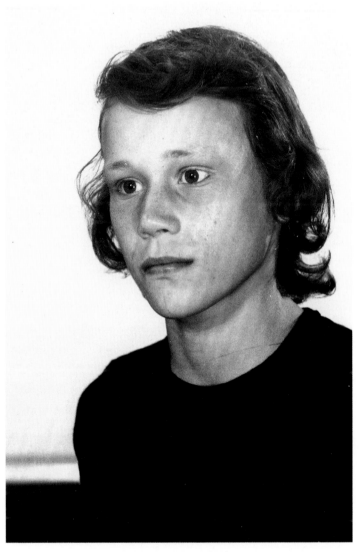

Marco at primary school.

Marco in his UVV kit at the tournament in France.

Ajax youth team in 1981.

Marco and his mother at the table, early seventies.

St Nicholas' Eve, early eighties. Marco (holding gift of a silver boot),
Carla and Stanley.

Marco outside the family home on Wagenaarkade, 2 May 1985.

Marco and his father at Lake Garda, early seventies.

CAVIA$

NIKE

MA[R]

R.C UTREG

le coq

e best SPORT[IF]

FC UTREST

V[B]ASTEN

funest

IN DE G[A]

CRUIJFF NR1 ooh, Serah, Serah

QUE CERA

F.C.U.

M[B] 10

le coq sportif

C

SKULLHEAD

BUNNIK SIDE

AV

UEF

BASTA - BOOMM

WE NEVER WALK ALLONE

{ blessure in ø pour moi jetzt }

LOKKERTJE, ZWERVER

D.B.E.

FUCK YOU !!

IK BEN DE BESTE!

KS

-ooo

F.C. UTREC[H]

NT GRE[E]N

FUCK OFF

Marco in his room in Johan Wagenaarkade, around 1980
(© UTRECHTS NIEUWSBLAD, MICHAEL KOOREN).

Marco and his father at home in Utrecht, around 1980 (© HARM DE GRIJS).

Marco with Ricky Testa la Muta in his Pro Patria kit, 1987.

Marco at Ajax, aged 17.

Marco doing national service, 1986.

Marco at the Under-20 World Cup in Mexico, 1983.

Marco and Dutch national coach Rinus Michels, 1984
(© FOTOPERSBUREAU WIM HENDRIKS).

Ibiza, summer 1985.

Aad de Mos, Kees Rijvers and Marco with the Golden Boot, '85–'86
(© TELEGRAAF, JAN STAPPENBELD).

Maradona's Napoli, where I scored from a pass from Ruud. It didn't feel like my championship though, because I had a different objective. For me every minute I played counted. I had to regain my match fitness so I could return after the summer. I had shown Milan too little of myself so far. Fortunately, Ruud had been attracting all the attention and it was really his title.

Five days before the start of preparations for the European Championship I had surgery on my broken cheekbone in Amsterdam. I arrived at the Dutch team's training camp in Noordwijk with a battered face and a massive bruise around my left eye, which turned a different colour of the rainbow every day. It was my visiting card.

On 1 June, 11 days before the Euros, we played a friendly against Romania in the Olympic Stadium. I came on in place of Van 't Schip after 60 minutes and played outside-left. We won 2-0, but I made little impact. Michels stuck with John Bosman as lone striker, with Gullit behind him. He had been successful with this in the run-up to the Euros, so why would he change things now?

After the match I met Johan just outside the stadium. He took me to one side and was quite unequivocal: 'You mustn't let yourself be misused by Michels, you're not an outside-left. You must play as a striker or you'd be better off staying at home.' He kept on about it: 'Why did he put you at outside-left? Why did you go along with that? You know you're a striker, don't you? You're the best striker there is. So what's Michels doing? If I were you, I wouldn't take the risk. If you play outside-left, there's a good chance you won't play well. And then people will have plenty to say.'

He was making perfect sense and it got me thinking. However, I hadn't been able to play at all for the last six months and everything I was doing now to get back to full fitness was so I could do better in the new season at Milan. In the end that was the most important thing for me.

I told him: 'I understand what you mean and I hear what you say. But I'm just glad to be playing again. All the training and playing I can do now can only be of benefit to me with next season in mind. Because I want to play well at Milan; that's what I'm obliged to do, after losing the whole of last year.'

In the days before the tournament I wasn't worried about playing in the Euros. I just wanted to get fit and that was how I felt as I got on the bus to West Germany.

GLORIFIED TRAINING CAMP

In that week before the Euros I just enjoyed the training. I had no trouble at all with the pressure. We often played a game between the starting line-up and the reserves, 10 v. 10 or 11 v. 11. The crazy thing was that the reserves, with Kieft and me, won nearly all those games. It was strange and Michels began to pick up on it as well.

I also did some extra training with Bert van Lingen and Monne de Wit, the physiotherapist. I wanted to get some hard yards under my belt, because I had a lot of catching up to do. Not every day, but I regularly did an extra session on my own in the afternoon after the collective morning session. Getting lots done. The other players noticed this, as did the coach of course. In any event I was making an impression. They were saying things like: 'Well, he's really up for it.'

And it was true. It was clear in my mind; I had no expectations because I was completely unconcerned about the Euros. Bosman was playing, I wasn't. I was simply there to get better. So for me it was nothing more than a glorified training camp.

Then came that opening game against the Soviet Union. I could see from the bench that we were playing well, but having no luck.

I came on half an hour before the end. It went reasonably well, but I didn't score. The Russians did though. A poor start.

Michels completely changed the team around after that. Out went the 4-3-3 and in came a classic 4-4-2. Schip was left out, Bosman likewise and Erwin Koeman came in. Michels had played Bosman and Gullit throughout qualifying, but that defeat changed everything. I had made an impression, perhaps in the last half an hour against the Soviet Union, but certainly in training, so I came into the starting eleven. Up front.

IN THE STARTING ELEVEN

When Michels included my name in the first eleven against England I knew it was getting serious. Only now were the Euros really beginning for me and it was no longer a training camp. My name on that piece of paper – that set the place on fire. Immediately there was a different mood. We had lost the first game and now the pressure was really on. We had to do it this time.

Playing in the final stages of a tournament is what you do it all for. It's what you've trained so hard for and what you've played all those matches for. But you never know what's going to happen and so there's always a certain tension. However, you need that tension; it helps you, it's what makes you sharp. As a professional you go through a process of increasing nervousness every game and gradually you learn how to deal with it. It's different for everyone and it's not something you can write down in a textbook.

I was often fairly tense before important matches because I was already going through the match in my head, seeing specific situations in my mind's eye. The skill for me then was to put the match 'away' for a while, to keep my mind off it as much as possible, while at the same time preparing myself for it. It was a dilemma. How do you relax in such a situation? How do you get any rest?

A game of cards or larking around with Schip would always help me. An afternoon nap. A distraction. Each of us has his own way.

One player will read a book, another will get overexcited. In situations like this I actually became a little quieter, a little more withdrawn. I would try to prepare myself down to the last detail, to ensure I didn't leave anything to chance.

But if you aren't tense enough, things can go awry, you won't have that sharpness. Then again, if I was too tense, I sometimes got cramp. And if I got cramp, that was it, I couldn't do anything. Some players can keep playing, but not me. Just get me off the pitch!

And now, England. I hadn't played for a long time, not in the starting eleven anyway. I didn't sleep on the afternoon of the Holland–England game. And I knew that all eyes would be upon us.

Someone who was well used to situations like this was Ted Troost, a haptotherapist (someone who uses touch to treat tension). He could soothe away the tensions in your body and straight away you felt fresh again. You didn't have to tell him anything; he could just feel what was wrong and what he had to do and afterwards you would feel calmer.

I had come across him at Milan through Ruud. He worked with other national team players too, but he wasn't allowed to visit our hotel during the Euros. The team doctor Frits Kessel had a problem with him. Ted was probably seen as a bit of an oddball, all a bit hocus-pocus, too alternative. They didn't want the press getting wind of him, because then the newspapers and TV programmes would all start asking questions that Kessel would have to answer. What's all this about then? What's Ted Troost doing exactly? Is it medically justified? They weren't at all ready for that at the Dutch FA.

Ted stayed in a different hotel, not far from ours. A few of us would go to see him and he would treat us one at a time, Gullit, Van Breukelen and me. The Dutch FA were paying for his hotel. Two years later, at Italia '90, when Rinus Michels, by then technical director at the Dutch FA, saw Troost entering the team hotel, he made a point of closing his eyes. He was saying: 'I haven't seen you, but you seem to be doing something useful for the players, so I'm not going to make a fuss about it. You have my blessing.'

Ted's an unusual character, a special individual. But he managed to do something to help me deal with the tension better, to get my body loose. That's what mattered, that it helped. Never mind all the rest, the song and dance that went with it. To be provocative I once said: 'So? Even if he just sits on me. If it helps, it's fine.'

What counted, just before England, was that I was fairly rested. Ruud was certainly weary; he had a very long season behind him. I hadn't, I was completely fresh. Everything was like new again. I had had to wait for eight months to be able to play football again. So yes, I was really up for it.

PRECISION WORK & SEA OF JOY

The relief that came with my first goal against England was huge, as you can see from the way I celebrate. That goal felt liberating. The tension had been so great. First match lost, then twice nearly going behind in the first half. This was the moment.

It isn't that I can still feel that goal physically, but I can see it vividly in my head. I think it's seared into many people's minds. Gullit went down the left and passed the ball with the outside of his right foot. I took it under my left foot with my back to goal. The ball instantly dead. Defender at my back, Tony Adams.

Then it came to the crunch. Lightning quick I turned on my axis to face the goal. With a quick chip I transferred the ball to my left foot, just out of the defender's reach. The incoming defender got a slight touch on my shot, so the ball ended up in the far corner, out of the keeper's reach.

It was pure instinct. At this level it's all instinct really, whether it's Tony Adams or someone else behind you. You subconsciously take in the information about his posture and how he's moving. That's automatic. You have to go past him. The second you move, your touch takes over.

At the very top the difference is infinitesimal, imperceptible, but nevertheless decisive. One player is a fraction quicker than another. They are both doing all they can to be the quicker. Or the more skilful. That's how it often seems. But sometimes the motor system or physique of one of them is just slightly better. The differences are minimal and only a few are decisive. Scoring or missing. The difference is in the detail. A better technique, greater perception, a faster reaction. One player brushes the ball with his foot just half a millimetre higher, in exactly the right place. Another touches the leather three millimetres further on, bringing instant disaster. One of them sets off a quarter of a millisecond earlier, because he sees things quicker, and is therefore in the right place at the right time, while the other one is a fraction late. It is aspects such as these that ultimately make the difference at the very top. Just like at this European Championship.

I ended up scoring a hat-trick against England. That was the greatest good fortune. When you're the one who does what all those orange shirts are willing you to do. When the stadium explodes and everyone goes crazy, when a country goes wild. I once called it a 'sea of joy'. There is a terrific explosion of joy anyway when you score, but a full stadium like that increases it tenfold. And when you know it's on TV as well, it increases a hundredfold. Then you explode.

The first of my three goals against England was pure relief, the second validation and the third bordered on the unbelievable.

REAL BITE AGAINST THE GERMANS

We moved to a different hotel for the semi-final against West Germany in Hamburg, which was good, a welcome change of scene. I remember watching the other semi-final, Italy v. Soviet Union, with John the evening before. A really dirty game, with lots of yellow cards and injuries. That's fine, we thought, let them finish each other off.

There was more tension surrounding the match against Germany. For many it was very emotionally charged, in part because of the Second World War but also because of 1974 of course. I had no time for that anti-German sentiment. I didn't feel it was relevant to my generation, because we hadn't really grown up with it. We knew what had happened, but our sole concern was the football.

When you're playing the host country and they're also the favourites, everyone is extra motivated anyway. Van Breukelen went completely nuts, getting everyone involved, while Frank Mill screamed loudly in his ear. You couldn't avoid it, everyone being a bit hyperactive.

In the first half we had a bit too much respect for Germany. They just had the edge and had a few good chances. After half-time we actually went behind, through that undeserved penalty. We immediately changed our game and seized the initiative; Koeman, Rijkaard, Van Breukelen and I stirred things up considerably as we picked up our game. It had a real bite to it, attacking and going in hard. The penalty I won was just as debatable as the German one, as the referee conceded afterwards, but Koeman converted it and so it was 1-1.

From that point on we began to dominate. On the pitch we felt we were getting better and outclassing the Germans. The score though stayed level. Then came the 89th minute. We had several players capable of making a good pass, Mühren, Rijkaard, Van 't Schip, and of course Jan Wouters. He had a real knack for putting the ball in just the right place. His pass to me was perfect. I had to slide, as it was the only way I could reach it, and I just got there. I toe-punted the ball as hard as I could and, wonder of wonders, the ball flew into the far corner.

I thought that Franz Beckenbauer, the German coach, made a great gesture after the game. He came into our dressing room and congratulated us: 'Well played, my compliments to you.' I was impressed. And we had played well. But even so.

That night we celebrated in Hamburg, though we kept it respectable. Our other halves were there too. We danced and for the first time saw the pictures from Holland. How the country had gone mad. What we had unleashed was incredible. Many people saw the match against Germany as the real final. Michels himself said as much later on. But for me there was only one final.

GIFT FROM GOD
Germany was fine, but I had my heart set on the main prize. We had something to prove against the Soviet Union after that opening defeat. In the days before the final I said: 'Holland have been runners-up a few times, it's time we won something.' That's how it felt, a great chance to write history.

On 25 June 1988, two hours before the final, we walked round the pitch at the Olympic Stadium in Munich. The same stadium where, in 1974, Holland had lost the World Cup final we really should have won. Michels had been the coach that day too. And there was a banner in the stadium that read: And on the eighth day God created Marco.

We kicked off at 3.30 and the game swung this way and that. With half an hour gone the ball was played forward high in the air. I could have headed it goalward myself, but heading it back to Ruud seemed a better idea. He really smacked the ball home with his head. 1-0.

The second half was barely ten minutes old when the cross came in from the foot of Arnold Mühren. He was without doubt a gifted left-footer, perceptive and sophisticated, but this particular ball wasn't one of his best. Actually, it was rather aimless. But it was one of those days when everything came good.

As the cross came down, I thought okay, for heaven's sake just smash it at the goal. I haven't got the energy to do anything else with it. Then I watched as it flew in. From an impossible angle. Behind Rinat Dasayev, at the time the best keeper in the world: 2-0.

A goal like that just happens. You know how you want to hit it to send it in a certain direction, but for it to turn out like that…

Once the ball had flown in, I was in a state of total disbelief. Wow, what just happened? You can see it in my face as I run back to my own half. I didn't believe it myself. Teammates asked me: 'What happened there? How did you do that?' But you can see I had no idea.

The strange thing about that goal technically was that I no longer had a full range of movement in my right foot. Since my ankle ligaments had been fixed in that operation in November '87, I had reduced mobility there and could no longer take on such a ball at full power. With a good ankle I would very probably never have scored that goal.

And ultimately maybe it was a kind of 'Divine Intervention', because of what happened to my ankle. I really do believe that. A certain balance between unfairness and payback. In a way that goal was a gift from God.

The game briefly became tense again when we conceded a penalty, but Van Breukelen saved Igor Belanov's effort. Half an hour later referee Michel Vautrot blew the final whistle.

Finally. Champions.

HERO IN SOCKS

After the final against the Soviet Union we carried Michels around on our shoulders. I got a little carried away. While he was suspended in the air, I removed one of his shoes. I was curious to see how he would react, what it would do to him, the great Mr Michels. When we put him down again, he was standing there in a single shoe and a single sock. A really childish prank, ha-ha. Actually I should have pulled his sock off too.

There were many things Michels did very well. He kept a tight rein on the training camp and ensured spirits remained high. He had really good communication skills and would put us in our place if need be. He was a character, let me put it that way. And to us he was also a man advanced in years, which commanded respect. He had achieved a lot as a coach, at Ajax and at Barcelona, so he was dyed in the wool and we appreciated that.

But when it came to tactics, well, I didn't see them then. And I didn't really see them later either. He just got us playing those practice games, 11 v. 11, or 10 v. 10, and then didn't say much. He just watched.

But we played football to win. It wasn't about the performance, but about beating our opponents. We had been absent from a few tournaments, so we played pragmatically, with no frills. The stronger we grew as a team, the greater the belief in our ranks. We had top players in good positions, like Koeman, Rijkaard, Wouters, Gullit and me. Good players in the right places gives you an edge and Michels managed to get the job done.

He started out with a 4-3-3 formation against the Soviets but very quickly ditched it after that game. Then we played an old-fashioned 4-4-2, with Ruud as a kind of free man and me up front.

We also had an incredible amount of good fortune. Against England the ball landed on the back of Koeman's head. A free kick from Glenn Hoddle hit the post behind Van Breukelen before going out. In the opening match we did have some bad luck, but against the Republic of Ireland a lot of good luck. I was actually offside when Kieft scored his goal. We started well, but the Irish were dangerous too, though it turned out all right in the end.

Michels later wrote a book about football and his 1988 success. I didn't think it was a good read as far as tactics were concerned. To my mind Cruyff was the one who really understood tactics, he was the one who could use them to make a difference. Michels was more of a man manager, a good coach.

INTERNATIONAL BREAKTHROUGH

The strange thing about the euphoria surrounding our winning the European Championship was that I immediately felt the need to bring us all back down to earth. An hour after the final I said: 'Let's not go overboard. Next week we'll all be back at the supermarket again.' Offering a little counterbalance to all the superlatives. And we still had the canal cruise and the visit to the Queen to come.

Exactly like that goal in the final. There were whole stories you could tell about it. We happened to play Germany in a friendly five months later and for fun I said: 'Give it to me again.' This time I think I put it 28 metres over and 23 metres wide.

Any search for an explanation of why everything fell into place for me in '88 is difficult, because actually it's inexplicable. It just happened. You do the very best you can, but it's not something you can make happen. You're a professional footballer by occupation and suddenly you get the chance at the highest level.

It can make you feel very nervous, but you have to deal with it.

I had been on the biggest stage of all for the first time. The whole world had been watching and I had risen to the occasion. I had been decisive, several times, in fact. For me it had also been unreal and suddenly everyone had started asking questions: how is it possible? How do you do that?

But it's still inexplicable. Everything just fell into place in '88. It's not something that happens very often – everything didn't fall into place at the World Cup in 1990. And by then I was supposedly a better player than I had been in 1988. It isn't straightforward in the way of: 'If I work hard, I'll achieve this.' There's always something unpredictable, some element of good fortune.

But maybe there's something in my character that helps, so that things end up going the right way more often than not. When I set my mind to something, I'm single-minded. I shut myself off from everything around me, even though I'm really no less nervous than anyone else.

It's the same with golf. When I'm putting, I'm just as nervous as the next man. I stand there shaking on that final putt. But then I shut myself right off. I don't get flustered. Technically anyone could make that shot, but mentally it's a completely different story. I shut myself off and think: this is the only putt that counts. And then I just pop it in, despite everything that's going on around me. Afterwards everything comes back into focus. You just cope with the tensions and the doubts and do what you have to do. But it's a struggle every time. It's all to do with mindset and having your eyes on the prize.

I believe those people who force their way to the top are trained mentally to win frequently. Take Roger Federer. Such a great champion. He can be emotional after a Grand Slam final. And I can understand that, because he too has experienced doubts after crucial poor shots. He has to get through that mentally. It's a struggle that gives you the strength to learn how to deal with those doubts. He fights his way through it and eventually very often finds a way to win. If after five hours in the final the tears sometimes flow freely, it's because of the total release resulting from that mental struggle.

When he became very emotional after losing the Australian Open Final in 2009, there was a lot of talk about it. But I understood exactly what had happened. I wrote him a short note to give him a lift. And to say that I understood. It was something I was sure he would appreciate.

For me the European Championship in '88 was just like a Grand Slam win after five sets and five hours. Such a release. Everything that had happened was also incredible. Ultimately, I had played a tournament that I could or should never even have dreamed of. I had scored five goals and three of them had been decisive.

If I'm honest, I had actually spent the 18 months leading up to that tournament sailing into a headwind and had then had the good fortune to suddenly find the wind with me, full in my sails. Because in the end this European Championship was my great international breakthrough, even though Johan had advised me not to go at all. He never actually mentioned it again. After the European Championship though he did make me a serious offer to go to Barcelona, where he had been appointed the new coach. I did think about it briefly, but in the end I declined because I still had to show what I could do in Milan.

PART II

AC MILAN, ITALIA '90 AND
THE BEST IN THE WORLD

1988–1992

PLASTIC BAGS AND TENNIS SOCKS

1987

There were quite a few things Ruud and I had to get used to in Italy. Wherever we went with Milan, the fans were always there in large numbers. They created a terrific atmosphere with their singing and their clapping. There was one song though that we used to hear wherever we went.

It was a short refrain that Ruud and I very soon came to recognize, but couldn't really hear properly. 'What is it they keep singing?'

'I've no idea, it sounds a bit like "Hugo Lasagne" or something like that.'

'He must be a real star, because we hear it at every ground.'

So we asked the other Milan players, who told us that, before they start singing, the fans everywhere chant '*Tutto lo Stadio*', which means something along the lines of 'All together now', to get everyone to join in, ha-ha. People would also regularly come up to me for an autograph or a photo, even if I was sitting injured in the stands. They would always tell me what they wanted me to write under the autograph as a dedication. 'For Claudio, with much affection', for example. In Italian this is: '*Per Claudio, con simpatia*'. Or '*Per Pietro, con affetto*', 'For Pietro, with love'. There were a few variations on this theme.

One day there was a group of supporters who all had this sort of request. The last one said: 'Please will you sign your autograph "*per esteso*".' I took this to be the name of a friend of hers so I signed the autograph and underneath wrote: '*Per Esteso, con simpatia*'. Perfectly done, so I thought. They began to laugh, so I asked: what's wrong? It turned out that '*per esteso*' means 'in full'.

My teammates also laughed at me once because I thought Emporio Armani was a brother of Giorgio Armani. It just goes to show how much I knew.

The Italians are far more obsessed with appearance than we are. This became quite clear in the early days. I remember that Ruud and I would arrive at Milanello with our toiletries in plastic bags and wearing tennis socks and trainers. The Italians did things differently. They wore highly polished leather shoes that matched the colour of their belts. Just as their socks matched their suits. And they kept their toiletries in a stylish leather case. It took us quite a while to get used to all this. They must have taken us for a right pair of country bumpkins, with our white tennis socks and our tube of toothpaste in a plastic bag. Something else that was completely new to us was that after showering they dried their hair with a hairdryer. Ruud and I had never seen this in Holland, men drying their hair with a hairdryer.

We used to have a hot meal at lunchtime at Milanello. Being Dutch we were accustomed to munch, munch, munch, finished, but there they took their time. The Italians would get themselves comfortable. More than that, they would even conduct entire conversations about the food. I remember Ancelotti talking about a special Parma ham that had to be carved in a particular way. They talked about how to prepare pasta, which sauce went best with it, and then how to prepare the meat. The others would ponder this at length. Whole stories. We wondered what we had let ourselves in for. What was this all about?

MILAN (2)

Barcelona turns red and black

24 May 1989

The crowd was moving ever closer to the bus in the streets around Plaça de Catalunya. The square itself was a sea of people. The driver was trying to manoeuvre through the masses, but sometimes he had to wait until the crush was past.

I was sitting by the window. Everywhere I looked I could see Milan fans and red and black flags. You could hear the songs through the windows of the bus. We knew that much of Milan had come to Barcelona, but no one had expected it to be on such a massive scale. The day before, when we had gone to train in the stadium, it had still been relatively quiet, with small groups of Milan fans here and there. But this crowd was unprecedented.

From time to time we looked at each other in the bus. What could go wrong? Nothing really, unless we failed to reach Camp Nou in time. But no one, except perhaps the driver, who was really getting worried, seemed concerned. We were Milan. Nothing would happen to us.

The day I arrived at AC Milan I realized it was a different world. Italy and Holland couldn't really be compared, certainly not at a sporting level. At Ajax football was a bit more laid-back, casual even. Of course, I'd had the chance to work with Cruyff, which was unique and beyond compare, but in terms of dedication and importance, being a professional footballer in Italy was much more than a job, it was a real vocation.

Just look at how much and how often they write about football in the papers. You couldn't keep up with it all even if you wanted to. Not long after arriving in Italy I decided to stop reading them, apart from anything else because the press sometimes had a rather casual relationship with the truth. I soon learned all the escape routes out of Milanello, so I could avoid the journalists. The press simply distracted me from what I was really concerned about: becoming an even better footballer.

The team was one of enthusiasts and their dedication was exceptional. That was something we shared. They loved the sport and they wanted to get the best out of themselves. Players like Baresi, Maldini, Tassotti and Costacurta, but also Donadoni, Evani and Massaro. And Carlo Ancelotti, who had come from AS Roma. They were all young men who lived for their sport. When they were eating, it was in the service of football. When they were resting, same story. When they spoke, they spoke about their sport. Everyone was dedicated and the outside world was a faraway place. Few outside influences found their way in.

I found myself caught up in this Milan culture. We lived as full-time professionals and had just one aim: to win matches. Nothing else mattered. I think this attitude was that great Milan side's greatest strength.

I thought it was wonderful to have nothing to worry about but football. Milanello for me was football paradise, where I was constantly trying to get better without distractions but with kindred spirits at a high level. That was the best thing for me, especially when I could finally join in training and matches again after that episode with my ankle.

That season I had already scored 19 times in Serie A and in the European Cup I had scored seven goals up to that evening in Barcelona.

As I stared out of the window at the crowds of red and black in the streets of Barcelona, I thought about the fact that the Milan fans had had to wait 20 years for this European Cup final. In 1969 they had beaten Cruyff and Keizer's Ajax 4-1, but there had been far less success since then. In all that time the fans had had to make do with memories of the glorious Milan side of the fifties and sixties, with the great Gianni Rivera.

In the years of Ajax and Cruyff and then of Bayern and Liverpool, Italian football had increasingly faded into the background, one reason being the ban on foreign players. But when I was at Lake Garda with my parents on holiday, the talk was always of Milan, Inter and Juve. We didn't know much about Serie A in Holland, but at Lake Garda I was aware that *calcio* (football) was on everyone's lips.

Once Maradona had made Napoli champions, all eyes turned towards Italy again. The ban on foreign players had been lifted and from 1987 Italian clubs were again allowed to play two foreigners, increasing to three in 1988. Silvio Berlusconi hadn't hesitated. He had bought Milan in 1986 and had huge ambition, which he backed up with targeted purchases. He had given the fans hope again after all the lean years and wanted to make Milan not just the best club in Italy, but the best club in the world.

On that bus I realized that it had only been three years since Berlusconi had acquired Milan. And until only recently, if you were a Milan fan, you would have considered this impossible: that this evening in Barcelona, 24 May 1989, we could become the best club in Europe. Obviously, staying at home in Milan in those circumstances was absolutely not an option.

It had been a strange year. After the European Championship in Germany I had returned to Milan with my reputation enhanced. I had also just been awarded the Ballon d'Or, ahead of Ruud Gullit and Frank Rijkaard, who came second and third. All eyes had been on me, but the pressure I put on myself had been far greater. I had looked upon my first year at Milan as a lost year, so I felt that I had to make up for it now. The '88–'89 season had to be my season. The good news was that Frank Rijkaard had joined us at Milan that summer.

The season before, Arrigo Sacchi must have asked me a hundred times what I thought of Frank. Frank's messy year, and the fact that he had signed two contracts at the same time, put doubts in Sacchi's mind, but there came a time when I had had enough. Every time I said he would be an asset, but how often did I have to say it? Fortunately, it finally happened. We could make very good use of a midfielder of his calibre at Milan.

I felt that Sacchi set things up very well defensively, but up front it was mainly Gullit, who ran for two. Pietro Paolo Virdis, up front alongside Ruud, was far less of a runner. I was delighted with Rijkaard's arrival. He really would add something to our attacking play, especially when he played alongside Carlo Ancelotti.

The bus continued to move slowly, but we were gradually nearing the stadium. We had already heard that it would be completely full of Milan fans. In part that was because we were playing Steaua Bucharest. The Iron Curtain was still in existence then, so only a few of their fans were allowed to cross the border. The Romanians had therefore returned nearly all of their tickets to UEFA, which had then made them all available to Milan fans. Even though the final was in Barcelona, a thousand kilometres from Milan by road, there was a real exodus under way. Fans had travelled by car, by plane, by train and by coach. No more than a few thousand Romanians were expected, the rest would be Milan fans. Just shy of 100,000 spectators in Europe's biggest stadium. I tried to imagine what kind of atmosphere that would create. A full San Siro was imposing enough, but this would be the absolute pinnacle.

It had so nearly all gone wrong in the second round against Red Star Belgrade. It had ended 1-1 at the San Siro. And in Belgrade, on 9 November, it proved to be our good fortune that the match was abandoned because of fog with Red Star leading 1-0. UEFA decided to replay the match in its entirety a day later, starting at 0-0. That was a stroke of luck. Ted Troost was flown in post-haste from Holland to get Ruud fit in time. I scored in the first half but Red Star immediately equalized. The two teams couldn't be separated after 90 minutes and extra time but we managed to hold our nerve in the penalty shoot-out.

Waiting for us after the quarter-final tie against Werder Bremen, which we won thanks to a penalty I converted, were the mighty Real Madrid, where Leo Beenhakker was the coach. In Spain we kept it to 1-1 with my equalizer coming midway through the second half, but the return leg at the San Siro was an historic night. We really turned it on and won 5-0, with Frank, Ruud and me scoring, along with Ancelotti and Donadoni.

It was a potent feeling to be part of such a strong team, one that had succeeded in putting our opponents under pressure quite so emphatically. Even when we didn't have the ball. After two seasons our patterns of play were increasingly natural. Sacchi's system was a strong one of course, but in the end the quality of the players was the deciding factor. It was the victory over Real in an ecstatic San Siro that had brought us here to Barcelona, to this final.

It had been a crazy journey from the Ritz Hotel to Camp Nou. You could see the astonishment on the faces of all the players. This was something out of the ordinary. Out of nowhere a sense of invincibility had emerged, the realization that something quite extraordinary was going to have to happen here this evening if we weren't to win. When we went on the pitch, we felt the same overwhelming sensation once more. The whole stadium coloured red and black, people going completely off their heads. Ancelotti said: 'Much can happen in life, but we cannot lose here.'

It was clear that this final could salvage our season. Early elimination from the Coppa Italia was one thing, but in the championship race we had had to concede to Inter, our arch rivals.

We were on top from the kick-off and were three up by half-time. We really did make each other play better, that was the strength of this team. Donadoni was outstanding, Gullit played well, Baresi, Rijkaard, Maldini and Tassotti too. In fact, everyone was on top form that day. In the end it wasn't really a match at all. We won by a mile. We were dominant. Ruud's 1-0 was just a tap-in after a bit of a scrimmage, but the other three were really good goals. Ruud's volley from the edge of the box was pure class.

The second goal, my first, was the header. I dived in front of my man, through the air, and hammered the ball hard into the left corner, across goal. A real cracker! The cross came from Tassotti, which was extra special.

In the second half I scored the last goal, after a lovely through ball from Rijkaard. I worked my way behind my man and shot into the far corner with my left foot: 4-0.

Afterwards it was alleged our opponents had been bribed. The Romanians weren't that well paid and being swept away 4-0 did look a bit suspicious, but it was utter rubbish. We were simply outstandingly good that day, with everyone so competitive. And of course, we had the fans.

Berlusconi, naturally, was on the pitch as well. It was his club. It had been his plan and now we were the best in Europe. He took great pleasure from that. Apart from the fact that he was chairman, he was also a real Milan fan. He was proud as a peacock when we hoisted him on our shoulders and afterwards he said it was one of the greatest nights of his life. That I thought was fantastic.

It says something about his passion and his single-mindedness. We celebrated long into the night in Barcelona, which for once had turned red and black.

500 GUILDERS

We weren't very well off at home and my father took all kinds of extra jobs to make ends meet. We weren't poor, but we did have to watch the pennies. For example, for a long time I, as the afterthought, didn't used to sleep in a real bed, but on a camp bed, a sort of foldaway thing. It was in my older sister Carla's room.

The evening before the European Cup final against Steaua in Barcelona we were training at the stadium when I ran into Roy van der Hart, son of old Cor van der Hart, the pro footballer. I knew Roy – he was in advertising and looked after advertising hoardings. He called me over at the end of the session and pointed to a spot slightly to the left of the goal in Camp Nou. 'See that advertising hoarding? The one with laser on it? If you score tomorrow, and then run past that advertising hoarding, I'll give you 500 guilders.'

The match had only just kicked off for the second half. It was 3-0 when I got that through ball from Rijkaard and slipped past the defender. I hit the ball cleanly into the far corner with my left foot. 4-0.

Suddenly, after that goal, that offer of Roy's flashed back into my mind. As a reflex I ran past that advertising hoarding of his. I thought: 500 guilders, thank you very much.

After the match I ran into Roy in the press room. 'So! I owe you 500 guilders, don't I?' he said. Before I had even picked up on what he'd said, he had slipped me the money.

MILAN (3)

'Forgiving is loving too'

Summer 1989

'I wish you every success and will always love you.' These were the words Liesbeth had left in a note for me on the dining table, before getting a taxi from our house to Linate, Milan's airport. She was heading back to Holland, just as preparations for the new season were getting under way.

Those were her last words after a weekend full of tears, when I had told her what was going on. I had finally been honest. I told her I had fallen for someone else who I wanted to get to know better. It came as a complete shock to her, that much was quite obvious that weekend, but she soon gathered herself and took off back to Holland.

When I returned to an empty house a few days later, without her, those words of hers came back to me with a jolt and affected me enormously. Those telephone conversations with that someone else didn't seem quite so compelling any more. I felt I couldn't just give up those three years with Liesbeth.

In Holland she moved back in with her parents and started looking for a job. She started making her own plans. That was really gutsy of her, to accept what had happened and simply pack up and leave. She made it clear it was my choice. My cage was open, as it were, but precisely because of that I was aware of all I had to lose and I missed her dreadfully.

After a couple of weeks I called her and said: 'I've made a dreadful mistake and I'm really very sorry. I knew at once I wouldn't be comfortable with that someone else…' There was no question though of her jumping on the next plane back to Milan. I had to be on my best behaviour for a while. But once she was back, things were fine between us again. Better than ever really.

The lovely thing about Liesbeth is that she really moved on from it all. She didn't harbour any resentment towards me. I think that in the end our honesty was our salvation. I told her what was going on and she was honest with me too. Later I came to understand that the ability to forgive is to love too. I felt extremely grateful that things were okay again. I started playing better football too. And that wasn't all. A little over nine months later our first daughter, Rebecca, was born.

I appreciate that I've been lucky in love. With Liesbeth. I hadn't had the best example from home and I had every intention of doing things better myself. I did follow my feelings in this regard, but you still need some good luck if things are to continue to go well with your partner. We're still very happy together.

Our division of labour was also very clear: Liesbeth concentrated on looking after the family and the home, while I earned our keep. We were both happy with that and it worked well.

In Italy Liesbeth was often alone and this of course was before the days of the internet and international TV broadcasters. Speaking the language was essential and she picked it up very well. What's more, we soon adopted the Italian lifestyle, including the lovely food. And that's remained the case ever since.

I consider myself fortunate. Strangely enough, I'm sure that this episode in the summer of 1989 brought us even closer together.

MILAN (4)

The stolen Scudetto

1989–1990

We had made an average start to the season, but in the spring we were on course for Milan's second national championship since the arrival of Berlusconi, Sacchi and us three, the Dutch contingent. The Napoli of Maradona, Giordano and Careca, known as 'La MaGiCa', were our main rivals, while Inter had also started well, with the three Germans – Klinsmann, Brehme and Matthäus – but we had left them behind in January and February.

We were on a great run, taking 21 points from 11 matches. It was still two points for a win then. On 25 February we beat Napoli 3-0 and cemented our lead. At least, that's what we thought. The league was going to be ending early that year because of the World Cup, which was due to be held in Italy that summer. At the beginning of April we still led Napoli by a point, with three rounds to go. Then strange things started to happen.

It began to look as though there was an inevitability about Napoli becoming champions. On 8 April they played a match at Bergamo that people still talk about today. It was 0-0 and deep into the second half when a coin was thrown from the crowd that hit Napoli's Brazilian Alemao on the head. He didn't initially seem to be in any trouble, but as soon as Napoli's physio reached him, a great to-do broke out.

If you look back at the pictures, you can see the physio saying to Alemao: 'Lie down, lie down.' Very strange.

Alemao was taken to hospital for observation. They really went to town, neurological examination, the whole works. In the end this incident led to the Italian FA awarding the match to Napoli, the rules stipulating a 2-0 win.

The second dubious incident came two weeks later. By this time we had assured ourselves of a place in the European Cup final again, having beaten Bayern Munich over two legs. If Napoli became league champions, and we won the final again, Italy would have two teams in the European Cup, which at that time was still for league champions only.

It very much appeared that this is what the Italian FA wanted to happen, despite our lead over Napoli in the league. With the incident at Bergamo and the two points they had been awarded by the FA, we were now level, although we did have a better goal difference.

On Sunday 22 April, with two rounds to go, we played an away game at relegation candidates Hellas Verona. I've never seen anything like it. The referee, Rosario Lo Bello, did everything he could that day to make sure we lost. He had a really busy day with the whistle.

At one point he gave me a yellow card for an innocuous obstruction. I barely touched my opponent. It was the umpteenth free kick he had given against us, so I asked him: 'What do you think you're doing?' He ignored me. Then, in protest, I took off my shirt and immediately received a second yellow, and therefore red. Rijkaard was also sent off not long after, again for two yellows, again contrived. And then Costacurta was sent off after seeing red. We had eight players left on the pitch. Sacchi too was then sent off. It was a very strange state of affairs and it felt like a put-up job.

Verona would rightly be relegated that season, while we were coming off a wonderful run. But that day, with our eight men, Verona ended up beating us 2-1. Cheated out of two points.

Napoli won a week later at Bologna and were then officially champions, ending up two points in front. It felt like a complete stitch-up. Even all these years later I get angry about it. We were robbed of the championship, at least that's what it felt like.

HOLLAND (2)

The scandal and the shame

Italia '90

For days I just stared out of the window into the enormous garden. Into nothingness. I was being completely unsociable. Everyone knew not to disturb me. I had no wish to watch any more of that World Cup, but most of all I couldn't bear to face anyone. We weren't far from Cannes, in the south of France, in a villa near the sea. Liesbeth was there too of course and our daughter Rebecca. Otherwise almost no one knew where I was and that was exactly how I wanted it.

I was embarrassed. We had disgraced ourselves at the World Cup in Italy. It was the first major setback in my career. Up till then nearly everything had turned to gold, a major trophy each year, the European Cups and a European Championship won. In 1987, 1988, 1989 and 1990, trophies all the way. But now this World Cup. It was a disgrace. I myself had played dreadfully.

In May that year we had won the European Cup with Milan for the second time in a row. At the end of 1989 Frank, Franco Baresi and I had been voted the best three players in Europe and, as European champions in 1988, we were among the contenders for the world title. That didn't mean we had one hand on the cup, but with the squad we had we were clearly capable of competing for the main prize. Things actually went wrong on every front.

It all started in qualifying, with Thijs Libregts as national coach. Ruud Gullit had had a lukewarm relationship with him for years after

Libregts, as Feyenoord coach, had spoken somewhat condescendingly about him in 1984. So it was no surprise that Ruud wasn't happy with him. The majority of the players' group didn't think he was the best man for the World Cup either. It didn't come to a head until after qualifying, in February 1990. After the friendly against Italy, Ruud, as captain, had taken a clear message to the Dutch FA on behalf of the team: 'The players' group wants Libregts to go.'

In response the Dutch FA summoned all the players together at the Schiphol Hilton Hotel on 25 March 1990, just before the team's departure for Kiev for a friendly against the Soviet Union. A notable presence that evening was the 1988 coach, Rinus Michels, only now he had a quite different job at the Dutch FA.

After the '88 European Championship Michels had left for Bayer Leverkusen, but he didn't see out the season there. In the autumn of '89 he had returned to the Dutch FA as technical director. The chairman of the professional football league's executive committee, Martin van Rooijen, had only taken office on 1 November 1989, in what for him, it later proved, was a difficult job, mainly because he had no footballing background.

At Schiphol, more than two months before the start of the World Cup, Michels and Van Rooijen on behalf of the Dutch FA committee wanted to hear from the players' group if they really were unwilling to continue with Thijs Libregts. The outcome was clear, as it had actually already been for a month. Michels had obviously been expecting this, because he immediately presented us with three names as potential replacements: Aad de Mos, who had been successful with KV Mechelen and was coach of Anderlecht; Leo Beenhakker, who was coach of Ajax and who had previously taken temporary charge as national coach; and Johan Cruyff, the coach of FC Barcelona. 'If we can get hold of one of these three candidates for Italia '90, will that be acceptable to you?' Michels asked. After consulting with the players I said: 'Johan Cruyff is the best of these three. So I don't want either of the others, I just want Cruyff. It's best if we all say now who we prefer and I think we should vote on it.' At this point Michels and Van Rooijen left the room.

The outcome was perfectly clear: eight votes for Johan, three for Beenhakker and two for De Mos. No doubt about it. The message to the FA was clear. Since Frank, Ruud and I weren't travelling to Kiev because of commitments with AC Milan, Ronald Koeman was given the task of delivering the outcome of the vote to Michels on behalf of the group around the time of the friendly against the Soviet Union in Kiev. This he did two days later.

For me it would be a dream to go to the World Cup with Johan as coach. He was doing well at Barcelona, while many of the players had won things at national and international level. What we needed was someone everyone had respect for and everyone would listen to. A strong personality. Johan was someone with the authority to fashion a team out of our disparate talents. He was also technically and tactically better than the other candidates. We needed someone like him. We all knew that.

Libregts was duly relieved of his duties and Rinus Michels got down to work. He would start by talking to Johan, we thought. We had every confidence because the players' group had been so clear. Then we forgot all about it, because we had lots of other things to think about. We were still fighting on three fronts with Milan and were very much in the race to win the European Cup again.

The bomb dropped late in April. We had expected Michels to consult with us once he had done his homework and sounded out the different candidates. But he took us completely by surprise.

At the end of April Michels called a meeting at the Van der Valk Hotel in Sassenheim. He would be there himself, along with Martin van Rooijen and five players: Ronald Koeman, Ruud Gullit, Frank Rijkaard, Hans van Breukelen and me. We were already there when the Dutch FA delegation walked in: Michels, Van Rooijen and, to our total surprise, Leo Beenhakker.

We'd thought we would be having a meeting with the Dutch FA about who the national coach would be and we took it for granted it would be Cruyff, our first choice. And here was Michels, presenting us with a *fait accompli*. He showed up with Beenhakker with all the usual formality and therefore deprived us of any opportunity to discuss it. Beenhakker was there, sitting beside him. We were told he would be introduced to the press a few days later.

We were astonished and highly incensed. Why Beenhakker now, all of a sudden? How come? Simply scandalous. Michels had put us on the spot and seemed concerned only with looking after his own interests. That's why I subsequently said in the media that Michels had just used us to get rid of Libregts, that he was going his own way and had ignored our wishes.

Michels' unexpected choice had an extremely detrimental impact on everything and everyone, up to and including the last minute of the last match. It was the beginning of the end for our World Cup.

At Beenhakker's introduction, on 26 April, Michels went to great lengths to portray 'the Milan three' in a bad light in front of the entire Dutch sporting press. 'The Milan attack is far too set in its ways and completely out of order,' he said. He also demanded apologies from me.

I had major doubts about Michels' role, but then maybe Johan had been difficult. Perhaps Michels had been in touch with

Cruyff after all? Because of those doubts and because Beenhakker's appointment was now a done deal, I subsequently offered my apologies. I didn't know what exactly had happened between Michels and Cruyff, nor did I want to be the cause of any conflict that would overshadow the World Cup. It was that very same week that Napoli went past us on their way to the championship in Serie A in such dubious fashion, so I wasn't feeling at my best.

But even with my apologies Michels failed to come round. In fact he went so far as to pour more fuel on the fire. He had a column in the *AD* newspaper, which allowed him to sow discord in the players' group through different channels. The three of us Milan players had the European Cup final to play, so when we arrived at the Dutch team's training camp seven days after the others, this was immediately portrayed in the press as 'prima-donna behaviour', as us feeling 'superior' to the rest and everything having to revolve around us. But we 'just' had a European Cup final to play. That was the sole reason.

While all this was going on, life went on at Milan. On 23 May we beat Benfica 1-0 in the European Cup final at the Prater Stadium in Vienna, Milan's second European Cup in a row. Joy unbounded. It was in any event a busy and special week because two days later Rebecca was born in Amsterdam. Wonderful, obviously.

When we reported to the Dutch training camp the following Monday, we certainly had mixed feelings after everything that had happened with the Dutch team over the last few weeks. It was a false start, which meant that Leo Beenhakker didn't have it easy. Both *De Telegraaf* and *AD* went on sowing discord in the squad between the 'stars' and 'the workers'.

But I can't really blame Beenhakker, it was beyond him too. We actually trained incredibly badly. It was really quite pathetic. In 1988 the B-team had often beaten the A-team during the preparations for the European Championship. This time the A-team was so much better every time we played, which wasn't the way it should be. In training terms it was far from perfect. At our request adjustments were made, but because the atmosphere was already so sour, things almost got out of hand on one occasion when Rijkaard and I squared up to each other. He kicked me, I elbowed him, he elbowed me, I kicked him. We started arguing because of our already heightened emotions and frustrations. Beenhakker intervened and made further adjustments. I thought: too bad, only now is something finally happening. Finally, we're going to be competitive.

Otherwise things between Frank, Ruud and me were fine. Ruud had had trouble with his knee injury before the World Cup, while Frank and I were super fit. We were very happy with Ruud as captain and point of contact. We didn't need to be in the forefront of things so much. It was clear though that all was not well within the squad. There were too many small groups and we were no longer a single entity.

Preparations left something to be desired too. Before the World Cup we spent time in a castle in Yugoslavia with an old-fashioned drawbridge. In the back of beyond. It was also incredibly dusty. I slept badly because of the dust in the bedrooms. And it was cold, even though we were due to play in the heat of Sicily and Sardinia. There was a work schedule, so we got up at six o'clock every morning, which wasn't very likely to put us in a good mood either. The atmosphere was rock bottom and then we had the first match to play.

In Palermo we struggled to a 1-1 draw with Egypt. We played poorly and were inconsistent. The second match, a few days later in Cagliari in Sardinia, against England, ended 0-0. We were lucky that two England goals were ruled out. The third game, on 21 June, was against Republic of Ireland in Palermo. Again we played badly.

With the score at 1-1 with 15 minutes to go, we shut up shop. This was because three draws would be enough for us to go through to the last 16 as the third-placed team in our group. But once more our play was lamentable. Mine included. I didn't play well.

Then came the last 16 match in Milan. At the San Siro. Against, as they still were then, West Germany. It was boiling hot, more than 35 degrees. In the second half I got dreadful cramp, partly because of the tension, but by then it already all seemed beyond us. Frank Rijkaard and Rudi Völler were no longer on the pitch because they had both been shown red cards.

They went 2-0 up. We had no chance now. Just before the final whistle Koeman made it 2-1 from the penalty spot, but it was too late. And then we could go home. I actually felt relieved the agony was at an end. Many other players felt the same, I think. Most of all I just wanted to disappear, it was such a disappointment. I felt I was one of the players responsible and that stayed with me for a long time.

Leo Beenhakker still talks about box 13, which he claims contains all the secrets of why Italia '90 was unsuccessful. But I think that box 13 is as good as empty. The tale of Michels, who ignored our desire to go to the World Cup with Cruyff, is the crux of the matter. Anything else is irrelevant.

Following Beenhakker's appointment we had said to each other: 'No complaining, lads. Shoulders to the wheel. We'll make a success of this World Cup regardless.' We did everything we could to turn the tide, to make the best of a bad job. We really did have a very good squad, the best in Europe. Four, five, maybe even six players of the very highest calibre.

But I felt that something had crept into the squad, which meant that we – the Milan players – were viewed differently, were treated differently. I couldn't put my finger on it, but I could sense it. I'm the first to say that as players we had a rotten tournament. That's why I was so embarrassed when it was all over and literally hid away in that villa in the south of France for a couple of weeks. It was my first major setback. And it had been on the highest stage too, at my 'own' San Siro.

Years later we found out that Michels had never been to discuss the job with Johan at all. He hadn't even bothered to try. And Van Rooijen had no idea who Michels had or hadn't spoken to. The executive committee had left the choice of the new national coach entirely up to him. It turned out he had only ever spoken to one candidate and that was Leo Beenhakker.

We'll never know what Michels' real reason was. But my sense is that he was scared that Cruyff would outdo him by making Holland world champions. That he would erase the success of Euro '88 by achieving something even greater. That Cruyff would perhaps perform better than Michels as coach. He wanted to prevent that, I think. Nothing more than a basic human emotion: jealousy.

MILAN (5)

The rift with Sacchi

1990–1991

The matter was finally settled in the massage room at Milanello. I was having a massage when Arrigo Sacchi came in to have a word with me. Or rather, to tell me something. To be honest I had long since reached the end of my tether when this incident took place, in the spring of 1991. We had worked together for three seasons, and something inside me snapped. It wasn't something that come out of the blue, though, it had been building up slowly but surely.

Sacchi is a lovely, decent man. The contrast between him and natural-born footballers was striking. He would stand there on the training ground with his big Ray-Ban sunglasses and spindly white legs, though he had little playing ability of his own. He was relatively inexperienced at elite football level, so still had to prove himself when Berlusconi took him from Parma to the great AC Milan. That was in the summer of 1987, after he had beaten Milan in a cup tie in an un-Italian way with Berlusconi looking on.

He had introduced a tactical system at Milan that worked. Everyone knew exactly what he had to do in every situation. Certainly from our second season, '88–'89, you could see these patterns in the matches. We could do them in our sleep. He talked about this system incessantly and explained it to me so often that eventually I thought: come on. I've got it now. And if I hadn't understood it by then, I never would. In the early days we had

123

difficulty understanding one another, because my Italian was no more than average and his English wasn't all that great either.

I must also be honest: I was used to Cruyff. No one comes close to him. But the fact that things didn't click with Sacchi wasn't just to do with our different views about football.

Tactics certainly played a part. The system I grew up in at Ajax was 4-3-3, with three attackers. An outside-left and an outside-right would provide the striker with good crosses. Sacchi played 4-4-2, with just two attackers and a very rigid defensive unit. He called his system revolutionary, attacking, and even gave it a name: 'zonal pressing'.

He was an unknown coach, so when he suddenly changed the way the great Milan played from what Italy was used to, he had to explain this 'new' system. He gave a lot of interviews and was on friendly terms with a good number of journalists, which helped. He had to sell his 'zonal pressing' as something special, something un-Italian.

As early as his first year, when my injury meant I spent the greater part of the season as a spectator, I could see that it really wasn't attacking at all. That block of four defenders was incredibly solid and effective: Tassotti, Costacurta or Filippo Galli, Baresi and Maldini. It's hard to imagine a better defence in the recent history of European football. People can still rattle off these five names in every corner of the globe. They were real winners. But, in spite of their great talents, they confined themselves to defending.

In front of them was another line of four. Carlo Ancelotti was one of the two central midfielders. A wonderful footballer, that's for sure, but he wasn't known for his ability to get around the pitch, partly because of his dodgy knees. He was a wonderful organizer though.

When Frank Rijkaard played alongside him the following season, something changed, because Frank was another graduate of the Ajax school and was used to popping up in the penalty area. Donadoni and Evani were also good midfielders, but in that first year I mainly saw two rows of four, who were really very good defensively. Not even a mouse would get through. And then we had Giovanni Galli in goal, so we kept a lot of clean sheets that season. Up front were the two attackers, in that first season usually Virdis and Gullit.

Against Roma I was on the bench. Gullit was racing up and down, working like a Trojan. He really did run for two. He had so much energy, it wasn't normal. But Virdis, the sly fox, wasted no energy on what Sacchi called forechecking; he just stood somewhere near the halfway line waiting for a good ball.

That afternoon Milan won 2-0. All the newspapers said this wonderful, new, un-Italian 'zonal pressing' system was really revolutionary. Sensational. That disturbed me because it wasn't. It wasn't attacking. It was mainly defensive. We won by defending well.

But anyway, I know how sport works: the winner is always right. I did note that the Italians weren't used to challenging authority. However experienced they were, no one disagreed with Sacchi. And certainly not in public.

However, as I used to do in Holland, I had my say after one of the early matches that first season. We had lost 2-0 at home to Fiorentina. I felt we hadn't been attacking enough, that Ruud and I had not had sufficient service from midfield. The newspapers made a huge song and dance about it. It was unusual for a player to question the coach's tactical plan in the media.

I was quite used to discussion. The Dutch anyway are not as respectful of authority as the Italians. But after that I mainly conducted such discussions behind closed doors, hardly ever in the press again. Not that I had changed my mind, but for the rest of that season I was concentrating on myself, on the pain in my ankle, the operation and recovery.

So when Milan won the Scudetto in 1988 after that wonderful victory in Napoli, thanks to an unrestrained Gullit outshining Maradona, Sacchi of course received all the plaudits for his revolutionary zonal pressing system. That's simply how it works. At the same time I knew that as Milan's striker I would be judged on goals, and nothing else. And for that I needed good service from midfield. To score you need good balls and support from midfield. And the discussions and meetings with Sacchi were almost never about that, which I felt was a real pity.

After Euro '88 the Italians saw me in a different light. I was pleased about Frank's arrival, as it gave me hope of a rather more attacking style of play. And through Frank I could give the rest of the team a boost. If the tempo was too slow or too few good balls were coming my way, I would have a go at Frank and then things would start to happen. Later he admitted that was how it worked with him. We would in fact become more attacking, but still the emphasis in Sacchi's training sessions was on the positions we should adopt and how to get hold of the ball when we didn't have it. Relatively little attention was given to what to do when we did have possession.

Apart from that Sacchi and I didn't hit it off personally, which happens sometimes. He would call me '*lunatico*' and related my behaviour to the phases of the moon. He found me hard to pin down and didn't understand me.

I found him nowhere near direct enough. He never took a hard line with the stars. If for example I wasn't running fast enough in a drill, he would shout at a young player: 'Hey, run a bit faster, eh!' But it was really meant for me.

I prefer direct confrontation. Honesty. My relationship with Mauro Tassotti is a case in point. I was up against him in a training session that first year. It was a one-on-one with no holds barred. On one occasion he was so annoying that I went in really hard. In response he kicked me. It became a heated exchange, and we ended up squaring up to each other with clenched fists, ready to lash out. Sacchi sent us both to the dressing room to calm down. While we were sitting there, on the wooden benches, we looked at each other and almost simultaneously burst out laughing. We could see the funny side. We were both hotheads and complete fanatics and recognized that in each other.

It's something that's often happened to me. Sometimes I have to clash with someone first to make a real connection, to feel something. Only then will something develop and grow. From then on there was a bond between Mauro and me that only grew stronger. We are still good friends and see each other regularly.

I didn't have that kind of connection, that kind of honest confrontation, with Sacchi though. It was all very pleasant, it was all very polite, and above all it was very often a sermon about tactics. We hardly ever just went ahead and played a game at training without interruption, without some tactical coaching points. Sometimes I just wanted a nice game of football, which is what you need from time to time as a player.

Sacchi was obsessed with the game and his system, he was fanatical. He would work on it seven days a week, day and night. When we stayed in a hotel before a match, the players in the room next to his would sometimes wake up because he was shouting in his sleep: 'Offside, offside', or something. That was a regular occurrence.

We were the best team in Europe, winning the Intercontinental Cup in both the '88–'89 and '89–'90 seasons. It's safe to say that we had the best team on the planet in those years.

When things weren't going so well at Milan after Italia '90, for the first time there was pressure. The '90–'91 season was a poor one for Milan. I felt the chemistry between the coach and the players had run out. And I didn't keep things to myself. At the same time my hunger to win trophies was far from stilled. Anything that was blocking the path to further success had to be removed. Even if that was the coach. That's how I am.

So when, in the spring of 1991, for the umpteenth time Sacchi came, unprompted, to explain something to me about tactics and my role in them, I blew my top. I had had enough. The only witness to that clash was the masseur.

I interrupted Sacchi in full flow and icily said: 'Mister Sacchi, let me say just one thing very clearly. You always say that we are so successful because we have worked with you, but I would put it another way. We haven't won all those trophies because of you, but in spite of you.'

A stony silence fell. Sacchi looked at me as if I had stabbed him in the heart with a dagger. He was totally shocked. He said nothing in response and left the room.

With the benefit of hindsight I should of course have done things differently, expressed myself in some other way. Sacchi didn't deserve this assault.

Sacchi then went and told Berlusconi he could no longer work with me and Berlusconi would have to choose between him and me. Berlusconi chose me. My preference was to stay in Milan. I was happy there, playing with the absolute best in the world. There was still so much we could win.

And then Berlusconi brought in Fabio Capello. Actually an inexperienced coach, but a former player, who at the time was a commentator on one of Berlusconi's sports channels. Once again it proved a great move.

MILAN (6)

'The San Siro is mine'

1991–1992

The start of the new season proved to be the dawn of a glorious era. I found it a revelation working with Capello, someone who mainly talked about football again. About ball possession, build-up, creating chances. Someone who was direct. A breath of fresh air. After a shaky start with a few drawn games, we went on a great run.

Capello's approach was a bit harder and tighter than Sacchi's. He took a firmer line with the media, but also the players, some of whom had to get used to it, including Baresi, Maldini and Tassotti. But if you looked at how we played and the results we got, you could see the difference. Milan won the championship three times in a row under Capello.

He took tough decisions and was prepared to go further than Sacchi. The hierarchy in the team had also changed since 1987. Ancelotti was a wonderful player, but now he was having a lot of trouble with his knees. Capello went for the young Albertini in that position. He had greater running ability and could also read the game well. We were none the worse for it, as Capello could well see. Ancelotti was upset, but he understood.

Capello had regular clashes with Ruud Gullit, where Sacchi had for the most part been complimentary to him. Ruud was having more and more problems with his knee and it was becoming obvious that he found it increasingly difficult to hit the same high levels of his early days. Under Capello he therefore began to feature less and less.

It had to come to a head at some point. One Saturday morning we were training for the away game against Juve. It was clear from the practice games that Ruud would not be among the first sixteen players, so not even on the bench. Training was followed by lunch, then a rest. We were due to leave for Turin by coach at 4.30. It was clear to everyone, except that Capello had forgotten to tell Ruud personally that he was not in the squad. At 4.30 there was Ruud at the coach, and it was then that Capello said: 'Sorry, Ruud, but maybe I wasn't clear, you're not playing. And you're not on the bench either.' Ruud was angry. 'Fine, but you didn't tell me.' So Capello said again: 'I'm sorry, maybe I wasn't clear.' Ruud did that deliberately, I think, because he was seeking confrontation with Capello. He wanted to settle the score.

We won the match 1-0, without Ruud. Painful, of course, but on Monday at the post-mortem everyone was back again, including Ruud. Capello said something about the incident at one point, something like he hadn't perhaps actually spelled it out, but it should have been clear nonetheless. All this unpleasantness led to upset in the dressing room. They did have it out later, but it was clear that something was about to change. That's when Ruud ended up going to Sampdoria.

Italy's high regard and respect for the AC Milan of that era under Capello only came later. Because we won the Scudetto three times in a row, the first time undefeated. But also because of our style of play, which made an impression in Italy. Under Sacchi we had won one title and two European Cups, and Capello built on his work. In five years under Capello we won four titles and another European Cup. The respect all over Italy after the work of both Sacchi and Capello was obvious. *Gli Invincibili*, 'The Invincibles', we were called.

It was honestly my best period at Milan. I was top scorer in Serie A with 25 goals, a total that hadn't been achieved in more than a quarter of a century. I believe I played 55 times under Capello and we never lost once. Bar the last one, after I hadn't played for months because of my ankle, my 56th, the Champions League final in May 1993.

That was also the time when the San Siro was increasingly feeling like my home. It was such an intense feeling, it was my hunting ground: 'I'm the boss here. The San Siro is mine.' The afternoons when I scored there always felt very special. All the tension would fall away and my football would have a free and easy feel to it. Playing football at the San Siro became a real pleasure.

The strange thing is that this sense of 'the San Siro is mine' stayed with me for years afterwards. Even after I had finished playing and came back to Milan from time to time. It has ebbed away only very slowly with the passing of the years.

'NOT IN MY AEROPLANE'

1991

Liesbeth was heavily pregnant with our second child when I flew to Rome with Milan on 14 December 1991 for the away game against Lazio. It was the last game before the winter break and we had remained unbeaten since Capello's arrival.

I'd made sure nothing would stop me from being with Liesbeth at the hospital in Amsterdam for the birth of Rebecca, two days after the European Cup win in Vienna, on 25 May 1990. It was incredibly special to be there. Afterwards I had to go straight to the training camp with Holland for Italia '90.

This time was different. Liesbeth and I had discussed it in advance. I would be there if I could, but if not, that would be fine too. Liesbeth was fully behind the decision. She was due around that weekend of 15 December and would give birth in hospital in Milan.

Late that Saturday evening, when we were already in Rome, I received a phone call to say her contractions had started. There were no more scheduled flights that evening and the only way back to Milan was to fly in Berlusconi's private plane. But Berlusconi was unequivocal: 'We need you tomorrow, Marco. So as far as I'm concerned you're not going back. Not in my aeroplane anyway.'

On Sunday morning, two hours before the match, our second daughter was born. I got a phone call with the wonderful news. We would call her Deborah. I was happy, really delighted, and Liesbeth sounded happy too. It was all good. So I went into the match with

133

extra motivation. I scored the equalizer and after the match dedicated the goal to my new-born daughter. That's a custom in Italy, dedicating goals, though it's not something I did very often.

What I didn't know was that Liesbeth was now having doubts about the name Deborah, because she realized it would be pronounced very differently in Italy and Holland. She wasn't happy about it, so that same Sunday evening she changed the name to Angela. We both thought Angela sounded better. It felt right. But I had already dedicated the goal to Deborah after the match and that was what was in all the papers on Monday.

It certainly had Berlusconi momentarily rather confused. The day after she was born we had Milan's Christmas dinner, our collective conclusion to the year, before everyone goes home to their families. He opened proceedings by congratulating the Van Basten family on the birth of our new child, Deborah. I immediately said: 'No, it's not Deborah, it's Angela.' He was completely thrown, ha-ha.

WHO GETS CLOSE?

1991–1992

It was our daily Milano Tre ritual. A glass of something at the end of the day, sitting out in the garden. Liesbeth would tell me about her day and I would tell her about mine. Sometimes it would be some little thing that sparked our conversation. Out in the street. On TV. Or something the children had done. We might have a lively discussion, or enjoy a companionable silence, but it was something I valued.

Some people like looking for adventure and seeking out new places, but I prefer going back to places I know. You know where you are, there's no need to settle in. I like that. I don't necessarily have to have the same room in the hotel each time, but I can find my way to the beach on Elba in my sleep. That's precisely what I find so relaxing. And isn't that what holidays are for?

I remember being on holiday in Italy with Liesbeth after signing for Milan but before I had been presented to the press. It was the summer of 1987. We went to the beach and I was soon recognized. The crowd of people wanting a photo with me and asking for autographs grew so big that Liesbeth, who was lying there quietly sunning herself, found herself completely covered in sand because of the ensuing commotion. It was really very embarrassing and not a little frightening too.

Frank and I often used to wait on the players' bus until Ruud had got off and caught everyone's attention, then we would quietly slip away through the side door. At Milanello there's a secret passage you can use to evade all the journalists, which brings you straight out into the car park. Not a lot of people know about it. Of all the Milan players I was the one who made the most use of it. I often found the attention of the press or the fans stressful.

I believe you perform at your best when your energy is at its peak. You get your energy from sleep, from good food, from living for your sport and from having as little hustle and bustle as possible around it. The sharper you are, the more you make the difference. You must avoid anything that drains your energy, as it reduces your ability, your flexibility, your power to give your all. It saps your strength and makes you weaker. I really believe that. So a healthy dose of selfishness is not necessarily a bad thing. If you look after yourself properly, you perform at your peak, which pleases the people around you. You're also able to give something back.

Liesbeth has never known anything else. When I first met her, I was regularly going to a hypnotherapist in Watergraafsmeer with Johan before a match. I had trouble with nerves before matches, so Johan suggested I go with him and give it a try. We took turns in the chair. The man waved his arms about a bit, walked around us but never actually touched us. After half an hour it was all done and we paid him ten guilders each. And the following Sunday I did indeed have fewer problems, so I went back again the following week. We kept going for a very long time. John van 't Schip went with us once. At one point the therapist went round behind him and suddenly began to moan really loudly and wave his arms about: 'Oh! What tension, what tension! Grrr. Grrr.' John was scared out of his wits. He wasn't impressed and never went back again, ha-ha. But I had no problem with it, it helped me. Johan also benefited from it and was always open to 'new' ideas like that.

Sometimes people like that end up in your private life too. Ted Troost became a sort of family friend of ours in Italy. I remember Angela crying a lot as a baby for the first six months. We suffered sleepless nights because of it. It was also really stressful. Eventually Liesbeth put Angela in Ted's big hands, with the words: 'Can you help us?'

Ted laid Angela on the table and suddenly smacked the tabletop hard. This startled her and she stopped crying at once, but you could see she was still very tense. Her body was rigid. Then Ted laid her on her front on his thigh. He said: 'Wait a moment, just trust me and watch Angela closely.' Initially all her muscles remained tense. But ten minutes later her arms and legs were hanging limply on either side of his thigh. She was completely relaxed and asleep and never disturbed our sleep again after that.

Ted had been spending a lot of time at Milanello with Ruud when I was having trouble with my hip. I think it was the spring of 1988. We started talking and he said he could have a look at it. In no time at all he had fixed it. That's how it all began. Later on we even sorted out a contract for him at Milan to ensure he received regular remuneration.

When he was around we would often go for a round of golf at the end of the day. There was a good atmosphere. His treatments were very effective. Haptonomy (a treatment in which tension is solved by touch) is certainly something different, because every individual and every situation is different. 'Everyone's body is unique and therefore responds differently,' Ted often says. He's a sensitive man.

He tried to make me feel I belonged there, even without the goals and the trophies. So then I relaxed. What he did helped me. I didn't really care how.

HOLLAND (3)

Taking a penalty

Euro '92

I was on the point of taking the penalty. The Denmark keeper Peter Schmeichel was standing on his goal line. I'd paced out my run-up. This would be my last kick after 120 minutes of football. Uncompromising football, because twice we had gone behind here in Gothenburg. But if we won we would be through to the final. All that remained was the penalty shoot-out. Five shots each. I knew my routine, I could hear my breathing, feel my heartbeat. It was noisy in the stadium, but I shut myself off. As I always did. I waited for the referee's whistle, but all sorts of things were going through my head. I had to set a good example. After Koeman's decisive penalty, I was second in line. Denmark had also scored their first, even though Van Breukelen had got a touch on Henrik Larsen's shot with his left hand. But it had made no difference.

Taking a penalty is a specialist skill, a speciality within football. At Milan I had been taking all the penalties for some years. I scored 21 before I missed one, against Parma. Taking penalties had become something I was skilled at. A penalty is a duel between one player and another. In effect you have two options. Either you choose one corner or the other before you take the kick or you wait and react to the keeper. I've tried both, but the more penalties I've taken and the more experience I've gained, the more I've dared to wait.

Waiting actually gives you the best chance of scoring, if you can anticipate fast enough. But it's also the riskiest, because however good your experience and preparation, there are always keepers who stand still. And then what do you do? Basically it's not something you're ever going to know in advance. Keepers aren't all the same either. Some will always dive one way or the other, others will sometimes wait a moment. They may surprise you if you decide to 'wait'. That's the problem. Because then you have no option but to kick the ball very hard into your chosen corner almost from a standing start, and that's not easy.

Recently at Milan I'd been taking them like this. It's difficult, but if you do it properly, it nearly always works. I always start with a little jump, a hop, so there's some momentum behind it and I have more time before shooting. And just before I shoot, I swing my shooting foot back. That's often when I see the keeper move left or right and when I still have control and can decide.

The option I choose will always depend on how I'm feeling at the time. It will depend on the match, on how I've been playing, on the opponent, on the atmosphere, on how I've been in the match. A penalty is also a moment of vulnerability. As a player you're on a hiding to nothing, because if you score you're only doing what you're supposed to do. The skill is to park the stress and rely on your tried and tested routine, your experience. If you've done all that and can then 'let it happen', then you've done the best you can. There's nothing more you can do and nor should there be.

What counted for me as I stood there in front of Schmeichel was the 120 minutes I had already spent on the pitch. Tiredness reduces the sharpness you need to wait all that time, to watch carefully and to anticipate very quickly.

It had been a strange tournament for me, because we had actually been playing better than in 1988. The match against Germany was convincing. We were 2-0 up at half-time, and really played them off the park. It ended 3-1. We had a strong team.

But I hadn't had the same leading role I had in 1988. In fact, I hadn't scored at all yet at this tournament. At least, I had scored, against the CIS (a transitional entity at the beginning of the post-USSR era), but that perfectly good goal had been ruled out.

The team though was good this time. Something had changed since Rinus Michels had made a visit to Milan. I had taken the initiative to get him talking to Rijkaard again. Rijkaard had retired from international football after Italia '90, but I knew we desperately needed him if we were to get anywhere at this European Championship. Fortunately, after that conversation with Michels, which I was part of, Frank was prepared to turn out for Holland again. And with that the problem around Italia '90 was resolved as far as I was concerned. It was time to move on.

As I started my run-up, eye to eye with Schmeichel, I'd made my decision. Say what you like about penalties, however long you spend analysing them, in the end there is never a hundred per cent guaranteed way. Right then I simply didn't feel good enough to wait, so I was going for the no-nonsense approach. I had decided before my run-up to kick the ball hard and low into the right-hand corner. And that's what I did. The shot wasn't particularly bad, but it wasn't very good either. Schmeichel dived full-length the right way and got to it. Oh, no, what had I done? Pah.

Then we had to wait. I was hoping, thinking that Van Breukelen was really going to have to stop another one. He'd got close twice, but everyone scored. All the Danes and all the Dutch. My miss was the decider. We were out. No final for us this time.

And yet it felt different from Italia '90. This time we'd played well, especially in the group games. Better even than in 1988, I think. And even though I was really fed up with my penalty miss, it did feel like something that's part of the game. I wasn't embarrassed like in 1990.

MILAN (7)

Complete abandon

1992

Every goal has a story. Like the one I scored at the San Siro against Sampdoria on 5 April 1992. Sampdoria were the reigning champions and we were on the verge of winning the title that year. It ended 5-1 that afternoon. When I scored my goal, to make it 3-0, the whole of the San Siro stood cheering. I too was really delighted, although the goal itself was nothing special. A neat rebound from a shot against the bar.

But Pietro Vierchowod, Sampdoria's marker-in-chief, was one of the best defenders in Serie A. My battles with him were always tough. We went in hard on each other, but always fairly. Even though we had beaten Sampdoria before, I had never scored against him. The papers kept tabs on it all and the fans were all in the know too. So when that goal finally went in there was pure joy in the stadium. And for me. Which was really odd, all that euphoria about what in itself was a simple goal.

Vierchowod really was a very good defender. As was Jürgen Kohler. Along with Bergomi and Ferri, at Inter. They were the most difficult defenders. If I scored against one of them, I was extra pleased, but otherwise I was never too concerned about my direct opponent. I didn't have much to do with them. For me it was always only ever about winning.

Not many players succeeded in putting me off my game so much that I overstepped the mark. Except that time with Pasquale Bruno of Torino. He was so obsessed with preventing me from scoring that he completely lost track of the ball and the state of the game. His sole concern was me and making my life as difficult as possible. It was very strange, but also very annoying. Then a cross came straight towards me, he ducked in front and kicked the ball into his own net.

I proceeded to do an idiotic little dance around him, just to show him how ridiculous his defending against me had been the whole time. He was apparently happier putting the ball in his own net than letting me score.

The Torino players weren't too happy with that little dance of mine, nor were the crowd. The whole Stadio delle Alpi turned against me and tried even harder to put me off. Capello took me off for my own protection, though I thought that was a bit of a pity.

On 13 September 1992 we played at Pescara. With 20 minutes to go we were 4-2 down, but then I scored three times and we won 5-4. The first of the three was a ball I took with my right foot, on the edge of the box, from a cross from the left, slipping it past the keeper into the far corner in a single movement. Technically it was a pretty good goal. As a striker you simply have to be able to hit a ball coming from the left with your right foot, with control and out of the keeper's reach. Done. So then it was 4-3.

The second goal, a few minutes later, was a bit more special. It was reminiscent of the one Johan Cruyff scored in the European Cup final against Inter. The ball came across from the right. It started high, but fell into the penalty area and landed on the ground near the penalty spot. I controlled the ball instantly with my right foot and then it was simplicity itself to put it wherever I wanted. I slipped it calmly into the corner. 4-4.

But the most important one, for me, was the last goal, a few minutes later. I set off with the ball, heading towards the keeper, though I hadn't decided what I was going to do yet. It was a situation I'd encountered hundreds of times before. The experience of all those hundreds of times was stored somewhere inside me. I'd missed chances and I'd converted chances. Everything came together as I advanced on the Pescara keeper. I felt so confident that I relaxed and simply let things happen. I just let my body take over. I waited and waited, until the keeper went to ground, then I chipped the ball over him. It floated into the Pescara net with a lovely graceful curl: 5-4. That gave me such a delightful feeling. I was floating on air.

As a striker, when you're bearing down on the keeper, on your own, you basically have three options. The first is to go past him, using your speed. If he comes out, you can effectively go past him at twice the speed. Unless there are any defenders running with you. They can complicate matters.

The second option is to take an early shot. The keeper will be expecting you to shoot so you must do so just before he thinks you will. You'll have the best chance of scoring if you shoot past his standing leg. That's often the near corner. You'll surprise him with the early shot.

The third option is to wait. You keep your options open for as long as you can. And because you take your time, and are patient, you can wait until the keeper goes to ground and then chip the ball over him. He can do no more than grab at thin air.

An example of this is what happened between me and Joop Hiele in that 8-2 match between Ajax and Feyenoord in 1983, when Johan was playing for Feyenoord.

You train every day, you play positional games, you do shooting drills and you play practice games, so this is something that comes up on a daily basis. If it's something you do a lot in training and it happens to you in matches too – you see it, feel it, experience it – then, in a manner of speaking, your database gets fuller and fuller. You often see players in their thirties playing smarter football. More often than not they make the right decisions, they know how to play a match, where they have to go. Physically, they have a better idea of how to deal with tiredness and how to prepare themselves. They also know when it's imperative they don't lose a ball. This is what makes older players so important compared with younger ones, who often have the energy and explosiveness, but haven't yet developed the same ability to read the game and lack the same perceptiveness.

In this respect strikers are a rare breed. They know how to score a goal. How it feels. A good outside-right or outside-left should be able to do likewise, with the right mentality. You can see how Arjen Robben for example has trained himself to do this, to score goals. It's something that pays for itself. As an attacking midfielder you need to score a number of goals a season. Donny van de Beek is a great example. A number 6 of course will find it's a different story from a number 10, but you have to make sure you get yourself in the box. And then you can score.

Keeping calm in your head at the moment you get into such a scoring position is really crucial. You can train yourself to do it. Jari Litmanen was a midfielder who was extremely good at this, he knew exactly how to outmanoeuvre a keeper. And the calm that Van de Beek of Ajax displayed when he received that wonderful through ball from Ziyech at Spurs in the 2019 Champions League semi-final, and had the nerve to wait, that's class. That's keeping calm in your head.

It's no surprise that defenders or midfielders find scoring difficult. Nor is it uncommon to see attackers who try to defend make the wrong decisions. Defending is a completely separate skill, a specialist position. As is goalkeeping.

It's strange to think that Zlatan Ibrahimović wasn't really a genuine striker when he came to Ajax. Later, when he went to Juventus, Fabio Capello showed him a video of my goals to make him understand that, with his qualities, above all he had to score goals. Because scoring goals is what makes the difference.

After that you can see how Zlatan became a clinical finisher, capable of dragging an entire team along in his wake, and having the mentality to become a leader. He was a champion at every club he played at from then on. It was also down to the fact that each year he became more professional. He became aware of the importance of goals. I see him as a very good example of someone who has understood the essence of the game.

You can see this same development in Cristiano Ronaldo. As the years go by you see him become increasingly aware of the fact that scoring goals is what decides matches and wins trophies.

Messi is the exception who proves the rule. He has something of the divine about him. He must have fallen into some magic potion as a child. Everything he does comes off. A player like him only comes along once in 50 years.

Sometimes I too had moments when everything came together. There was a Milan match at Lecce, on 25 March 1990. We won 2-1 and I scored the winning goal. That in itself was not unique, but the way it happened was.

I received the ball on the right-hand edge of the box and ran towards our outside right. I slipped the ball to him with the outside of my left foot and he went in the box. I turned and sprinted goalwards, where I got the ball back. A one-two then. And I tapped the ball into the net: 2-1. Normally I would have played it with the inside of my right foot, but this was so relaxed, so spontaneous. I was playing here with complete abandon.

It's all about making the decision to let things happen, letting go of your control. As a striker you are usually super focused. At least I am. And sometimes, when you're a good way into your career, you do just let things happen, and the results can be fantastic.

MILAN (8)

San Marco

Autumn 1992

In the autumn things were going so well that the newspapers started coming up with superlatives for me. They called me *Il Cigno di Utrecht*, 'the Utrecht Swan'. Elegant, but mysterious. 'San Marco' also cropped up for the first time. *Ghiacciolo* was another, 'cool as a cucumber'. That was a reference to how I converted penalties. Usually, anyway.

In November 1992 I had been performing at the top level at Milan for 16 months or so. Nearly everything was going my way. I was prospering in the freedom and the new hierarchy under Capello. I passed the hundred-goal mark for Milan and for the first time was compared with Gunnar Nordahl, Milan's Swedish striker who reached the same landmark in the 1940s and '50s, and also José Altafini and Pierino Prati. It was a great honour to be on that list.

It also said something about the level I had reached in the autumn of 1992. The match against Napoli on 8 November, in the famous San Paolo Stadium, ended 5-1 to us, with me scoring four. On 25 November IFK Gothenburg visited the San Siro. It was 4-0, and I scored all the goals, the third with an overhead kick. Everything I touched turned to gold.

That month news came that I had won the Ballon d'Or for the third time. Now I was level with Johan Cruyff and Michel Platini. I won despite the 'unsuccessful' European Championship and despite Barcelona winning the European Cup. It was that conclusive apparently. Further endorsement came the following month when I was also named FIFA World Player of the Year.

What hardly anyone knew was that I was still having trouble with my right ankle all the time. After every match, especially when the pitches were cold and hard. The pain never went away. And I wanted to do something about it. San Marco or not.

MILAN (9)

The best in the world

Autumn 1992

On 7 December I was voted FIFA World Player of the Year. Votes were cast by the national coaches of 171 countries. I received the award from Sepp Blatter in Estoril in Portugal. It was only the second time the award had been made. You could say that I had achieved my goal then, being the best, but of course I wasn't satisfied yet. I never am. But it did set me thinking. How had I succeeded in reaching the top? Being the best footballer in the world feels really special. It had been an unusual journey. It was always a case of waiting to see how far I could go: UVV, Elinkwijk, Ajax, Holland, Milan. Each move had been a small step. And each time I had to wait to see how it turned out.

The European Championship in '88 was my great international breakthrough. The summer when everything fell into place. I had the wind behind me, after a really miserable period with my ankle. After that European Championship I was also regarded differently at Milan. I had decided a major tournament, expectations were higher still, my ankle was performing again. I had to stand up and be counted.

The 1988 Ballon d'Or had been based on the European Championship, not on the national title or the European Cup, because I had only played a small part in the title and we hadn't won the European Cup. So I remained critical of myself. There was so much more that I wanted.

What had I shown anyone at Milan so far? Unsurprisingly, I thanked my father, Johan Cruyff and Ted Troost.

My time at Milan was yet to come. That season we won the European Cup in Barcelona, the greatest trophy in Europe. A title in Italy. Top scorer in Serie A. After the unsuccessful Italia '90 campaign we reached a very high level under Capello at Milan. We played many wonderful matches in those years at Milan, won the Cup, won titles. When all's said and done, that was really special.

Some players who go abroad don't realize it, but initially you're seen as an interloper. You're there at someone else's expense. You have to start by earning your place. Once you've done that, you're beginning to get somewhere. And if you can help your new club win, then you're making a difference. You win together, and if at some point you actually become the most important player in the team, then your teammates are incredibly grateful to you. And that's what happened in those years at Milan. Together we were very strong and outstandingly good. Each player had his own role.

I really did become half Italian. If I hadn't got injured, I think I would certainly have carried on playing at Milan until 2000. I had no need to leave, definitely not. I was happy there, despite the lure of Cruyff and Barcelona. I could play football nice and freely. I was lauded in Milan. It wasn't going to get any better.

I had navigated my way to the top of the pyramid. I always did everything I could to perform to the best of my ability. That may sound easy, but it's not. Because all sorts of things have an impact on your performance. Every tiny decision. What you eat, who you meet, which parties you go to, how late you go to bed.

Everything, and I mean everything, can have an impact on your performance.

In my experience whatever you don't do is even more difficult to keep up than the things you do. Having the discipline to let things go is a very important factor. The biggest of all maybe. Going out. A party. Going to visit someone. A glass of alcohol. The list is endless. And that's where you can make the difference. You have to live by it. Not 99, but 100 per cent. That's dozens of decisions a day, year after year. Discipline makes the difference. Look at Cristiano Ronaldo. When he gets home he does some underwater cycling to loosen his muscles.

An attitude, a lifestyle like that comes from the drive to be the absolute best. And where does that drive, that ambition, come from? It's an interesting question and is different for everyone. Often you have no idea. With Maradona you can see that his background was an important driving force because his family came from a very poor district of Buenos Aires. He wanted to give his family a future. But what was it that drove me?

Naturally, it wouldn't be strange to say that from an early age I wanted to show my father what I could do with a ball. I received a lot of approval from him for my performances on the pitch. That can motivate a child. In addition, I've said I was trying to escape the unhappy situation at home and found joy on the football pitch.

What also played a part, if I'm honest, is that I really wanted to be financially independent. Not that we were really poor, but money was always a consideration. Money gives you independence. I very much wanted to be free to do as I pleased. That was a really important driver for me.

Only later, when I was actually financially independent, did I also come to value intellectual independence. When you can also have freedom of thought, freedom of emotion, that maybe is worth far more.

PART III

THE ANKLE

1992–1998

ANKLE (2)

St Moritz

21 December 1992

I was nervous, which was a little odd given the splendour of this place. I'd flown here in Berlusconi's private jet and was being treated like a prince. The beds were bigger and wider than in Holland, the food was wonderful and the view of the Swiss mountain tops was superb. The Klinik Gut in St Moritz was known as one of the best clinics in Europe, but still I felt uneasy. After four years I was going to have surgery on my ankle again.

I was going only for the very best. It was only a few weeks before that I had been voted FIFA World Player of the Year, which was unreal, although not entirely without merit, I think. I had turned 28 just two months before and I'd already won four titles, three European Cups, two Intercontinental Cups and a European Championship. And I was far from finished yet.

But all the same: hospitals and clinics, however lovely, always expose your vulnerability. However successful the last four years may have been, my ankle was still often swollen after a match. I could reckon on a good two days' pain, especially when it got cold and the pitches were harder.

It was me who had wanted this operation, despite club doctor Tavana having tried to discourage me. The club would have much preferred me to delay the surgery until the season was over and complete this wondrous time with Capello first. We were still unbeaten since his arrival. But I decided to go through with it. I wanted to get this troublesome ankle of mine sorted out. Given the success of my previous surgery, it was logical to go back to Dr Marti again. He knew my ankle better than anyone. In addition to his work at the AMC, he also had this clinic in St Moritz, no more than three hours' drive from Milan.

The aim once again was to 'clean out' the ankle and remove bone fragments. They, as Dr Marti had explained at the pre-op three weeks before, cause constant inflammation. They can damage the cartilage if they find their way between the bones. And you have to be very careful with cartilage, that much I already knew. We could have waited, but I felt the winter break was a good time. And Tavana would be there in the operating theatre representing both the club and me.

Dr René Marti had let everyone know I would be having surgery at his private clinic here in St Moritz. He was the number one ankle specialist in the world, but it did him no harm of course to count me among his clients. That's the way it is. Marti was a flamboyant man, once a ski instructor, and proud to be on friendly terms with the cream of the dance and sport worlds. It was no surprise when the AMC took him to Holland to set up the department there from scratch.

It was the morning of 21 December 1992 when I was collected by two nurses who pushed my bed down the wide corridors to the anaesthetic room. Marti, exuding confidence, came to shake hands with me. Tavana was a little more reserved, but also shook my hand. He wished me good luck.

When I awoke, I had no idea what discussion had ensued over my head during the operation, how heated it had become and what had ultimately happened to my ankle. Nor did I yet know that this operation would drastically affect my career, in fact it would change my life completely.

What I did know was that two days later something rather surprising happened. I had distinguished visitors at my bedside in the form of two of Italy's absolute leading figures. Like them, I was still of course uncertain about the outcome of the operation.

In the morning Berlusconi came to see me. The hard-working, ever energetic businessman. The inspiration. He had some words of encouragement for me, delivered from the end of my bed in the manner in which he managed Milan and his business empire, full of force and conviction. He was 'the prince', the leader of a young guard of successful business people. His presence at my bedside and the respect he showed me filled me with pride.

Much to my surprise, I then had a visit from Gianni Agnelli the same afternoon. Just like Berlusconi, he had a second home in St Moritz. But I hadn't expected the top man at Fiat and chairman of Juventus to be at my bedside. Agnelli had something of the 'King of Italy' about him, a real aristocrat and intellectual. He oozed wisdom and calm. His visit to me was special enough, but so too was what he said to me: 'We made a huge mistake. We should have bought you in 1987. I thought you'd like to know that.' He said these words very calmly, full of admiration. It touched me. A great man, and he said that to me.

The next day I was barely awake and still getting over the anaesthetic when Marti came in to tell me the operation had been a success, that he had removed many fragments of bone and that, in order to gain good access, he had also had to saw through a piece of bone. He said that recovery would probably take four weeks, but he'd agreed with

Tavana they would tell the outside world six weeks to leave some room for manoeuvre. It was difficult to take it all in.

I was looking forward to Christmas in Holland with friends and family. On crutches, maybe, but even so. More than anything I was looking ahead to my recovery in January, getting back on the pitch in February and scoring more goals at the San Siro.

This would all prove to be an illusion.

ANKLE (3)

Going for a walk in the North Sea

February 1993

We covered the last 200 metres to the beach in thick anoraks. Ted had parked the car as close as he could. There wasn't a soul about on this bleak day in February. As soon as we got out of the car the westerly wind blew me back a step or two. As Ted had predicted, there was a light on in the beach bar: The Sea-Breeze. How appropriate. Ted went in first. Behind the bar was a woman clearing up, otherwise the place was empty.

'Gentlemen, how may I help you?' She didn't recognize me. Ted did the talking. He knew I liked that. It was keeping me out of the wind, though not for long. I was supposed to have bare legs. Or at least, bare ankles.

Ted asked if we could get changed and leave our things there for a while. She said that was okay. We took off our shoes and socks and swapped our long trousers for shorts. We left our things in a corner, put our jackets back on and I walked silently behind Ted, back onto the beach in our bare feet. Again the wind took me by surprise.

He had started the day before, when I was at his practice in Rotterdam and he had examined my ankle. As always he did this with the utmost care. 'Marco, this ankle needs rest,' he said. 'It's overworked. I only have to look at it and it starts sweating. How long has it been like this?'

I explained that after the operation in St Moritz the pain had been different. Sharper, more piercing. With every step. That wasn't how it was before the operation. Then I had only had problems after training or a match, and then it had swollen up, but now it was red, swollen and sweaty all the time. The scar from Marti's knife, over the entire inside of my ankle, was still clearly visible. While it had healed over, it was also red and swollen.

Ted sighed and said nothing, as he made his way around the rest of my body with his hands, routinely but sensitively, as I had come to know. But something told me he only had half his mind on it, as if he could sense what was actually going on. After 20 minutes he suddenly said: 'We're going to the sea tomorrow morning. When the tide's in. We'll go for a walk in the sea, you and I. That's something we have to do.'

The cold, shifting sand was a relief for my ankle. We walked to the water's edge and stepped in. Each wave washed over our feet and calves. We started walking. Heading north. Ted on the right, me on the left, closer to the breakers. On the left the water, on the right the sand. The water splashed against my calves. I could feel the sand beneath my feet suck away as the water flowed back. We walked on. The wind was fierce and cold, but the seawater was colder still. After the shock of the first ice-cold waves, I was slowly losing the feeling in my feet. As I sank a little way into the sand, the pain was a good deal less, but after a quarter of an hour walking in the sea, I did have a sense of relief all round.

The huge breakers drowned out everything, but we didn't have much to say to each other anyway. We just walked. One step at a time. If Ted said it was a good idea to walk in the sea to give my ankle some rest, then that's what we did. Ted had been right so many times. He didn't need to explain it to me, I trusted him. He knew my body best.

The further we walked in silence, the more the pain eased. And the more the pain eased, the more I noticed our surroundings. I saw the crests on the waves before they crashed onto the beach. I saw the gulls hovering motionless above the waves.

I had been fully focused on my ankle since the operation at the end of December. On the pain I hadn't known before. The sharp, nasty pain. How many sorts of pain were there actually?

Suddenly Ted tapped me on the shoulder. 'Shall we turn round?'

I nodded. The water was washing over his ankles too, and his knees were wet. After 20 minutes we were back at the beach bar and went inside. The woman glanced up from behind the bar. 'I'm sure you'd like something now?'

Ted mumbled something that sounded like: 'Let's dry off first.' He produced two towels from somewhere and gave one to me. 'I'd like a hot chocolate. How about you?'

'Lovely.'

He asked me to rest my leg on a chair. Then he sat down on the chair next to it and looked at my ankle without touching it. He nodded in approval. 'We'll do it again tomorrow.'

ANKLE (4)

My last match

26 May 1993

It was a night to forget. The Champions League final between AC Milan and Olympique Marseille didn't go the way we were used to. Losing a European final was a completely new experience for us. For the first time in history, in fact.

I had been on the pitch twice since my operation at the end of December. Everyone wanted it so badly: Berlusconi, Capello, Tavana and me, of course, most of all, but as Tavana had predicted, recovery was taking far longer than we hoped. It was gruelling. The ankle seemed to be super sensitive. It swelled up for the slightest reason. And since December I had also been in constant pain.

Very often I didn't train with the others. I would work on a side pitch or in the gym. I often felt just as much of an outsider as in my first year at Milan. It was terrible not being able to train with the squad, not being able to play. But in Capello's second year Milan ended up reaching the Champions League final and naturally he wanted me there.

I wanted nothing more, but the pain had flared up very quickly each time during those two matches, restricting my movements and therefore my speed around the pitch. I tagged along in the cup against AS Roma in March and it wasn't much better against Ancona in May. I did score with my head from a corner and was delighted with the goal after all the misery, but what I didn't know then was that it would be

163

my very last goal. Even though I had a particularly bad feeling about my ankle after the surgery.

I had been back to Dr Marti, with Ted in tow. We had lots of questions, but even Marti was unable to explain why the recovery was taking so long. After a few months Milan were very annoyed about how slow the rehab was. I too, after months of sticking at it, with no appreciable change in the condition, felt I'd gone as far as I could with Marti. He just kept saying that I needed more time to recover and that rest was the best policy.

In the absence of any improvement, the idea emerged of approaching the Belgian doctor Marc Martens. He had operated successfully on my meniscus in 1989 and was also well known at Milan through his treatment of Ruud Gullit's knee. Ted also recommended him. At my first appointment in Antwerp, just before the Champions League final, Martens gave his opinion on why my previous treatment hadn't worked. He said he was an expert in cleaning out ankles like this. After the final he would operate on my ankle again.

The closer the final came, the more convinced I was that I would never be able to play in it without painkillers. In agreement with Milan's doctors and Capello I then made a radical decision. For the first time in my life I played with an injection. My whole right ankle was completely numb throughout the match. I didn't have much to show for it though. Two crosses and a shot on goal. Maybe I looked good now and then, but I was short of finesse and strength.

It was strange playing with such a numb ankle. Capello took me off in the 85th minute, something he wouldn't normally have done. I didn't understand why, he'd never substituted me before, and I'd never lost a match with him. That evening we did lose. I felt really bad about it. Because of the result, because I had managed to do so little and because of the prospect of another operation. I walked off a football pitch in an official match for the last time. Though I didn't know it then.

By the strangest of coincidences this final was in the same stadium where I experienced one of the greatest moments of my career. The Olympic Stadium in Munich. How painfully ironic life can be sometimes. My light in international football both started to glow and was snuffed out here. How uncanny. And all that in less than five years. All I had to look forward to after that night in Munich was my wedding to Liesbeth. It was set for 21 June, two weeks after Martens' surgery.

WEDDING

21 June 1993

There was no European Championship or World Cup and the league had just ended, so it was finally on. I was on crutches after Martens' operation, but that didn't make our wedding day any less special.

Our friend Alphons Peters had organized everything down to the last detail. Liesbeth had got involved, but I had kept out of it. For me things like this always only start getting real nearer the time. Liesbeth had urged me to look for a wedding suit in Italy, but I ended up buying a classic three-piece suit, with pinstripe trousers and a waistcoat, just a few days before from Tip de Bruin on Nieuwendijk. She 'just' had her dress made in Haarlem, after looking all over Milan without success. She looked wonderful. Rebecca and Angela, then three and two years old, were the bridesmaids. They particularly liked their dresses, but otherwise didn't understand much of what was going on.

The ceremony was in the morning at Castle De Haar in Haarzuilens, a beautiful location. Through my membership of the De Haar Golf Club I had come to know Baron Thierry van Zuylen van Nyevelt de Haar, a keen fellow golfer. After a few rounds together, Teddy, or Ted, as he was known, invited Liesbeth and me to an annual tournament held at his country estate in September. He always used to invite all kinds of VIPs and other worthies from around the world to it, including the likes of Brigitte Bardot, Gregory Peck, Jackie Onassis, Maria Callas and Roger Moore. We took part twice. Really the idea was that all the guests would stay in the castle during the tournament, but we preferred to sleep at home in Badhoevedorp. Nevertheless, we very much wanted to get married at Castle De Haar. Ricky Testa la Muta and Ruud van Boom were my witnesses, while Liesbeth had asked two friends.

The press gathered outside the castle and photos were taken after the ceremony. The rest of the day we had our own photographer and someone else from Milan, but otherwise just friends and family around us, which was very nice. The press were kept well away by security. For reasons of privacy, but also for reasons of security. An army of security people had been drafted in because of Berlusconi's presence. There was no way the press could get in. Most went home disappointed, with few sensational photos. Much of the comment in the newspapers, in particular *De Telegraaf*, was about how they hadn't been let in. They felt it was inappropriate and 'old-fashioned' to keep it all behind closed doors like that. I was very happy that it had been organized so securely.

Dennis Heijn, another friend, had arranged a helicopter that took Liesbeth and me for a flight over Badhoevedorp, Schiphol and Utrecht. They waved to us from the control tower at Schiphol, and air traffic was even stopped briefly. They put us down in Maarssen, at the Wilgenplas, a Michelin star restaurant where we ate lunch with our guests. This was also where we met up with the Italians, who had flown in by private jet that morning especially for the wedding: Berlusconi, of course, plus other Milan luminaries, Galliani, Capello, Tassotti and Tavana.

The party in the evening at Kasteel de Hoge Vuursche in Baarn was nice and relaxed. Alphons had arranged for Paul de Leeuw to be the special guest. He had become a big star in Holland, although this had rather passed us by. People went completely wild when he sang *'Vlieg met me mee naar de regenboog'* (Fly with me to the rainbow).

Everyone sang at the top of their voices and did flying impressions, what a madhouse it was. Paul sang another song that was very appropriate for Liesbeth and me: *'De vleugels van mijn vlucht'* (Wings of my flight). The words were so poignant, then and now. She really is the quiet strength in my life.

Later, when we were in our bedroom, we both had a good laugh about how everyone had gone into such raptures over Paul de Leeuw. Until that day we had never heard of him and his rainbow.

ANKLE (5)

The Ilizarov apparatus

June–September 1994

The apparatus had 22 pins going through my leg. Actually it was a kind of frame all around my lower leg. The Ilizarov apparatus, of Russian make, was fitted in June 1994.

As the December 1992 operation hadn't gone well, I had finally looked at treatment options beyond Dr Marti late in the spring of 1993. My ankle remained painful and swollen. AC Milan were very unhappy about it too.

The Belgian doctor Marc Martens was to be my new saviour. In June 1993 Martens had told me at his practice in Antwerp: 'Marti's approach hasn't worked for you. I'm going to sort it out for you now. I know how to clean out your ankle.' He had even conducted open discussions about it with Marti, through the newspapers. Martens presented himself as someone who knew exactly what to do. But again there had been hardly any improvement following the surgery. I ended up waiting for a year, in the hope of some progress, but in vain.

In the meantime I kept searching, even trying alternative therapies. Acupuncture, for example. There was a special Chinese practice on Biltstraat in Utrecht where I went with Ted Troost a few times. With those needles in my ankle, and hot coals against them. They did make my foot a little less swollen, a little less stiff. The practice also gave me some herbs, which I had to put in hot water at home and then put my foot in for half an hour. I even did this at

Milanello. I would walk around with a plastic bag with this herb soup in, while the others were at training. It did help a little. My ankle was less swollen, but the pain was still there when I moved it.

Then there was a brief moment of hope. In May 1994 we suddenly had some success with insoles and I felt slightly less pain. I briefly imagined that I might be able to go to the World Cup in America after all. But it proved to be a ridiculous idea, a mirage.

A year after Martens' 1993 intervention there was absolutely no prospect of improvement. Then, in June 1994, he said to me: 'There's something else we could try and that's the Ilizarov apparatus. They use it for people with achondroplasia, dwarfs. To make them taller. Pins go through your bones and are connected by a frame on the outside. Every day you pull the pins the tiniest bit further apart, by turning a wheel, so that in the course of a few months your bones also move slightly further apart.'

In my case we were talking about my shinbone and my ankle bone. Pulling these bones apart with this apparatus would create space between them where new connective tissue could grow that could act like cartilage. This could eventually replace the damaged cartilage so I would feel less pain and be able to move better and play sport again. That was the idea anyway. Martens clearly said before the whole procedure: 'It can't get any worse, you have nothing to lose.'

On 14 June 1994 they fitted the apparatus around my leg, 22 pins through my bones, in my shinbone and my foot. I had to clean it myself with alcohol and cotton wool three times a day. The places where the pins came out of my leg, through my skin, could become infected and so I had to disinfect them. A horrible job. They were open wounds, so there was a constant flow of muck coming out.

In those three months my lower leg became completely infected three times. Within a few hours I would have a fever of 40 degrees and would have to dash off to Antwerp, to the hospital where Martens was, for medication and observation. I couldn't drive a car myself with the frame around my leg, so Ted and Liesbeth both acted as my drivers.

Now, all my hope, after 18 months of misery, was invested in this apparatus. So I wanted to stick with it. After six weeks one of the pins broke off. That was excruciatingly painful. Then I had to go to Antwerp again, as fast as I could, to have it put back into my bone.

I had told Martens I wanted to stop. 'You're halfway there,' he said, 'keep going. It'll be worth it.'

So I kept going, although I slept very badly because the frame around my leg made it almost impossible to move. Every day I had to turn the wheel very slowly, two turns, to pull the bones apart.

The time before the Ilizarov may have been really awful, but those three months with that apparatus around my leg were absolute hell. Constant pain, not being able to sleep, all the cleaning and then the infections, the broken pin and the fever.

When Martens finally removed the apparatus from my leg in Antwerp, I thought the worst was over. But there was much worse to come. Once the apparatus had been removed, my ankle gave me no support, I couldn't walk, I couldn't do anything.

Like the dancer Nureyev

In Italy they saw beauty in the way I moved, they felt my style was graceful. That's why they called me The Swan. There's also an Italian children's book, a fairy tale about the Utrecht Swan, *Il Cigno di Utrecht*, based on my life in football. I think it's really special that children have that read to them at school.

Silvio Berlusconi would sometimes call me Nureyev, after the famous Russian ballet dancer, whose dancing was peerless. According to Berlusconi, I danced at the San Siro. At home in the hall I have a large painting based on Nureyev. An elegant dancer in red and black, Milan's colours. The style appeals to me. Without any frills.

The Dutch TV show *Studio Sport* once made a programme comparing my movements on the football pitch with those of a ballet dancer. The ballet guru and choreographer Rudi van Dantzig and Johan Cruyff discussed the similarities and differences between elite ballet and elite football. It's a compliment to be compared with a top dancer. It was very interesting, and the visuals were excellent too. You saw elegant movements of mine at De Meer, match images with classical music backing. And they arranged for a top ballet dancer, Clint Farha of the Dutch National Ballet, to dance in an empty Ajax stadium. It was called *Feints*. That was exactly what Berlusconi meant by his comparison with Nureyev.

What they all found so wonderful was that my style was so upright. Though I didn't quite see it that way. As a sportsman I think you really have to be closer to the ground, with a low centre of gravity, like Messi, Cruyff and Pelé, for example. They all look far more elegant, because they have a masterful way of moving. But I couldn't get as close to the ground. I couldn't bend my ankle so well after the operation in 1987, so I was always a little more upright in the years afterwards. Nevertheless, a great many people found my style very attractive. The perfect combination of coordination and balance.

ANKLE (6)

Night in the playroom

Spring 1995

It must have been getting on for four o'clock. I didn't think I'd woken anyone up this time. As I returned to the bed on my knees, I knew exactly what I had to do. I pushed myself up and back with my left leg, so that I ended up sitting on the bed and then I could lie on my back.

It had become routine. It was the least painful way, as I had learned over the last few months. Now that I was sleeping in the playroom, the others in the house weren't disturbed by me so much. I no longer needed to get down the stairs. That made a difference. Time and pain. But I was having trouble with myself. And increasingly with my thoughts.

Now that I was lying on my back again, I could focus on my breathing. Since the removal of that Ilizarov apparatus, the pain had been constant. The painkillers I got from Dr Tavana were nearly all gone, though I wasn't taking them as often. I didn't like those tablets. I wanted to know how it really felt.

I laid my hands on my stomach. An aura practitioner, Bert, had told me I had to try to shift my attention when I was lying on my back. My hands on my stomach, breathe deeply and then shift my focus from my ankle to my stomach. Away from that 'stiff leg'.

I tried it for a few minutes, but my ankle refused to be ignored. That was something else I now knew. I carefully turned onto my left side and touched my ankle very gently, another set ritual, as a kind of check. Swollen and sweaty, painful to the touch, however gentle I was. No change there then.

Lying down the pain was at least bearable; it was more of a nagging pain, but standing on my right foot was simply impossible. I just couldn't do it any more, not since Ilizarov.

Over the last few weeks more and more negative thoughts had been going through my mind. Nocturnal struggles in my head, even as I tried to calm and distract myself. Sleeping was very difficult. I was often not at all physically tired because I was hardly doing anything during the day. I couldn't burn off my energy. Only on the exercise bike did I sometimes succeed.

At least my tossing and turning wasn't keeping Liesbeth awake any longer. One parent having sleepless nights is more than enough with two young girls. Not that I could do much with Angela and Rebecca. I still couldn't take even a single step, so I wasn't much use to them. I sometimes felt a millstone around Liesbeth's neck. I hardly ever went outdoors. It took such a lot of effort, using the crutches all the time. I also found it embarrassing; I didn't want people to see me like this. So I would spend all day in front of the TV. Liesbeth handled it well, but it was amazingly difficult for her too. It was all so hopeless.

First, I had to calm my head down. This maelstrom of thoughts always came at night. Once I had crawled back into bed, after that trip to the toilet, I knew what was coming. Sometimes I would think all this was a punishment. That I had to pay for my drive, my pride, my great ego. For years I had just wanted to improve, play football at a higher level and earn more. With that great urge to get to the top and become more important, I had come a cropper big time. And now I was stuck. Bert tried to help me understand it better. He told me I had to be more flexible. Less stubborn than my father. Draw more on my softer, feminine side. A different mindset. And then relieve the stress on my ankle through the right hormone balance. Through breathing exercises, for example.

Writing things down might help as well, he said.

But as I lay there alone at night, none of that helped much. I would wonder what was really going on. I couldn't stand on my right leg and the muscles on that side had also begun to waste away, after three months of Ilizarov and eight months of crutches. I would compensate with my left leg all the time. Over the last few weeks I had been having some trouble with my left knee as a result of all this compensating. One problem led to another, but I wanted to understand it. Understanding helped me. I don't like losing control. So I reflected, tried over and over again to understand it. And as I lay there puzzling, my whole body would start sweating and sleep would seem even further away. I could feel the stream of negative thoughts coming when I lay down. They would overwhelm me, grab me by the throat. They were thoughts that were not helpful to me. Sometimes I thought I had bone cancer, because of the hundreds of X-rays of my ankle. Did anyone reassure me that this wasn't so? Or I thought that the screws in my leg had caused such a mess that I would never again be able to walk normally. That I was crippled. And then the sweat would break out and I would just lie there. I felt so powerless.

There was nothing optimistic I could set against my negative thoughts either. I was 30 and unable to walk. I was the father of two children, but couldn't play with them. I had been a celebrated sportsman, but couldn't even go for a walk round the block. I had trusted two doctors, but things had just got worse. What kind of future did I have? What were my options?

So I tried to restore calm to my head. I turned onto my right side and stared at the table with the board games, Monopoly, Goose,

Risk. I tried to think of the board games I used to play with the boys in my neighbourhood, tried to summon up some positive images. Bert had also said: 'Think about something positive if you're having negative thoughts.'

Board games normally cheered me up no end, but when I thought back to the table tennis table in Henri's garage, the leaping and the smashing, all that now seemed so far away. I couldn't even walk. Even what would normally make me happy wasn't helping me now.

It was also very tiring, just reflecting on my own thoughts. According to Bert, in my head I had magnified the problem with my ankle out of all proportion. I had to bring it back to something more realistic. But that wasn't it. That really wasn't it, because nothing had helped for two and a half years. Things had simply got worse.

Ted had dragged me all over the place. To the sea, to an acupuncturist, to the aura practitioner. Bert, that is. Liesbeth had recently even been to a Jomanda healing with a friend for me. 'Who knows, it might help, you never know.' It was well intentioned. As was what Ted did. But none of it made much difference. Nothing had helped.

A few months ago Ted had even wanted to take me to India, to some alternative healer or other in an ashram. But I had said no to that, it would have been a step too far for me.

Perhaps it was because I was a bit out of it, but I did find Bert's story interesting. It was about mindset, about looking at your injury differently, about flexibility and stubbornness. And standing firm.

Perhaps it was complete nonsense, but I did want to go back again. He came over as a smart guy. Sensitive. And it couldn't do any harm. He also came up with the breathing exercises. Next time he wanted to talk about my childhood. Oh well. It was all incredibly woolly, but okay, the regular doctors hadn't got me anywhere either.

So who was I to reject this out of hand? Who knows, it might help me a little, though it seemed terribly little that night.

Suddenly I remembered a phone call from Tavana. Last week, I thought. Liesbeth had answered. Tavana had very cautiously asked whether there had been any improvement. Liesbeth had answered for me. No, she said. Nothing, none at all.

Since that phone call I had occasionally thought about my contract with Milan. I was still being paid, but I hadn't played for two seasons now, since I had extended my contract by three years. That was all incredibly generous of Milan, but last week I had increasingly been thinking I had no desire to benefit from Berlusconi's largesse for another season if a return to football was so far away. I had shown my face at the final against Ajax, the month before. It had been painful, though I hadn't let it show.

Then a new thought started rising to the surface of my consciousness, something almost intangible. A fragment. But deep down I knew what it was. A vague outline, but increasingly concrete. I didn't yet dare think it out loud. It was big. It was very painful. But there was also something I liked about it. Giving up. Letting go. Surrendering. The next day I would phone Berlusconi and tell him. It was hopeless. I would never be coming back. It was over.

ANKLE (7)

Dying swan

18 August 1995

I was running and it was actually going rather well. Running at speed I mean. Okay, it was a jog, but even so. I'd started by walking – 10, 20, 30 metres – and then picked up the pace. And now I was maintaining my speed. Jogging. It had been a while.

It was quite a decent distance. All in all an exhilarating lap. And strangely enough I felt absolutely no pain. Stride by stride, running as though in a trance. Almost on autopilot. And in my ordinary clothes too – jeans, pink shirt, brown suede jacket.

As I ran I would occasionally raise my hands. Then I would clap for a moment. That went well too, in a flowing motion. I repeated the clapping a few times, as I ran.

I knew it was the thing to do, but it was also the way I wanted it to be.

Even though I knew this place well, I didn't feel comfortable. Despite the tremendous applause, I felt alone. I felt the emptiness, but continued my lap because I felt I had to. It was almost over.

I didn't really want to be there at all. This wasn't how it was supposed to be. I shouldn't have been running around here in my ordinary clothes while the others were standing still, in the centre circle. This was where I should have been sprinting. Scoring, first and foremost. For years to come. Conjuring up gems of goals on the grass of the San Siro. My grass.

I didn't want this. Not now. I still had so much more to give. There were still so many goals I wanted to show to the world. There was still so much I could win. This was only the beginning.

It felt silent, despite the 80,000 fans and their applause. Even though I could hear them chanting my name and see their banners.

For years I had had pain in my ankle, but that day the pain was gone. In fact, all the pain was gone. Numb, stunned, defeated, I didn't know how to describe it. Unreal. It was as though I wasn't actually there. I was running. And I was clapping. And everyone just kept singing, shouting and clapping. It was shaking. This stadium. My stadium.

Suddenly it hit me. As clear as day. It struck home. In front of the 80,000. I was witnessing my own farewell. Marco van Basten, footballer, was no more. You were watching someone who had ceased to be. You were clapping for someone who no longer existed. I ran and I clapped, but I was no longer there.

Perhaps it was because it was such a spontaneous event. That's why it had taken so long to sink in, but this was it. I had never wanted to believe that this moment would really come. My surrender.

Grief rose from the depths of my being. It caught me by surprise. The singing, the applause, forced their way through my armour-plating. I wanted to howl, but I couldn't start crying like a baby. I forced myself to remain calm. All under control, as I wanted to be, as I felt I had to be. I've always been able to do that if I really wanted to. This time was no different.

I ran. And I clapped. But I showed nothing of the pain. I could see my teammates, still waiting in the centre circle, full of emotion. Even more strongly I felt that the whole stadium was filled with grief. For what had been. For me. For who I had been. I was on the verge of tears, but I showed nothing.

I stopped running and clapping. My lap was at an end. Something had changed. Something fundamental. Football had been my life. I had lost my life.

That day I died as a footballer. I had been a guest at my own funeral.

ANKLE (8)

Liberation

February 1996

After that summer of 1995 and my farewell at the San Siro, I couldn't really sink any lower. We moved the family from Milan to Monaco and were regular visitors to Holland. There was still hardly anything I could do and the pain was there every day. I had completely had it with doctors, though I did get into conversation with Niek van Dijk, ankle specialist at the AMC, that autumn.

In November 1995 I told him the whole sorry tale. I had had three years of pain in my ankle, and after the Ilizarov apparatus it had got so much worse that I could hardly do anything. Walking was painful, I couldn't play golf, I couldn't play tennis, and football of course was completely out of the question.

Van Dijk was from a new generation of doctors who used new methods. He came up with the idea of keyhole surgery for ankles. Problems can be fixed without needing to open up the ankle. Even though he had learned his trade from Marti, his approach was completely different.

Van Dijk later helped many with his keyhole surgery, including Messi, Ronaldo and Zlatan, but for me this approach came ten years too late. The technique simply didn't exist back then. According to him, I was the only professional footballer he ever had on his table who had to stop playing because of the consequences of torn ankle ligaments.

'There is really only one solution,' he said. 'I will make one further attempt to clean it out. The chance of it making any difference is just one per cent, but you never know. It can't do any harm anyway. And if it doesn't work, and we'll know within a few weeks, I recommend fusing your ankle.'

Van Dijk took one look inside my ankle with a microscopic camera. He was very honest: 'Your ankle is in a very poor state. This really can't go on any longer. I think we need to fuse your ankle. Go away and think about it.'

The bone was now such a mess that it was becoming porous and beginning to look like an Aero bar. If I were to put any pressure on it, it could snap apart. 'We must be careful,' he said, 'because the joint is in such poor condition. I normally see people in their eighties with an ankle like this. They're the ones who have complaints of this kind.'

That was the ankle I had now. That's what the wonderful doctors had managed to do. I was 31.

The benefit of fusion is that your ankle stops getting inflamed. You no longer put the joint under excessive strain because there's no friction. The ankle is no longer swollen, though movement is limited. Finally, some calm comes to the joint and, if things go well, the pain slowly goes.

Finally, here was a doctor who told it like it was. I honestly hadn't known that such an option, fusion, even existed. For the first time in years I felt we were getting somewhere.

Van Dijk was now the number one ankle specialist in the world, although reputations rarely meant much to me now. For me it was more about the approach. He examined my ankle and decided it was affected by dystrophy, a kind of post-traumatic stress in the joint. The swelling, the getting hot, the sweating, the inability of the ankle to relax. It concerned him because it had been so longstanding. Van Dijk said: 'This has to stop. I understand that you can't go on this way, we need to do something.'

Fusion sounds simple, but it's actually major surgery. What it boils down to is that the top tarsal joint of your ankle ceases to be a joint. Your shin bone is screwed to your ankle bone and after a few months the bones grow together. The result is that there can be no movement between the bones and the whole cartilage issue becomes irrelevant. After the keyhole surgery Van Dijk was more certain than ever that the cartilage had almost entirely disappeared. It was bone on bone, and probably had been for more than a year. Hence the dystrophy and the pain.

He left the choice to me. Fusing your ankle is for the rest of your life. It's a sacrifice. There's no going back. He said: 'You'll be paying a price to be pain-free. You must think about it carefully.' I found it very difficult to work out what I would be able to do with my ankle afterwards. I really wanted to do some sport again, but it was also a kind of surrender. Giving in to the painful reality that my ankle was wrecked. I couldn't bear it, acknowledging the failure of my ankle.

At the same time I no longer had any choice. The pain had brought me to my knees. The sleepless nights, staring at the ceiling. My irritability, purely because I couldn't do any exercise to burn off my energy. Since Ilizarov it had been unbearable. After eight months of crutches and painkillers it had simply got worse. Sport was still out of the question and there was no prospect of improvement.

I took the plunge at the beginning of February. On 14 February 1996 at the AMC Dr Van Dijk fixed my shin bone to my foot with a few big screws. It sounds very graphic and it was. It was fused.

After ten weeks of plaster, to let the bones grow together, the pain was gone. My ankle was completely fused, no friction, no movement, but no pain. I couldn't believe it. Naturally, I wasn't allowed to do much to begin with, so I tried not to be too euphoric, but I didn't hold back either. It was liberating. For the first time since December 1992 the pain was gone.

Every morning I expected the pain to return when I got up. 'I'm sure it will start hurting again when I walk on it today.' But no. The wounds from the operation healed and for the first time in years my ankle was relaxed again. I had limited mobility, I couldn't move my foot as I had before, but the bottom tarsal joint was still functioning. So I hadn't ended up with a club foot. I had to get used to it, but as the months went by I gradually learned how to get around with my fused ankle.

We were living in Monaco at the time. As soon as I could, early in May, I even tried a gentle game of tennis. I had met someone there who had just had surgery on his back, Gerard Iwema. I can still see us on the centre court at one of the most attractive tennis clubs in Europe, right by the Mediterranean Sea. Gerard and me. Our standard when we started was enough to make you weep. It was certainly a case of the blind leading the blind, ha-ha.

But it was the first time I had gone out to play sport again, for a simple game of tennis. It was really wonderful. I had been indoors for so long. Miserable, sitting on the settee in front of the TV, sleeping in the playroom, stumbling to the kitchen to get something to drink. Now and again on the exercise bike, but that was it. Real sport was so far away. That tennis with Gerard, however limited, felt a bit like the light at the end of the tunnel. Liesbeth said later that the dark cloud around me began to lift when I was able to play sport again, however little I could do.

So I was doing a bit of tennis and also playing golf again. That became my new passion and I really enjoyed it. Football was a non-starter with my fused ankle, but I thought it was wonderful being outside, feeling the sweat and playing matches again. Even when I lost. When all's said and done, since the fusing of my ankle, it was as though a miracle had happened.

It had been a difficult time after that Ilizarov apparatus. A dark chapter. And now that it was finally over, for the first time in years something lovely, something bright, something sunny reappeared. I could burn off my energy again, I could breathe again. I felt liberated.

The wonderful thing about Monaco is that many of the people who live there like doing their own thing, so it was a place where I could be reasonably anonymous. It became a bit more cheerful on the family front too. In May 1997 our son Alexander was born there. After two daughters we now had a son as well. We were delighted.

When I started playing sport again, of course there were new obstacles. Playing golf, my ankle stopped me from completing my swing fully, but I learned how to compensate for it. It wasn't ideal, but physically I could handle it, so it soon stopped being an issue. And then I could give it everything, all my energy. It was a new world.

Later on, Van Dijk told me I had almost scared him out of his wits because I was supposed to rest completely for ten weeks after the operation, to give the bones the time they needed to grow together. Before then everything was still too fragile for too much pressure to be put on the recently fused joint. After twelve weeks Van Dijk's mother-in-law phoned him to say he should switch on the TV. He did so and couldn't believe his eyes: an indoor footvolley tournament in Aalsmeer, and who should be there, playing a game in the sand with someone else, against Ronald and Frank de Boer? Yes, me!

Van Dijk told me he had gone white with fright, but on reflection he decided: this guy is testing his limits. Playing sport so soon and so intensively was risky. He hoped the telephone wouldn't ring. And fortunately it didn't. It remained silent. Eventually he was able to heave a sigh of relief.

It was a risk perhaps, but I felt totally liberated. I couldn't believe I had my body back. I wanted to enjoy it to the full right away, despite its new limitations. The pain had gone, it felt like a gift. I wanted to know how far I could go.

In the end Van Dijk was the only doctor who really helped me. I'm eternally grateful to him for that.

In the summer months we sometimes went to Juan les Pins, to the beach. It wasn't far away. Once I saw a group of guys playing footvolley. I went to join in because I had less trouble with my ankle in the sand. My only problem was pushing off, but I could make up for that with my great feel for the ball, ha-ha.

After joining in a few times, I got talking to a Frenchman aged about forty. He was exceptionally good, and really stood out. He was well built, technically excellent and hugely gifted tactically.

We were in international company, with Brazilians and Argentinians. Many players took part each day, but he was far and away the best. His name was Jean-Claude. I asked him what he did for a living and he told me he worked at Nice airport, in baggage handling. Removing cases from the belt and taking them away. Hard, mind-numbing work. 'Well, you have to do something,' he said.

But he was so good at footvolley, he won all his games, so I asked him why he hadn't been a professional footballer.

'I had a great future in football in front of me,' he said, 'until I tore my cruciate ligament at the age of sixteen. The long recovery period that followed got in the way of my professional career.' A lot of bad luck with his knee finally forced him to give up on his dream. He had had trouble with it for years and only much later did he start playing a bit of footvolley on the beach at Juan les Pins. Now he was enjoying himself again and he also felt the return of that desire to be good at something. And he had indeed become really very good.

On the way back from Juan les Pins to Monaco I couldn't get the image of Jean-Claude by the baggage belt out of my head. This was a man who had lost his whole career, who had never been able to become a professional footballer. I had at least had the chance to play at the top level for ten whole wonderful years. That was when I realized that my glass wasn't half empty, but half full. That I should be happy and grateful that I had the chance to experience all those fantastic moments in my football career. I also thought back to the time when I stood in front of the mirror at Milanello and thought: it can't end here, can it? I still have so much I want to show the world.

In the car going back to Monaco I was suddenly struck by a very powerful thought. I could keep complaining that I had lost half of my career, but at least I had had half of one. And in that half a career I had also had the good fortune to experience many wonderful things. It was a real eye-opener.

PART IV

FINANCES AND THE COACH

1998–2009

FINANCES (1)

Christmas in the dark

2001

We had been living back in Badhoevedorp for three years. We had left
Monaco in 1998, mainly for the children's sake. We wanted them to go
to a Dutch school and grow up in Holland.

It was a week before Christmas when I heard Liesbeth call from
downstairs. There had just been a ring at the door and she sounded a
little panicky. And Liesbeth doesn't panic easily. Hardly anything ever
alarms her. I raced downstairs two steps at a time. She was standing
in the hallway with a large blue envelope in her hand and a rather
troubled look in her eyes. 'They've frozen everything, the man said.
Including all our bank accounts.'

'What do you mean, who have?'

'The tax people. Look.' She pushed the thick envelope into
my hands.

When we opened it, we saw the amount in bold print at the foot
of the page. The demand was incredibly high. Far more than we could
ever pay. The tax authorities were freezing everything. My throat felt
like it was being squeezed and the muscles in my legs were tensing up.
We did of course still have money from my time in Italy – although I
hadn't touched a ball in nearly nine years – but this meant that I now
no longer had access to it. It made no sense to us at all.

In the months that followed I spent hours in tax offices and with
lawyers. I did my best to understand all the financial jargon, but it was

very difficult to follow in any meaningful way, let alone understand
it properly. Sometimes I yearned for the time when I was still playing
at Ajax and every week would drink coffee with Cor Coster, my
first agent. A flamboyant man who had seen a lot in his time and
sometimes perhaps sailed a bit close to the wind, but in my time with
him I at least never ran into any problems.

When I got my first contract as a player at Ajax, I wanted things done
properly. Cruyff always talked a lot about football with young players,
and now and again about things like this too. It was through him
that I came into contact with Coster, his father-in-law. He lived in a
wonderful building on Nassaukade. I often used to go and see him
on a Friday morning. His wife would bring the coffee and Uncle Cor
would start telling these brilliant stories. About business, but also
about life. Later on he would take me to AC Milan as well. Johan had
wanted to keep me at Ajax for another year, but by then I had been top
scorer in Holland three years in a row and had won the Golden Boot.
So Coster could see opportunities. Unsurprisingly. I liked him.

I will never forget our first time in Italy, in the summer of 1986,
when Silvio Berlusconi received us at his country estate. Cor Coster,
Apollonius Konijnenburg and me. Apollonius had set up the contact.

We were royally entertained. It was a huge complex, each room
grander than the one before. 'Don't let yourself be overawed, Marco,
let's stick to the plan. He's just trying to impress us,' said Cor. I had to
chuckle because I could see he was a bit nervous. I loved it all though.
Berlusconi showed us his library, a splendid room. Again Coster
whispered: 'Don't let him dazzle you. We'll only sign the contract if he
offers us the amount we want.' At one point he had me in stitches. He
just kept up the idle chit-chat as Berlusconi carried on with his guided
tour. Berlusconi even played us the Milan anthem, the new club song

he had had composed, and what's more sang along with it. In the end Berlusconi did exactly what we wanted, so all of Coster's nerves had been for nothing.

A few months later, in Amsterdam, Berlusconi gave me a watch as a gift, which was great, but not of course why I'd signed a contract to play abroad. He had big plans for Milan, that was the main thing, and was putting a lot of money into the club. And I was indeed going to be paid handsomely. I signed a preliminary contract with Milan in the summer of 1986 and the signing-on fee I received from Berlusconi, a few million guilders, was deposited at a bank in Switzerland. When I actually went to Milan a year later, I signed a routine contract.

Some time later we did actually declare the money held in Switzerland to the authorities in Italy. You could apply for a kind of tax amnesty, which was very common in those days. If you had earned money somewhere that hadn't yet been declared, this amnesty allowed you to pay a certain amount in tax and a relatively small fine. This then as it were 'legalized' the money for the Italian tax authorities.

Coster arranged everything properly, but with the contracts getting bigger and bigger in the years that followed, in 1989 he had brought in a large international law firm. From then on he worked with a lawyer. It started well enough, but soon she began driving Coster up the wall. She wanted everything done strictly according to the letter of the law and in every last detail and he felt she was increasingly taking the lead in the partnership. He said he wanted to bring the relationship with her to an end, but I was very happy with her.

It was very important for me that everything was arranged and recorded correctly. I wanted everything to be entirely proper and within the rules. No problems. I wanted to be able to sleep easily. I had seen how things could go completely awry with Johan and that

Michel Basilevitch, his Belarusian adviser. Johan had handed over all his earnings to invest in a Spanish pig farm and lost everything. It was the first time he did anything without Coster knowing about it. Coster apparently said afterwards: 'The only thing Johan can do now, without me, is go to the loo.' In the end he had to start all over again. That's partly why he carried on with football all those years. Same old story. And I really didn't want to go through that myself.

Coster eventually asked me to choose between him and the lawyer. I thanked him for the services rendered and then switched over completely. From then on the lawyer looked after all my affairs. It maybe cost a bit more, but at least I knew it was all above board.

Reality unfortunately proved to be rather more problematic than all the fine words led us to believe. Liesbeth and I believed we had everything nicely sorted. Until we sat on the settee together and opened the envelope that afternoon in Badhoevedorp, in late December 2001.

THIS TAX DEMAND, FROM THE DUTCH TAX AUTHORITIES, TO BE PAID BY MR VAN BASTEN IN FULL BY 31 DECEMBER 2001: 32.8 MILLION EUROS.

We had imagined our Christmas with the children rather differently.

COACH (1)

How I came back into football

2002–2004

After my ankle had been fused in February 1996 and I was fully
focused on my recovery, between 1996 and 1998 I slowly came back to
life in Monaco. Finally, free of pain. Playing sport helped, but football
was a long way off. I hardly ever watched it either. *Studio Sport* wasn't
shown there.

During the 1998 World Cup I did once sit in the stands with
Danny Blind at Holland v. Argentina in Marseille because it was
being played only two hours from my home. It was the game with
Ortega's bizarre header against Van der Sar and that important goal
from Bergkamp. I was sitting on that side of the stadium. It was a really
fantastic goal, but it didn't do much for me. I mainly remember the
headache I got from the hours sitting in the blazing sun.

It was around that time, during World Cup qualifying, in 1996 or
1997, that Guus Hiddink asked me to be his assistant. He already had
Koeman, Rijkaard and Krol as assistants and he felt I was the perfect
fit for that group. We discussed it on the golf course at Mougins, but
I didn't do it in the end. I had absolutely no interest in it. I had left
football far behind.

As soon as I could finally walk pain-free again, I mainly played
golf. Walking was no longer a problem and my ankle didn't swell up
so quickly. I played a lot in the Monaco area. Back in Holland I joined

the Noordwijkse club and started playing rather obsessively with some people I got to know there. For me just for fun is never enough. I want to keep winning.

Since I had a handicap of four by this time, I was able to take part in a qualifying tournament for the Noordwijkse club's first league team and to my great surprise I earned a place as sixth player. The team played for the Dutch championship, a kind of golf premier league, but at amateur level. I became even more obsessive about it. In 2000 we became champions of Holland. The year after we were in the final again, but lost narrowly. It was a lovely time when football was briefly out of the picture. The fun of playing in a league grabbed me again, but not being a natural golfer, it took me a lot of effort to keep my standard up. It wasn't long before I stopped playing in the league.

At that time I was also seeing more of John van 't Schip again. There had been a period when we hadn't seen so much of each other, but we had always been good friends. First in our time at Ajax and later in Italy too, when he was playing at Genoa.

He had become coach of FC Twente and early in 2002 I went along to watch a training session. John was really enthusiastic about the work and was doing fairly well with Twente. Afterwards the thought did cross my mind: might this be something for me too? It was the first time I had felt this way. I noticed that little by little my initial reticence was beginning to disappear. Especially when John was subsequently sacked, because Twente were losing too many games, and we had the idea of maybe doing something together in the future. But I would have to do my coaching badges first.

I had enrolled with the Dutch FA to do my coaching course in the '02–'03 season. But in May 2002, during a friendly match with the 1988 European Championship side against RKC, I tore my cruciate ligament. It was one of the first times I had been back on the pitch. After no more than a minute I took an outswinging ball from John Bosman on the outside of my foot. As I turned, on that bone-dry pitch in Waalwijk, it felt like a safe door slammed shut on my knee. A dull pop. It was terribly painful.

I was really fed up. I needed to take it easy for six months. In the end the recovery took nine months. Luckily I was no longer a footballer. A week or two after the operation I got a mechanical device for my leg to keep my knee moving that I used three times a day.

So I eventually did the Professional Football Coach course while rehabilitating from my cruciate ligament operation. It wasn't ideal, but there was no other way.

Normally, you were supposed to do Coach Level 3 first, followed by Level 2 and then Level 1, but I went straight onto the Professional Football Coach course. Ronald Spelbos and Wim Koevermans were the instructors. I had played with both of them, so that worked out well. They made it fun, not preachy at any rate and they really tried to help me. Initially, I had wondered what it was they were going to teach me at the Dutch FA's headquarters in Zeist. But apparently there were certain gaps in my knowledge and I needed extra support.

At the time Cruyff was advocating giving former professional players 'that diploma' straight away. He thought a course like this for former pros was nonsense. I didn't agree with him. I really needed that year and in my view ex-professional footballers should go on two courses: the Coach Level 1 course and the Professional Football Coach course. You need time to switch over from thinking like a player to thinking and acting like a coach.

Overall I found it all really interesting. Running a training session isn't something you can do straight off the top of your head.

Preparation, leading meetings, creating line-ups, choosing tactics, all these things were new to me. And they are things all professional players have to learn if they want to become a coach. At the same time I had been away from football for years, so I needed a refresher. For example, I didn't know the names of all the players in the Eredivisie by a long shot.

When John became coach at the Ajax Academy, I did a placement with Ronald Koeman's first eleven. Zlatan Ibrahimović kept daring me to do things at training. Can you do this? Can you do that? That was all well and good, but I could do very little with my ankle and my recently repaired cruciate ligament. I realized at once that I could never be a coach like Cruyff, who joined in with the Rondos, went in among the players and was at least as good. And Cruyff was my role model. So that was painful. A real limitation.

I remember when I started the season with John at the Ajax Academy. I had passed the course with flying colours and for the first match at home against the Vitesse Academy I was on the bench as assistant coach. In no time at all we were 2-0 down. What's happening here? I thought. It was all going so fast, I was really taken aback. Then came the question: 'So what do we need to do?'

John of course was rather more used to it than me and was already preparing a change, before I had even begun to understand what the problem was. Ha-ha. Simply the idea that you had to do something instead of just watching was completely new to me. And I didn't see it; I realized that I wasn't yet used to watching a match tactically with a view to intervening quickly.

But managing the Ajax Academy with John soon felt quite natural. And I was comfortable on the sidelines. We knew each other really well. To start with he was head coach with me as his assistant, but halfway through the season we swapped places. I started leading the training sessions, holding meetings and making final decisions during matches. That was certainly very different. Great experience too.

It was an unusual time with Ronald Koeman as head coach, Louis van Gaal as technical director and John and me at the Ajax Academy. Louis has by nature always had something of the schoolteacher about him, so the two of us – just like Ronald – had to give him an account of what we were doing each week. Every Tuesday John and I would be in Louis's office. Which was fine in theory, but one Sunday after the first team had suffered a defeat, it was fairly unruly in the coach's office. Ruud Krol was there, Tonny Bruins Slot, David Endt, Koeman, John and me. And Louis. There was a noisy, disorganized discussion going on and the atmosphere left something to be desired. Suddenly, out of nowhere, Louis shouted: 'And now everyone be quiet. It's pandemonium in here. This really won't do!' A bit of a rant. But Koeman was head coach and we were in the coach's office, so we were all rather taken aback. 'This isn't communicating, it won't work like this,' Louis continued and he left the room with a hint of indignation.

The next evening we had an Ajax Academy match, and the following morning John and I were back in Louis's office. During the meeting that followed he began to question me fairly critically: 'Why did you do this and that?' He felt I should explain things better, communicate better with the players.

He'd gone too far. 'Excuse me, no, all you're doing is preaching,' I said sharply. 'For no good reason you embark on a rant while you're in the coach's office, and you're technical director. Ronald's the coach. You startled us all. That's a strange way of communicating!'

Louis was clearly incensed. Who did I think I was? He started to call me 'assistant'. When we had finished, after an hour, he opened the door. Next to his office were the general offices, with doors open, where all sorts of people worked. As we left he said to John: 'And take your assistant with you.' Everyone could hear, which was precisely what he wanted. I gave him a look as if to say: aren't you the funny one.

FINANCES (2)

Everything was for Bassie

September 2002

I was on the exercise bike, going through my workout programme, as so often in recent weeks. Five minutes at 180 watts, four at 140, six at 190. And another five at 180. Finally, eight minutes at 130. I read my heart rate off a monitor strapped tightly round my chest. As usual, I made a note of the figures on my notepad. Heart rate, wattage, distance, minutes. As I have done all my life. It was calming to have figures on paper. The pad was nearly full. I was sweating. More than normal, though it was no warmer than usual up here in the attic. A heart rate of 195, that wasn't so good.

Why hadn't I heard anything? Why weren't they calling me? They knew I followed the news, didn't they? That I had seen on the news that share prices had now reached an historic low and recovery was nowhere in sight? They also knew that the planes flying into those towers had had an effect globally, didn't they? They had to look after my money? Invest it wisely? The last few times I had looked at my statements, it had left me feeling worried.

Yes, I had said they could invest aggressively. I had wanted a different approach from before, when Alexander Jurgens, my Dutch-Swiss friend from Monaco, managed my money. An annual return of around 4 per cent on average. Nothing wrong with that, you might say. Nothing reckless.

Back in Holland I had heard from friends and people around me that a return of 10 to 14 per cent per year had now become quite common. What was I doing with my money in those safe Swiss investments? Time and again they would tell me how I was missing out on opportunities right under my nose. So yes, I got carried away, I'll be honest about it. I was seeing dollar signs in front of my eyes. Initially, I transferred two million euros and eventually everything, another 20 million plus. That was at the end of 1999.

They had people at the bank who knew about these things, didn't they? Who would do what was best to protect my capital? Who would call if something was wrong? You would expect that, surely? I hadn't heard anything from my lawyer either, although she wasn't directly advising me on my investments. Yes, Alexander had warned me, but I hadn't listened to him.

It had been gnawing away at me for weeks. The day before, I had for the first time summoned up the courage to do a search, online. I was no expert, but I wasn't born yesterday either. However, seeing those figures in front of me gave me a fright. The Amsterdam Exchanges Index had nearly halved since I transferred that 22 million to the ABN AMRO Bank to invest for me. I started to sweat. Then I went and had a good look at my own statements. That's not something I would ever normally do, I always left it to my lawyer. It gave me a headache and I slept badly as a result. I said nothing to Liesbeth because she usually left things like this to me.

After that hammer blow of a tax demand the previous Christmas, I'd well and truly got the wind up. We were now in discussions with the tax authorities, and the worst of the danger seemed to be over, but there was still a huge demand hanging over my head. Major errors had been made, that much was now clear, but who had made them was still uncertain. I had less and less confidence in it all.

I said as much in passing to Perry Overeem, who was well versed in financial matters. He gave a meaningful nod, but was otherwise noncommittal. Liesbeth and I had recently even begun to wonder whether I shouldn't seriously start looking for work again. There was something surreal about that because we had never actually had that sort of conversation before.

I put my notepad on the cabinet next to the exercise bike. My heart was in my mouth. I mopped the sweat from my brow and picked up my phone. I could still see that chap in front of me. I searched for ABN Asset Management and saw again the sparkling Oval Tower in front of me. At the time it had been a brand spanking new building next to the ArenA Stadium in Amsterdam Zuidoost. In the spring of 1999, a five-man delegation had extended every courtesy to my lawyer and me there. It had been as classy as could be.

It was the place, a VIP explained to me, where all the new, very wealthy clients were received, or rather, pampered. At the time returns were skyrocketing and they could promise everyone the earth without blinking an eye. Not only that: I was rolling up with – at the time – 50 million Dutch guilders in my back pocket. In new money, nearly 23 million euros.

Hallelujah! It was as if our dear Lord Jesus Christ himself had just wandered in. Oh yes, we really would like to manage your money. You want a high return? No problem. Of course, we spread the risk. We invest in 20 different funds. Our commission isn't the highest in the financial world and we will of course keep a close eye on your riches for you. Blah, blah, blah.

They also wanted me to be a kind of Sports Desk ambassador, as Richard Krajicek was at the time. ABN AMRO's Sports Desk ambassadors like Krajicek advise the bank how to optimize its service to athletes. I politely declined. After all the pretension and inevitable champagne, I had the business card of a rather more reserved man shoved into my hand. He had stared rather diffidently straight ahead throughout the meeting and wasn't so taken with all the jovial hand shaking. I liked him.

But otherwise it was an entirely bizarre set-up. Again an abundance of lovely neckties. But it was disappointing, with the benefit of hindsight, that I subsequently heard little more from these people. And that a large part of my capital had undoubtedly disappeared into thin air. Why hadn't my lawyer sounded the alarm? I was paying her enough, a nice bill from her every month. Ever since 1989.

And then he answered: 'ABN Asset Management'. He had clearly become well practised in bad news calls in recent months.

'Mr Van Basten. Good to hear from you. We've been through some extremely tough times, the last year and a half. You won't be surprised to hear that. Your capital hasn't come through entirely unscathed, I'm afraid to say, I can't put any gloss on it. We have left all your holdings as they are, and haven't taken the loss yet, however serious, in the hope that prices and – of course – your capital recover. We've been in a status quo situation for six months now. It's now September 2002. A year after the very biggest of crashes since 1987. So we're hoping to start building up again in the coming months and years. To keep the recovery going–'

'I'm sorry to interrupt you. But, to be honest, all these fine words are all very well. I just want to know what the damage is. What's left of the nearly 23 million I invested with you three years ago. If I withdraw it today?'

It all went quiet for a moment. It was as if he had to swallow hard. He hadn't expected this response. It wasn't the way he talked

BASTA

either. But there was no way round it. Even after the silence though he stayed on script.

'Mr Van Basten, I won't beat about the bush. If you decide to withdraw all your deposits today, and to give up all your holdings, and not wait for any recovery…Then, from your original investment of nearly 23 million, what you currently have left is…' – more silence – 'Um…a little less than 13 million euros. If you decide to go ahead…' – another pause – '10 million euros will immediately, permanently and for ever, evaporate into thin air. So please, please do think about it very carefully.'

When I stood up I had to grab the handlebars of the exercise bike. A dizzy spell. For form's sake I would still consult my lawyer. But I had already made up my mind. If I withdrew my money now, I would at least still have that 13 million. If I left it where it was, anything could happen.

Who was to say that more planes wouldn't fly into some towers somewhere? Or that there wouldn't be more attacks? Or that the stock market wouldn't take another nose-dive for some reason? No, I would take my losses. As soon as possible. Salvage what was left. With that amount I could at least survive. With my family. That's how it felt.

You've been an incredible dope to have been taken in this way, Bassie. Absolutely not 'everything is for Bassie'. Ten million vanished. Everything *was* for Bassie. I would put that 13 million back in the safe hands of Alexander, the one I could depend on. I went downstairs. Towel over my shoulder, water bottle in my hand and 10 million lighter. I was going to look for Liesbeth.

DO YOU BELIEVE IN FAIRY TALES?

2002

Perry and I had played golf together for a few years. And we also played a lot of tennis. We had met at the wedding of my schoolfriend André van Vliet in 1998, when I had just got back to Holland. In fact, André introduced us by saying: 'I think the two of you should play each other at golf. You're both nuts about it and both so ridiculously obsessive.' He could easily have added pig-headed to that.

At the first hole and after the very first stroke we found ourselves discussing the lie of Perry's ball, which had landed close to a fence. It was about precisely where he could play the ball from. And with or without a penalty stroke. Perry felt the fence was an 'unnatural element of the course', in which case you're allowed to place the ball slightly further away, without a penalty stroke. But I said: 'That fence has been there for ten years, so it's part of the course. It's a natural element of the course.'

So there we stood. Both of us super stubborn. The very first time we had played golf together. We even summoned a marshal to adjudicate for us. It was my home course, in Noordwijk. And I thought: this guy isn't going to tell me what the rules are on my own course. And Perry stood his ground just the same. In fact, in those early days, we had a regular battle of wills. Things could have ended very differently between us.

I will never forget the day we went to play tennis at a tennis centre in Nieuwegein, and I didn't play at all well. On the way there I was stuck in a traffic jam for an hour, then I was swept off court 6-0, 6-1. On the way home I spent another hour stuck in a traffic jam. Then he had the nerve to send me an email with a hint of sympathy. Something like: 'I got really lucky, it wasn't your day. And you got stuck in the traffic jam. I'm sure you'll do better next time.' Now, that's not the sort of thing to say to me. I wrote back: 'Stuff and nonsense, I don't need your sympathy.'

That shows what I'm like. But Perry's just the same. At the time we were obsessive about improving. Not for fun, but to win. That's all that mattered. Occasionally we would go out to eat with our wives, but mainly we played sport together and discussed all manner of things along the way. And even then we wanted to be proved right. Let's just say that I saw a lot of myself in him. But he was clearly better at business. Far better, I'm glad to say.

When I found myself in this financial mess, news of it trickled through to Perry. Increasingly, I was telling him things as we played. Especially when that tax demand landed on my door mat. He also picked up something about the investments I had. I knew he had built up a company with a workforce of almost a hundred. In 2000 he had asked me to open their new office building in Houten. Sometimes I would go there on the spur of the moment to have lunch, a bit of a chat and play table football with the young people there. It was fun, but around the turn of the year 2001/2002 I had major worries on two fronts. That demand for 32.8 million in particular was a bolt from the blue. Years before I had, let's not forget, hired an expensive firm to prevent precisely this sort of thing. I paid them stacks of money for their work, so that I could at least be sure no issues would arise and I could sleep easily. Or so I thought.

But no. On 1 January 2002 I awoke with the Dutch tax authorities on my back. It all had something to do with the way I had relocated from Monaco to Holland with regard to tax. Something had gone very wrong there. Though I didn't yet understand what.

Afterwards you might wonder how so much could have gone wrong with everything under the guidance and supervision of my lawyer. Was she right to rely on the tax expertise of others? Was it preventable?

What had happened was that a large international tax consultancy that my lawyer had hired specially for the purpose had come up with what they felt was an ingenious arrangement. And what did they come up with? Or rather: what did one so-called brilliant individual come up with? A complex arrangement with interest paid in advance, a variant inspired by a certificate of prepaid interest often issued by banks at the time. Only in this case it would be issued by my own limited company.

Broadly speaking, while I was still living in Monaco, I would transfer my private capital to my company set up specifically for this purpose, thereby acquiring a huge claim against the company. In the loan agreement set up for this the interest was paid in advance over a long period, ten or even twenty years, on a compound interest basis. As a result this claim rose to a sum four times higher than my deposit. This increase in value could be repaid by the company tax free once I had migrated to Holland, they thought. Wrong.

It was entirely legal, they told me. But it was a complete mystery to me and I left that sort of thing to my lawyer. Under her supervision I almost 'blindly' put my signature to the tax consultants' advice. It was all very complicated and time-consuming. I still wouldn't understand it now. But anyway, I trusted it. They told me it was fine and that the structure was okay. That was undoubtedly her belief at the time as well.

I don't know if you've seen *The Wolf of Wall Street*. It was – I later understood – a bit like in that film. In the financial sector at the time everything was enjoying skyrocketing growth. People were coming up with one brilliant new financial product after the other. They were earning a lot of money with them and from them. The specialists we spoke to about it later called the arrangement 'innovative and potentially brilliant'.

It all seemed so perfect, but they had made a grave error. Or actually two, as I later found out. The first was that they never sought a second opinion on the plan, the arrangement with the certificate of prepaid interest. Given how great a financial risk it was, you might think this was necessary and a good idea.

The second error was what really ruined this arrangement. Or rather: ruined me. They had registered the limited company set up for this purpose in the wrong country, in Holland. If I had lived in a country with a tax treaty with Holland, this demand would have been made impossible.

But now the Dutch tax authorities could investigate fully. And they did. It turned out they could now tax me and they did so straight away. Since my advisers had submitted an incorrect return, I received a 100 per cent penalty, with interest on top. The demand eventually came to almost 75 million guilders.

With the benefit of hindsight you could say that I should have simply paid tax on my future interest income. That I should have done the same as everyone else. Then I wouldn't have had this problem.

For the first time I began to have serious doubts about whether a lawyer was the right person to continue looking after my affairs. That was because the tax matter was slowly becoming clearer to me, but also because the investment issue had been allowed to drift somewhat.

In the meantime I was telling Perry more and more. He seemed very well informed and gave good advice. At his suggestion I then made an appointment to discuss the tax problem with my new tax adviser, Pieter Asjes of PricewaterhouseCoopers in Amstelveen. I knew far too little about the matter and shied away from it. So I asked Perry to go with me. After Pieter and I had spent about half an hour talking at cross-purposes, because my understanding really was so poor, Perry felt he could no longer sit by and listen and fortunately started to get actively involved too. As a result it ended up being a useful and constructive meeting, with the conclusion that it would be best if we were to aim for a compromise that was reasonably acceptable to me. And the prospect of a demand that I could at least pay. If all went well.

For the first time since that demand just before Christmas I was beginning to feel more relaxed again, and above all relieved. From then on – spring 2002 – I started to involve Perry more and more in my affairs. In the end, in 2005, we were able to reach an agreement with the Dutch tax authorities acceptable to both parties. The tax consultancy that had previously come up with the brilliant 'certificate of interest' eventually paid a substantial sum because of the errors they had made. They accepted their responsibility. That was fair, but to my mind it was also something of an admission of guilt. However, I had also been naive. Twice in quick succession I had been penalized for my own negligence and gullibility. I had relied too much on the advice and opinions of my advisers and lawyer. But yes, it was an area of which I had absolutely no understanding. It was so far removed from football. That was precisely why I had these people, to shield me from this sort of trouble.

By mid-2006 the partnership with my lawyer was coming to an end, because I eventually felt that Perry was better and more of an all-rounder. More resolute as well. He sank his teeth into my affairs like a pit bull.

I asked him to become my manager. My lawyer was clearly unhappy with this because now she had to report to him and send in her invoices for verification. Nor was I happy that she kept sending me new invoices for her legal remedial work, for things that I felt had in part occurred under her supervision. Tensions ran high between them during the negotiations about a change in my contract with the Dutch FA after the 2006 World Cup.

But whatever, I'm certainly immensely pleased that Perry crossed my path, because in the autumn of 2006 another financial disaster was looming.

COACH (2)

How I became national coach

2004

The way I eventually became national coach is actually rather an odd story. I came to the attention of the top brass in Zeist as a result of a refereeing howler. We were playing away at FC Twente with the Ajax Academy in the last 16 of the Cup. The match was suspended when unrest broke out among the supporters in section P just before a throw-in for Twente. But on the resumption, 20 minutes later, Twente were given a corner instead of the throw-in. From it N'Kufo scored the deciding goal, 1-0, which was how the match ended.

It was the knock-out stage, so we were out. I was livid. It was just wrong and went completely against my sense of justice. The goal should never have stood, the TV pictures proved it. So we lodged an appeal in Zeist. Our chances beforehand appeared slim, but I made a passionate case. Henk Kesler, Director of Professional Football and a lawyer, was among those on the panel.

In the end we lost the case, even though everyone knew it wasn't a legitimate goal, but being right and getting justice are two different things. Nevertheless, I think that Kesler thought: So! That Van Basten, you can't push him around. He stands his ground. Interesting. Later on I felt this was a factor, shortly after the European Championship in Portugal, when Dick Advocaat was hounded out and Kesler went in search of a new national coach.

On 15 July 2004 John and I were back on the training pitch with the Ajax Academy, starting our preparations for the new season. I looked at the photos again recently. The Dutch team had had a dreadful European Championship, but we were about to embark on another year with the Ajax Academy. Suddenly all sorts of things started to happen.

Kesler flew to Barcelona that week, to see Johan. I learned later that's where my name first came up. I don't know exactly how, but they were both enthusiastic. And then immediately afterwards – through Jaap de Groot – *De Telegraaf* also started to mention me as a serious candidate. Then everything went really quickly. Kesler called to ask whether I was willing to go and talk to him.

John thought it was fantastic. A wonderful idea. A great opportunity for him too. I was shocked initially. On the one hand it sounded fun and exciting, it massaged my ego, but when it got serious, I thought: wow, you don't really mean it, do you?! It was just too soon. I felt I would have to do things for which I was still completely unready. I was only just beginning to find my way with Ajax's reserve team. Getting used to the job. I wasn't yet fully trained as a coach. Coaching is something you have to learn on the job. You have to get a lot of miles under your belt and then you have to wait and see whether you get any good at it. Whether you can really add something. So all I could see were difficulties, bumps in the road, complications. I said as much to John. But he remained enthusiastic and optimistic. Johan too, and *De Telegraaf*. Initially, I was carried away by it all, I have to say.

But I made it clear to him, when we first talked about it really seriously at his house: 'John, be serious! I can't just go from nothing to national coach, can I? Really, what are you talking about?' But John said: 'Oh yes you can…I can help you!' His position was clear. 'We can do it,' he said, as I kept saying: 'I think it's far too soon.'

I kept expressing my doubts and John introduced me to Erik Reep, who worked with Willeke Alberti. She said she got on well with him. When Liesbeth and I arrived at the Van 't Schips', the room was full. Daniëlle, Willeke and Joop Oonk were there. Along with Erik Reep.

I was unsettled by it all and again expressed my doubts. They told Reep to 'go and have a chat with Marco'. So he and I went off into a separate room. 'Would you enjoy it?' he asked.

'Yes, I would. But I think, no, I really don't feel I'm ready for it at all.'

'No? But you know plenty about football, don't you?'

'Yes, I think so, but there's a lot more to it than that. And that's what I'm nervous about. I don't know if I can *handle* it.'

'Well, if problems arise, I can sort them out for you. In principle, when people feel stress, I'm all in favour of relieving it. So you can share it with me. And then we'll relieve it.'

Once my playing days were over, Ted Troost had slowly disappeared from my life. And then along came this gentleman, a mental coach. 'Listen. Don't worry about it,' he said. 'I'll make sure you feel all right.'

Afterwards I thought: oh, boy. It's getting more and more difficult to say no. Johan says I have to do it, *De Telegraaf* says so, John says so. And Erik Reep says it will be okay.

As Liesbeth and I drove back to Badhoevedorp together, she just looked at me as if to say: are you sure? But she tended to leave decisions like this to me.

Perry, who was only just beginning to become involved in my affairs, had no idea yet of what was going on behind the scenes. These emotions, these doubts, had remained neatly tucked away up till then. This was the first time 'they' had shown themselves. As long as I didn't say anything to anyone, I was the only one who knew about this anxiety. So yes, I let myself be carried away.

In the back of my mind I was thinking about the financial setbacks we had suffered shortly before, the outcome of which was still not entirely certain. If everything went against us, as national coach I would at least have a source of income again. That certainly wasn't the main reason, as I had really only started with John at Ajax because football had begun to appeal to me again. And because I liked it there with him. I was beginning to enjoy it again, even though I wasn't as good at it as Johan at that time.

But okay, when the Dutch FA came calling, it boosted my ego. And my wallet came into it a little as well. I would have some money coming in again and that was fine, what with that stock market disaster and the tax demand that was still hanging in the air.

Of all the people who had previously acted as my sounding board – Johan Cruyff, Cor Coster, Silvio Berlusconi and Ted Troost – three were out of the picture. The only one still on the scene, Cruyff, was a great advocate of this plan. In Barcelona Johan had told Kesler he should take me. And Kesler of course thought it perfect: Van Basten national coach, Cruyff sounding board.

It wasn't that I didn't have the guts to say a categoric 'no', but I was being pushed in one direction. And if I'm honest, I secretly wanted it too. It was an exciting adventure, but even so I had mixed feelings. I had so little experience that I didn't know what I didn't know.

The attraction was the stuff of high adventure. I was just afraid that I was completely unprepared. Another factor was that the people around me didn't yet have a good picture of me as a coach. I don't think they knew me well enough for that. New players, new coaches, new tactics and new trends had all completely passed me by.

And it was a strange time, with all that drama in Portugal: Van Hanegem saying he wanted to thump Advocaat. Dramatic PR. And the end of an era: Jaap Stam was retiring, Kluivert, Reiziger, Overmars, Frank and Ronald de Boer. Important players. The World Cup in 1998 and the European Championship in 2000 had been good. In 2002 they hadn't even reached the World Cup finals, and in 2004 there was a lot of discontent. The atmosphere in the Dutch camp wasn't good. So the Dutch FA was looking for something new and my name popped up.

John and I went to see Johan in Barcelona. I expressed my doubts to him too, but Johan simply responded as Johan does: 'What are you worried about? Is there anything to be worried about? And those who criticize don't understand anything about it. I'll help you.'

John would help me, Erik Reep and Johan too. So I thought: then I have to do it. I naturally felt it was a huge honour and challenge to be national coach, my sense of honour and pride were a big part of that. But at the same time I had my doubts and feared I was completely unready for it.

One day I went to see Kees Jansma, who was living in Maarssen at the time, to ask him to be press officer. I said: 'Yes, it means you're going to have to work with this greenhorn.' To which Kees replied: 'Be allowed to work with you, you mean.' Having Kees on board, along with the old hand Hans Jorritsma, honestly made me feel a little better at that point.

When I got down to work I found there were many very good things too. I was introduced as the new national coach in Zeist on 3 August. The presentation speech about my ideas went well. No big deal. The Dutch FA was relieved to have someone who came across calmly behind the table and the press were happy with me too. I put things well and didn't say anything out of the ordinary or get emotional. How helpful that can be, that calm exterior.

And when you sign on the dotted line, that's not stressful at all, because everything's still a long way off. It was only a day or two before I really had to start that that feeling, that stress, started to close in. The ever-present inner need to win. Tuesday 17 August, in Stockholm, the day before the match against Sweden.

Back in Barcelona Johan had explained how we should play. 'Keep it simple. Just 4-3-3 with a defensive midfielder.' He made a few other tactical points that I made a note of. I was trying to use him and his instructions to gain a little wisdom. Johan was the great man after all. At the presentation he had been officially appointed consultant to the Dutch FA, so the Football Association was providing support on all sides.

Yet despite everything we set off for Stockholm rather underprepared. We didn't even have an analysis of our opponents' playing style. We knew the players, but lacked a comprehensive report. In the lead-up we had mainly been concerned with our own players. It was only at the very last minute that we started thinking about our presentation on the Swedes to the players' group. On Monday evening, two days before the match, we were up until two o'clock in the morning with an overhead projector and a printer getting everything ready.

The night before the match against Sweden, I couldn't sleep. The moment at which I had to perform as national coach, to make my debut, was getting closer. That got to me, which meant I found it difficult to sleep. It felt like I had a final to play.

I lay there staring at the ceiling. I could feel the tension creeping into my body. Sleep seemed to be becoming a futile exercise. I got up, had something to drink, watched a bit of TV and went back to bed with the light off, but it just got worse. I stared into the dark with my eyes wide open. I looked at my phone. It was nearly 4.00am.

That night I called Erik Reep for the first time. Even though we had formally added him to the Dutch team as mental coach, his presence was mainly for my benefit. Reep came to my room at 4.30 in the morning and we talked. He tried to help me relax and get some sleep. I did eventually get a few hours' sleep, but it was still a bad night.

After that I was able to function okay and be reasonably normal and do everything I had to do. But it was a warning: this isn't great, it's not right. The thought then came to me: okay, that was the first time, and for someone with a new job it's logical to feel some tension at the start. It was still all new. In due course it would go.

The sleepless nights before a match never went away though. Since we only met up four or five times every six months, I could live with it. Once a month up to the winter break. You sometimes have three intense days or a full week when you have two internationals one after the other. In between times I was able to recover reasonably well. Ten days together, then three weeks of calm. I always recovered mentally as well, plus I had the time to evaluate everything at my leisure.

But the closer the match came, the more the tension grew. Until the ball started rolling, so to speak. I had a lot of help from Erik Reep, especially in those first few months. He had been formally brought in for the team, so he was at the first big meeting at Huis ter Duin in September. I had told him: 'Stay in the background a bit. You're mainly here to observe. Later you can maybe say something individually to a player.' But when we arrived in Noordwijk on the day in question, there he was, dressed in a Native American outfit at the entrance to the room where all the players went in. Complete with grass skirt, an enormous feather headdress and an axe in his hand. It was a bizarre scene. I was taken aback because this wasn't exactly what you would call 'staying in the background'. He welcomed everyone in person wearing this outfit. Later that afternoon he did in fact give a very good and useful presentation in his ordinary clothes, but it wasn't long before we ended the partnership with Erik because he hadn't delivered what we had expected. There were no hard feelings.

COACH (3)

Battle of Nuremberg

World Cup 2006

I'd not expected it at all, but once the tone was set, there was no going back. We were unlucky with the referee Ivanov, who was extremely nervous and completely unable to control the match. The Portugal coach, Felipe Scolari, didn't help either. He constantly poured fuel on the fire by working on the referee and winding up his players. The Portuguese are sometimes a bit smarter and wilier than us in inviting fouls, manipulating the referee or getting cards shown. They're known for it. Craftier. Portugal and Holland have also always been well matched, maybe because they are both too small to count among the big countries and too big for the small ones.

Our preparation had been the same as usual. Regular and clear instructions to the players. We also had youngsters like Wesley Sneijder, Robin van Persie, Arjen Robben, Mark Van Bommel and Giovanni van Bronckhorst. No dummies, they were streetwise.

The first yellow was shown to van Bommel after two minutes but things started to go really wrong after seven minutes when Khalid Boulahrouz planted his studs full on Cristiano Ronaldo's upper leg. A fairly rash challenge. It brought tears to Ronaldo's eyes and Khalid was lucky to get away with a yellow. But the tone was set. From then on it was up to the Russian referee to keep the match under control, but it wasn't Ivanov's day. Not at all. That became clear incredibly quickly. The match degenerated into what was later dubbed 'the Battle of Nuremberg'. After the game FIFA boss Sepp Blatter would say that Ivanov should have shown himself a yellow card, so poorly had he refereed. You could easily write a whole book about this match alone.

After 23 minutes Portugal scored. Maniche. A well-judged shot after a clever combination through the middle, Cocu's sliding tackle coming just too late. The ball flew into the net out of Van der Sar's reach: 1-0. Ten minutes later, at the other end, Robin van Persie's double samba on the right-hand side. A wonderful move. He was suddenly free with the ball, six metres to the right of the Portuguese goal. He had a number of options. A deciding moment. This could keep Holland in the game.

Robin had become an important player for Holland. I had first come across him some time before.

On 15 April 2004 Van Persie had played for the Feyenoord Academy against the Ajax Academy at *De Toekomst* (The Future), the Ajax youth complex. He had been temporarily returned to the Academy by Bert van Marwijk, head coach at Feyenoord, because they had fallen out.

I was still Ajax Academy coach with John van 't Schip at the time. There was a very big crowd at *De Toekomst* that evening and Robin had all kinds of abuse hurled at him, but he kept going and even provided the assist for the equalizer.

As soon as the final whistle went, an agitated group of fanatical Ajax supporters invaded the pitch and cornered Feyenoord players and coaches. All the TV cameras were soon disabled by the fans. Blows fell on various Feyenoord players, while Feyenoord coach Mario Been had to sprint away because someone came at him from behind. Robin van Persie was the troublemakers' main target. John and I tried to intervene to protect the Feyenoord lads. Ajax player Daniël de Ridder also helped Robin. With our help he was finally able to escape to the dressing room, but it was terrible. Robin said he had been really scared. A few ringleaders were given community service, but this was a real embarrassment for anyone well disposed towards Ajax. I later heard from Robin that Arsenal's chief scout was there that evening and that after the game he had told Arsenal coach Arsène Wenger: 'Go and get that Van Persie. He's made of the right stuff.'

A few months later I became national coach and Robin went to Arsenal. He was only with us that August against Sweden, but I didn't give him any playing time. He needed that year to establish himself at Arsenal. I selected him again at the end of the following May. In the meantime he had performed well under Arsène Wenger at Arsenal. He made his debut for us against Romania. A few days later, against Finland away, Robin came on as a sub, played really well and scored. It was abundantly clear that he was a great prospect for Holland. A natural talent, gold for Holland and his club. I realized that in Finland, where we won 4-0. He began to settle at Arsenal. I also had a very good relationship with Wenger, who was happy to groom him for the highest level.

Robin proved to be a great asset for us during the World Cup in Germany too. In our very first match, against Serbia and Montenegro, he made a decisive deep pass to Arjen Robben, who put us 1-0 up.

In the second match, against Ivory Coast, Robin opened the scoring with a free kick that he hit so hard and with such precision that the Ivorian keeper just didn't see it. Robin didn't hold back, screaming on the touchline. A primal scream, from very deep.

That was a scream I understood very well. The bond between players, or between a coach and a player, can get stronger if there has previously been friction, if you have been through something together or if you've given each other a piece of your mind. If you've shown your vulnerability. What happened between Mauro Tassotti and me or between Cruyff and me, for example.

I had a good bond with Robin. But he didn't bring us back into the match against Portugal after his wonderful move, the samba. He missed. It just goes to show that your influence as coach can only go so far. That turned out to be even more so as the game in Nuremberg unfolded. There was a crucial turn of events just before half-time. Portugal's Costinha received a second yellow card for deliberate handball, so Portugal were a player down. It was half-time, 11 v. 10 in our favour, but we were 1-0 down. The referee had very clearly lost his grip on the match. During the interval we told the players in no uncertain terms: 'Be careful. The Portuguese are wily. Don't go getting a second yellow. Be alert. Use your head.'

Ten minutes into the second half we made an attacking substitution, because we were still 1-0 down with 11 v. 10. Rafael van der Vaart came on for Joris Mathijsen. So now we were left with just three defenders. Eight minutes later, believe it or not, Luis Figo went theatrically to ground in front of our dugout, as Boulahrouz stuck out an arm in a challenge. Second yellow, so red for Boulahrouz.

Now I had another problem, because I only had two defenders on the pitch. I had to make another change straight away. Four minutes later I took off Mark van Bommel and brought on John Heitinga. Mark wasn't happy about it, but I had to do it. Mark and I had also been through a lot together before this World Cup, though I didn't feel they were experiences that strengthened our bond, as with Robin. The same probably went for Mark too.

On 4 June 2005 the Dutch team had played Romania in Rotterdam. A crucial qualifying match.

It had been agreed before the game that Mark would not cover if we lost the ball. But when the Romanian number 8, Dorinel Munteanu, started causing problems with defence-splitting passes, we decided to change our tactics. From then on Mark did have to cover. From the touchline we told him several times before half-time that he had to cover their number 8, Munteanu. But this he didn't do.

We waited until half-time and once again, away from the din of a full stadium, we stressed to Mark: 'Stay with the number 8, because when we lose the ball, he's causing a lot of problems. It's your job to prevent that.'

The second half was barely five minutes old when a completely free Munteanu again delivered two defence-splitting passes in the direction of their strikers. Again this caused lots of problems in our defence. There was no sign of Mark close to Munteanu. Okay, obviously still not clear enough... So, off he came.

I did though select him again in the run-up to the World Cup. In the spring, once qualifying was over. He played in the warm-up games and I picked him again at the World Cup, in a more attacking role. But the atmosphere between us was never really good again. I couldn't get through to him, we never had a proper talk and so the air was never cleared. That was partly down to me. The trust was gone. After that World Cup in Germany he said he didn't want to play under me any more, that he was retiring from international football. To be honest, I don't really blame myself too much for that.

But anyway, Mark ended up watching from the bench in that World Cup match against Portugal. It was 10 v. 10 with 20 minutes to go. A few minutes later Dirk Kuyt broke free and set off alone towards the Portuguese keeper Ricardo. It was the best chance of the match so far, apart from Cocu's shot against the bar. But Dirk shot straight at the keeper. Chance squandered. Just before time we brought on Jan Vennegoor of Hesselink, a last-ditch effort, but he didn't score either. Ivanov then sent off Deco and Giovanni van Bronkhorst, after their second yellow cards. So then it was 9 v. 9, but there were no more goals.

And then it was over. Portugal were through to the quarter-finals, Holland on their way home. After the final whistle there were tears for Edwin van der Sar, who knew that his last World Cup was over.

When I looked at the ratio of chances, 22 to 9, in our favour, it made me scratch my head. We were unable to score even once from those 22 chances, however much the match got out of hand. Ruud van Nistelrooy sat on the bench next to me throughout the game, all 90 minutes. He was the striker who had scored most in my time as national coach, 15 times. The fact that he didn't come on was down to the bizarre way the match unfolded, but there was another reason why he hadn't been in the starting line-up.

John and I had not been entirely happy with his game either in the run-up to the World Cup or as it got under way. We took him off in each of the first three group matches. At training the day before the Portugal match Ruud blew his top. He cursed John and kicked a ball away, with everyone listening and watching. I knew at once this was one of those moments when you as a coach immediately lose your credibility if you don't do something. What he did really wasn't on, I felt. I immediately sent him off the training ground.

Straight after training there was a press conference where I said that Ruud wouldn't be starting the next match because of his behaviour that morning. So the press knew before Ruud himself that he wouldn't be playing. That wasn't smart of me. This simply made him angrier and I had to start with my best striker on the bench.

Six months later, in December 2006, the air between Ruud and me was finally cleared. Initially, he had also had enough of playing for Holland with me in charge. As captain, Edwin van der Sar had urged me to go and talk to him after the World Cup. So I flew to Madrid and Ruud told me his side of the story. That was actually the first time we'd had a good, open discussion about the whole 2004–2006 period, but mainly about the World Cup in Germany.

It was only when I was with him in Madrid that I learned how our grumbling about his game and the substitutions had affected his self-confidence. And how his game had suffered as a result. As he was a goalscorer aiming for the top scorers' list, it was terrible for him to be taken off. So he went around hugely frustrated and this all came to a head during training the day before the match against Portugal.

What I also didn't know was that he really looked up to me, because I had been his childhood idol. Similar to how I had looked up to Johan. I also pushed him hard, just as Johan had pushed me. Except I didn't know exactly what he was thinking. And he didn't know what I was thinking. We hadn't forged a bond then and things went wrong. If we'd had that bond during the World Cup in Germany, things would have been different, I'm sure of that. Now I've got to know him better and come to appreciate him very much as a person. He's very passionate, open and honest. A really fun guy. Later on, during my NLP (neurolinguistic programming) course, I learned a lot about communication. About non-verbal communication, but also about the helicopter view, which you can use to put your emotions to one side. It allows you to step back and observe the situation from a distance. As a coach you can say: we're both angry, what's going on here? Both standpoints must be heard. Can we resolve this in some other way? In retrospect, that would of course have been far better.

Once I had cleared things up with Ruud in Madrid, and he had made himself available for Holland again, I was very happy. Mainly because we had resolved our differences. In the end we had a great time together with Holland. After we ended that conversation in the players' lounge at Ciudad Real Madrid, we were approached by David Beckham. He had been patiently waiting a short distance away for a quarter of an hour because he wanted to have a chat with me and ask for my autograph. I was surprised. Such a great and well-known player.

'The Battle of Nuremberg' still has the dubious honour of the record 12 yellow and four red cards in a World Cup match. The match going off the rails like that came as a total surprise to me as a coach; it was a strange course of events. It ended 9 v. 9 and eventually became a match you honestly feel rather embarrassed about when you look back at it. But when you coach, your main aim is to try and find a way to win the game. Now though it was time to go home. It was then that Holland and I, after a flawless qualifying campaign, with nothing but compliments, would come under heavy fire.

THE CHRISTMAS SPEECH

December 2006

I drove into the car park at Hotel Huis ter Duin in Noordwijk for the annual Christmas drinks with all the journalists who followed the Dutch national team. Some 25 or 30 of them, from all the mainstream media. They got a bite to eat, a drink and a speech from the national coach in an 'informal setting'.

I wasn't in the mood for it at all. And that wasn't just because of what had been happening around the Dutch team in recent months, since that match against Portugal. The change in mood, the scathing articles. No, there was something else that had been bothering me for days. And to be honest I was really worried. But I couldn't tell anyone about it that evening at the Christmas drinks. I had to keep it to myself.

The mood around the Dutch team had changed completely after the World Cup, as though the Portugal defeat was the starting gun for many journalists to explain to their readers and viewers in great detail what was wrong and what had actually not been going well for two years. The tone had changed and they aimed their barbs at the man responsible. The national coach gets the blame. I know that. That's how it is. The winner's always right, for the loser everything's wrong. Hardly anything is any good any more.

I shut the car door and walked to the entrance. Normally, I would be waylaid by journalists here. Not today though, because they were guests themselves and were being feted. Some of them had made the effort to put on a nice jacket over their denims. The man in a suit at the entrance greeted me with a nod. I had to keep reminding myself that for the next two hours I had to give no thought to the letter from Italy, though I knew it would be hard.

It was being suggested in the press, now that two players with a PSV Eindhoven background, Van Bommel and Van Nistelrooy, had retired from international football, that there were too many Ajax people on the staff and that therefore we were unable to assess players objectively. What nonsense. I really thought this was a load of rubbish. What had not helped in creating this idea was Edgar Davids' letter to the editor in *Voetbal International* shortly after the World Cup. He had been responding to a remark I had made at the closing press conference. I had been asked why I hadn't taken him to the World Cup. Well, he hadn't been involved for 18 months, for good reason, we thought. 'I don't pick Jan Wouters any more either, do I?' I had added, tetchily.

Edgar took exception to this, which is why he put pen to paper. I can well understand that he wouldn't like it, that it even made him angry. Nor was it entirely tactful of me to put it that way, but at the same time I thought it was a little over the top of him to write a letter about it. What was it actually all about? We'd watched him play four or five times in the autumn of 2005 and he hadn't convinced us then.

Clarence Seedorf was someone else who hadn't been involved for two years. All of a sudden that was an issue too. I found all these comments left a rather nasty taste in my mouth. It's best not to read them and not to watch the programmes, but it's part of your job and to some extent you have to keep abreast of the prevailing opinions and emotions. And then the negative ones often stay with you.

So that evening we were going to have a 'convivial' get-together to 'bring the curtain down on the year in an informal setting'. I would really have preferred not to be there. But anyway. The news that Perry had received two days before didn't help either. As soon as he had received that phone call he had driven straight to our house in Badhoevedorp to bring us the bad news. As we sat around the kitchen table, he said: 'We thought we were over the worst, as far as financial woe was concerned. But I fear it may get even worse.'

I kept my distance from the journalists and went straight over to John and Rob, who were chatting to Kees Jansma and Anja van Ginhoven. Kees and Anja were worth their weight in gold, keeping the press quiet and at a suitable distance. Kees slapped me on the shoulder, grinned his broad grin, looked at me with a twinkle in his eye and said: 'So, Mandela. Ready for the big speech?' I mumbled something unintelligible in reply because I could feel the stress beginning to flood through my body.

I'm not a natural talker, I'm more of a listener. I can do it, but mainly in answer to questions. Like an interview. Presenting is a completely different kettle of fish. But it was part of my range of duties, so there was nothing else for it. Often, when I have to speak, I can feel the tension disappear from my body after a sentence or two. Luckily, I had put the speech together with Anja and decided that I would express my surprise at the change in mood in the last six months. A waitress served me an espresso. I added some sugar and calmly leaned on the standing table next to Kees and Anja.

Kees took the floor in that casual, yet serious way of his. He introduced me and I walked to the lectern, straightened my grey jacket, took the sheet of paper from my inside pocket, had a sip of water, and waited till the room went quiet. Facing me were the press, a few people from the Dutch FA and the national team staff. The journalists were very much in the majority.

Good evening, everyone.

Last year I stood here just after the draw for the 2006 World Cup. The general feeling was that we had been drawn in the 'group of death'. How different the mood was then!

Full of good heart and with great self-confidence, all of us – players and staff, but also supporters, colleagues and press – counted down the days to the World Cup in Germany. There was belief in the qualities of the players and the technical staff. The experience gained during our good qualifying campaign, where we qualified for the finals unbeaten at the expense of Romania and the Czech Republic, made us – players and staff, but also supporters, colleagues and journalists – believe that there was much we could achieve in Germany.

Our preparation for the World Cup went smoothly. The results matched the high expectations of players, staff, supporters, colleagues and the media.

And then, finally, the World Cup itself.

And that's how it was. The mood had been excellent because we had won nearly everything, despite the major rebuilding of the Dutch team following the retirement of many of the former regulars. We even broke Rinus Michels' old record, I later learned. He had remained unbeaten in his first nine games as national coach. For me the count had reached 15. So everything in the garden was rosy. We had to move on with a new generation. There was barely any mention of the players who still could and were willing to play but who I didn't pick. We also started well. After the dramatic European Championship in Portugal, the mood surrounding the Dutch team had been poor. We had the support of Cruyff and therefore of a number of prominent media.

There had clearly also been a barrier to personal attacks on me, thanks to a status foisted upon me after my time as a player. One that had perhaps simply become enhanced while I was completely off the radar in the years that followed. The 'San Marco' label, one I had never asked for myself, was a kind of extra protection for me, as a novice national coach. But since the World Cup in Germany those days were finally over. If you go out of a World Cup after such an unpredictably crazy match, that can happen. But the press saw it very differently. And the public went along with it in the end. You wouldn't hear me say the football was great. Or that I was a wonderful coach. The results in themselves were excellent, up until that crazy match and that theatrical referee.

Victory in the first two group matches against Serbia and Ivory Coast. True enough, with hard work and not much beauty, but even so, we won. And we were through to the next round after just two matches. Who would have thought? An outstanding performance in a group that had been dubbed by many as the 'group of death'. And against Argentina, match number three, we achieved a creditable draw, with many changes on both sides. So far, so good.

But then. Sunday 25 June 2006. World Cup second round. Portugal v. Holland. What followed was a bizarre match. More chances for us than the Portuguese. But also 12 yellow and four red cards!! A referee who had an off day. In short, we all know the outcome. The dream was over. Losing hurts. It hurts all of us. Players and staff, supporters, colleagues and journalists. But how do you deal with it? Do you seek confrontation? Do you lash out at those around you? Or do you try to process the disappointment in a good way and learn from it?

Yes, I know. I couldn't bring myself to talk stuff and nonsense. I was holding up a mirror to the journalists. That's right. Was that allowed? Or was I supposed to let all that rubbish wash over me? Look, I can understand how some people might snigger when someone in a lofty position comes crashing down. That's only human. I understand that, but I'm allowed to respond to it at a personal level as well, aren't I?

No one in the room knew what was happening at the time, that there was a huge financial claim from Italy hanging over my head, that Berlusconi had for a long time kept himself out of harm's way in 'Operation Clean Hands' because he was prime minister. But that since he had lost his political immunity, the investigating magistrates had started delving into his financial past, as they had previously done with all the big business figures in Italy. And now it appeared that things hadn't been entirely proper in the Milan days. Many players had received apparently lucrative image rights contracts. Me among them. I think my salary at the time was the highest of all, so I was very much the fall guy, to put it bluntly. The Italian tax authorities' claim against me personally was 33.6 million euros. Higher even than the Dutch demand I had just settled. Good grief. What an unbelievable mess. And there I now was, giving a nice little talk. If only they had known.

The tactics were a disaster.
The changes were calamitous.
The Van Nistelrooy 'affair' unwise and certainly not smart.
Boulahrouz unfathomable and Van der Vaart unforgivable.
Sneijder inconceivable.
The list goes on.
No style.
No policy.
No attacking football.

The technical staff too inexperienced.
Consultant Cruyff impossible to follow.
Director Henk Kesler, who wanted to break my contract, in
a muddle.

Is it all really so bad if we – players and staff, but also supporters
and colleagues – are constantly chastised by a number of journalists
in the media?

Two and a half years ago we began a difficult job. We wanted to
play recognizably Dutch football again.

Many new players had to be drafted in and even so we achieved
good results. Okay, there's still not enough good, attractive football,
but we are working on it.

I was glad that we weren't in a group with Italy for Euro 2008, as Perry had said that for the time being I couldn't travel to Italy. With such a big claim the risk of arrest was very real. It was a serious business.

He explained it in simple terms. There was no problem with my first contract in Milan. Things went wrong with my second three-year contract, and its extension by a further three years. It seemed they thought they were being very inventive. From that second contract I received around ten million guilders per year, one million of which was my salary. On that I paid standard income tax in Italy. The other nine million was put by for payment at a later date. That was officially the fee for my image rights. After my time at Milan that nine million per year would be deposited in my image rights company account. The company would be registered in a country where you don't have to pay any tax on income of that kind, such as Monaco, so that the whole fee would be tax-free for my company.

In the end I had felt it reasonable and fair, on account of my lingering injury, that Milan should not pay me the money for the final year of my contract, so we were talking about a total sum of 45 million guilders. Nine million guilders per year over five years. That money was paid to me by a company that exploited my image rights. And that's what the investigators had stumbled across in their investigations.

The problem though wasn't the source of the money, but the ratio of salary to image rights fee. It was fairly out of kilter. Your salary was supposed to be far higher than your income from the image rights. Unless you hardly played, but were used constantly for TV advertising and other commercial activities. But that wasn't the case with me. We realized later that it would have been far safer if the ratio had been the other way round. It really was asking for trouble.

They had spent more than six months working on it together. And with so many financial experts, the people who came up with the arrangement, and the lawyers, you could be forgiven for thinking that good, foolproof contracts would have been drawn up. They had guided me through the process of finalizing these contracts and I wasn't alerted to these potential problems or dangers. Maybe they had, but that hadn't stopped them letting me sign them. In the end I had signed them all blindly without properly understanding the risks, but that will no longer come as any surprise to you.

Now that 'Operation Clean Hands' had brought all this to light, they went after perhaps the biggest fish of all: Mr M. van Basten of Badhoevedorp. Because no one had earned as much as I had in those years at Milan. I was probably the best paid footballer in the world at the time.

The overdue income tax on the 45 million guilders, plus interest and a hefty fine together made up the 33.6 million euros they were demanding. To be paid within six months.

And now. Again we're well placed in the qualifying campaign for Euro 2008. In fact, the situation is similar to that in the autumn of 2004. The Dutch team is still unbeaten and has qualification for the final stages in its own hands. We have a good squad.

A group with many players aged 23 or under. I'm also very much enjoying working with the staff and players and it's a very professional set-up. The mood internally is excellent. But we – players and staff – realize that there are still one or two areas for improvement, in performance in particular.

With this in mind we can look forward to the future with confidence. A future in which we continue to follow the path we embarked upon two years ago. Untroubled and unflappable. With the aim of achieving good results by playing attractive and dominant football. With the same approach and choices, the same attitude and the same conviction as at the start of our adventure.

Great times lie ahead of us. Despite the fact that the mood, for some of the outside world, is completely different from a year ago, when I stood here before.

There was some perfunctory applause. You could hear them thinking: yeah, sure. They were thirsty and each returned to their own table, where the drinks were served and they each had someone of their own to talk to. Fine. I walked to the table where a still mineral water was waiting for me. Kees said: 'Well done, Marco. You held up a mirror to them.'

Henk Kesler joined us and said: 'Nice work. It doesn't always have to be so deferential, does it?'

A few months earlier I had finally parted company with my lawyer. She had carried on working for me after the investment debacle and the situation with the Dutch tax authorities around the turn of the century, but after the 2006 World Cup, when my contract with the Dutch FA was re-evaluated, the communication between her, Perry and the Dutch FA was again so awkward that Perry said: 'I can't work like this, Marco. I cannot and will not look after your interests in this way.'

So he had forced me to choose between him and her. It wasn't a difficult decision, although I did find parting company – she had after all been looking after my affairs since 1989 – difficult from a personal perspective. It had been a long time and we had been through a lot together. We had become friends. But the decision was clear. That had been, would you believe, in September, just three months before. And then this happened.

Perry told me that my tax adviser had received a call from a senior official at the Dutch tax office who was in a quandary about the assessment. Not just because of the amount, but also because there was a tax treaty with Italy, which meant he was obliged to collect the assessment from the Dutch resident whom it concerned: Mr M. van Basten of Badhoevedorp. Yours truly.

After two mineral waters and some perfunctory chit-chat, I shook hands with everyone at my table, wished them all a Merry Christmas and set off for the main door before a journalist could buttonhole me. Time for a swift exit.

MR SEEDORF'S BOWLER HAT

17 November 2007

I was glad to have press officer Kees Jansma with me because no one would have believed me otherwise. It was after the narrow 1-0 win in the Holland v. Luxembourg match on 17 November in Feyenoord's De Kuip Stadium. It meant we had finally qualified for Euro 2008.

After the European Championship in Portugal in 2004 I'd had to make a fresh start with the Dutch team. A new crop of talent was emerging, with Van der Vaart, Sneijder and Robben, although they were mostly attack-minded players. Only one or two of the 'oldies' carried on.

Clarence Seedorf was someone I hadn't picked at all in my first two years as national coach, but when his form at AC Milan began to pick up in the '06–'07 season, I decided to call him up. I wanted to see him close at hand, at training and in matches, even though previous national coaches had found it difficult to find a place for him in the Dutch team. I finally gave him a chance because the likes of Sneijder and Van der Vaart were having occasional injury problems.

Having called him up again, I picked Seedorf to play in three friendly matches. In September I gave him a fairly long run-out as a sub against Bulgaria and then put him in the starting line-up in three qualifying matches: Romania away, Slovenia at home and Luxembourg at home, in October and November 2007.

Romania away was the first match in the qualifying campaign for the European Championship that we lost. Not that I want to lay that at his door, but it didn't help. John and I talked about it a lot at the time. In the end, after we had watched him for a while at training and in the matches, we decided we had better options in midfield. So he wasn't our first choice for the attacking midfield positions and we mostly went for Wesley and Rafael. But okay, in the circumstances and because of his good form at Milan, Clarence got a spot in the starting line-up in those three games in the autumn of 2007. This gave him the chance he so eagerly sought and that he felt he could lay claim to.

Straight after the final whistle of his third game, the 1-0 against Luxembourg in Rotterdam on 17 November, with one more qualifying game to go, Clarence asked for a chat with me. He wanted to talk that evening.

Kees Jansma arranged a room and in the end stayed for our chat. The last qualifying match, Belarus away, was coming up in four days' time. In Minsk. A great opportunity for him, now he was getting chances to show what he could do, even though we had already qualified. An opportunity for him to secure a spot in the final squad for the Euros.

To my surprise Clarence started by saying he was pulling out of that last match because he wanted to concentrate on upcoming important matches with Milan. Then he launched into a tirade. Before these last three games in the starting line-up he had for the most part had to make do with substitute appearances and he found it incomprehensible that I didn't pick him all the time. He felt he deserved more of a chance and was convinced that if I gave him that chance, we would be a very strong contender for the Euros.

I can't remember his precise words, but in essence it came down to: 'If you let me play, then we'll do well in Austria and Switzerland. The team will be better.' It was all designed to make clear to me that we had a great chance of becoming European champions with him in the starting line-up.

I was utterly dumbfounded. I really was giving him every opportunity to play in the team. So far he had been far from convincing. A defeat to Romania, a mediocre win against Slovenia and 1-0 at home to Luxembourg was not an impressive performance. So the game against Belarus away was another chance for him to convince me, to convince us.

But he believed he had already proved himself. That he was better than the players who did have a starting spot in this team because he was playing for Milan in the Champions League and Serie A. 'What more do I have to prove?' He felt it was totally ridiculous; his ought to be the first name on the team sheet.

I was really very surprised and responded by saying that I had given him three chances in a row. And the fact that he was now pulling out of the last match wasn't making a very good impression on me.

Kees and I had listened to him open-mouthed. What struck me was that he was acting more like a businessman than a 'footballer'. Mr Seedorf was wearing a full three-piece suit and at the end of the discussion he went straight outside, where a Mercedes with its engine running was waiting for him. There was a driver at the wheel who was to take him straight to the airport for a flight in a private jet, probably to Milan. He had a briefcase under his arm and an umbrella in his hand. Only his kit bag marked him out as a footballer. As he walked to the car and Kees and I stared after him, I was thinking: he may not be wearing a bowler hat, but it wouldn't look out of place.

Once the Mercedes was out of sight, Kees said to me: 'It's a good thing I was here too because I would never have believed that people would have the nerve to talk about themselves like that.' He couldn't believe what he had heard. And in the end I too was especially pleased that Kees had been there because otherwise no one would have believed me when I told the story.

But whatever Mr Seedorf, or Clarence, looked like, it was what he did on the pitch that mattered to me. And there he wasn't really making the team any better. He kept saying he did, but we really didn't see it that way.

As national coach you have to make choices. And I have always made those choices based on football and tactics. Nothing else matters to me. If people want to draw all kinds of other conclusions from it, so be it.

ALONE IN MINSK

22 November 2007

It was Thursday morning. I was sitting in the departure lounge at Minsk airport, waiting for the return flight to Holland on the morning after our defeat to Belarus. It had been dramatic: snow all round the pitch, minus six degrees, empty stands. Absolutely no atmosphere, and what's more – and this was the worst bit – one of my worst matches as national coach.

The newspaper headlines had already been sent through to me. They did nothing to cheer me up. I had gone to sit by myself in a corner of the departure lounge. Some distance away from the rest of the staff. And away from the players. I saw Dutch fans putting their luggage on the belt. I felt awful. John and Rob Witschge didn't think I should be so hard on myself because it was only four days ago that we had qualified for the Euros in Switzerland and Austria. They were in a great mood, defeat or not, but I saw things differently.

I hate losing. I feel the responsibility resting entirely on my shoulders and put myself down completely: I'm not creative enough, not clever enough, not prepared enough, simply not good enough. I'd failed. Losing to Belarus, in strange circumstances. Thoughts like that had kept me awake that night, so I was feeling rough.

There had actually been a good deal of discontent around the Dutch team for the last 18 months. In fact there had been little right with the team ever since that weird match against Portugal in the World Cup.

There had been a lot of criticism, a lot of frustration and clearly the mood in the newspapers and on TV had now spread to the public. For the first time there had been the occasional call for me to go. Wasn't it time for a different national coach?

Overall the qualifying campaign record had not been at all bad: eight wins, two draws and two defeats. But that made little difference. There was a lot of criticism of the way we played and the many changes. There were reasons for that, but that didn't make much difference any more. The Dutch team had been an easy target since the World Cup in Germany.

That's why this defeat in Minsk was another really painful moment I had to endure as national coach. As if the critics had been proved right after all. I didn't need anyone around me acting with forced cheerfulness. I felt alone. Strangely, it seemed as if everyone at the airport was avoiding me. As if I was infectious. I recognized the situation, from my playing days. If the coach was having a difficult time, you kept your distance from him.

Suddenly I realized what it was like. What Sacchi must have felt, when his days at Milan were numbered in 1991. Or what Beenhakker must have felt at Italia '90. Or Aad de Mos at Ajax, on the bus back from that defeat at Haarlem. Now it was my turn. And it felt rotten.

The match haunted my thoughts that night, even though there had been nothing at stake. Not for us and not for them. What difference did it actually make? But it did indeed make a difference.

It hadn't been a sparkling autumn for the Dutch team, but it hadn't been a bad one either. It had actually started very well against Bulgaria in September 2007. Ruud van Nistelrooy was back and scored on his return. Four days later we had a fairly difficult game in Tirana against Albania, but Ruud saved us in added time: 1-0.

Marco with the Intercontinental Cup, Tokyo, 1989.

Johan Cruyff with Marco during his rehab, February 1988
(© VOETBAL INTERNATIONAL).

Frank Rijkaard (third), Marco (Ballon d'Or) and Ruud Gullit (second), 1989
(© PRESSE SPORTS/OFFSIDE).

AC Milan celebrate victory over Steaua Bucharest in the European Cup final,
24 May 1989 (© PETER ROBINSON/EMPICS/PA PHOTOS).

Marco and Liesbeth, Antibes 1990.

Marco in Tokyo for the Intercontinental Cup, 1989.

Marco just after his operation at Amsterdam's Prinsengracht Hospital, 1987
(© NATIONAAL ARCHIEF, ANEFO, BART MOLENDIJK).

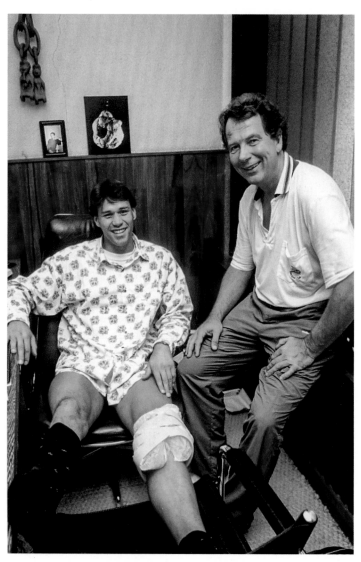

Marco and Ted Troost, around 1990.

Marco, Liesbeth, Rebecca and Angela at
Marco's thirtieth birthday, 1994.

Marco and Liesbeth's wedding, 21 June
1993 (© FOTOPERSUREAU PETER SMULDERS).

Marco, Liesbeth and Silvio Berlusconi.

Marco's parents on his wedding day in 1993.

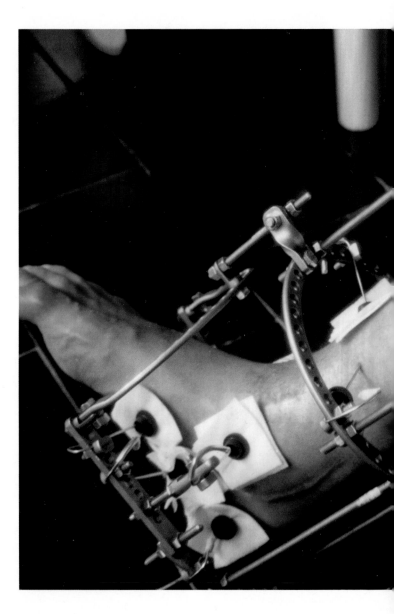

Ilizarov apparatus around Marco's ankle, 1994.

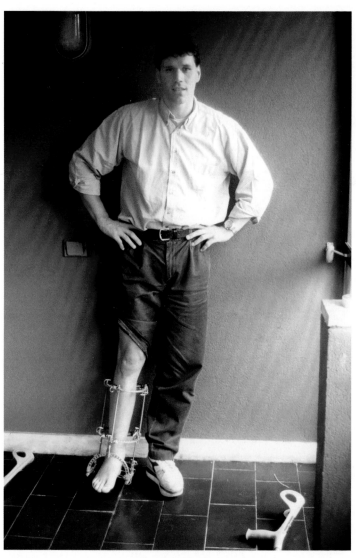

Marco with Ilizarov apparatus, 1994.

Marco with Dr Martens, 1994.

Farewell at the San Siro, 1995.

Marco as Dutch national coach with John van 't Schip.

Johan Cruyff, John van 't Schip and Marco (© MARCEL VAN DEN BERGH).

Group photo after golf tournament in Italy, including Filippo Galli, Mauro Tassotti, Perry Overeem and Dennis Heijn.

Marco with his friends (left to right) Ruud van Boom, Henri Relyveld and André van Vliet.

Marco with the children, Monaco, 1997.

Family photo from 2016.

The press immediately had harsh words at the ready. And that spread to the public. So when we lost 1-0 in Romania in the October round of matches, our goose was cooked. It was our first defeat in nine games and we still had everything in our own hands, but once you're a sitting target, things can move quickly.

A few days later, at home to Slovenia on 17 October, we took an early lead, but our game just didn't get going after that. It wasn't sparkling. We didn't run riot. The Eindhoven crowd started to grumble and for the first time the chants were aimed at me as well. They were calling for Foppe de Haan, who had just won the European Championship with the Dutch youth team.

Just before full-time we made it 2-0, our seventh win in ten qualifying games, but we didn't get the crowd back on our side that evening. They went home moaning.

At the press conference afterwards I had made do with few words. We hadn't played well, which was true, but at the same time we were only one win away from qualifying for the Euros. Against Luxembourg. And we did that four days before Minsk.

No problem, said John and Rob. We're going to the Euros anyway, aren't we? But for me it felt different. I can handle criticism, even if things are going badly. But when the press, and therefore often the public too, see things in a far worse light than they actually are, there comes a time when it can become unreasonable. Then they're playing the man. I had some difficulty with that. I took it badly.

You're dragged through the mud. Everyone pitches in. All and sundry. It's like being put out with the bins. You just get treated like dirt. It's like being in the stocks, like they used to do on the village square.

I knew that it should actually be something to enjoy, taking a talented group to a European Championship. But at that point it felt like a jar of misery. And all this when the biggest problem of the year had just been resolved. The Italian tax affair. Perry had thrown himself into it wholeheartedly. He had flown to Italy five or six times to confer with the tax authorities, Milan and our Italian lawyers. He had then had in-depth analyses done, both by them and by our tax specialists in Holland.

Eventually, he had a full grasp of the ins and outs of the matter. We could then embark upon the legal battle with the Italian tax authorities, with the lawyers believing we had a roughly 75 per cent chance of winning. The case would take years and therefore certainly cost many more hundreds of thousands of euros, but if we were to win, then everything might be waived.

But there was also a 25 per cent chance of losing. Then we would have to pay the full 33.6 million, plus the additional lawyers' fees incurred. I had 13 million euros left of the 25 million I'd taken back to Holland with me ten years before. That simply wouldn't work. So I risked lifelong bankruptcy.

Perry started talking to the Italian tax authorities. He threw the kitchen sink at them. He pleaded a certain ignorance and incapacity on my part when I had signed my contracts at Milan. He said that the advisers and lawyers had set up this arrangement and guided me, that I was a footballer in my twenties who couldn't possibly be held responsible for this sad state of affairs, that I had acted in good faith and that I had even signed the contracts rather blindly.

When we were in talks with them and the risk of arrest had disappeared, I had once gone to Rome with Perry myself to talk to the Italian tax authorities in person. We also spoke to AC Milan about the likely consequences. In the end it was clear to everyone that the best option for me was a settlement with the Italian tax authorities. At the end of it all we reached a settlement of 7.5 million euros. Still a huge amount of course, but in the end one I could live with.

I'm not one for offering profuse thanks, but Perry was well aware of my gratitude. We both knew that without his efforts and expertise I would have been in a very different position. Considerably more poverty-stricken in any event. However miserable I felt about this defeat and the criticisms, this was worth its weight in gold.

While all this was going on, Ajax had put out feelers to me through Perry regarding their head coach position. Shortly after 'Minsk' we would spend an evening having an 'informal chat' with John Jaakke on behalf of the club's Supervisory Board and Maarten Fontein on behalf of the board of directors.

The idea of being able to work with players on a daily basis instead of seven times a year, as with the Dutch team, did appeal to me. I was curious to know what Ajax would have to say. But first I was going to write down my own thoughts on how I would want to be coach of Ajax. What I would need to make a success of it. I should ignore the press for now. They would pounce on me soon enough at Ajax.

I saw the players, the fans and the staff from a distance. It may have been that I was extra sensitive in Minsk, not least because my mother had died shortly before.

MR PEEKABOO

October 2007

Right at the beginning she had actually spent a short time in a psychiatric unit. My mother, who up till then had been perfectly normal, was now mixing with people with mental health issues. It was really awful. A strange experience. You wouldn't believe what poor souls there were in those units. All of a sudden my mother was one of them.

But later, even in the nursing homes, we would see all kinds of people who had lost their way. Who had lost their memory or who were suffering from dementia, or both. They would be in some home or other and they must have been wondering: what am I doing here?

I visited her regularly in the years after her initial admission, even when we were living in Milan, but it was difficult because even then she had lost her memory. She barely recognized me, if at all. Sometimes still just a very little. So yes, it was a very strange kind of contact.

I would go to the home with Liesbeth and there she sat, surrounded by strangers. I would say hello and give her three kisses, but there wasn't really any recognition. We would sit there. A quarter of an hour. Half an hour. Time passed so slowly. They had some of that weak coffee. An old-fashioned tablecloth and some plastic flowers.

My mother wasn't really there any more. She'd gone. That's a lesson I've learned. That what matters is the spiritual contact you have, the essence. Only now that was gone. I was with her, but it was only her physical shell. And that shell had changed too. The medication and the sitting around doing nothing had led to her putting on weight. She could still talk, but she didn't really talk about anything. What she did say was mostly fairly random, although very occasionally, out of the blue, she would say something about the old days.

'How are you, Mr Peekaboo?' She said that to everyone. You can talk like that to anyone. It doesn't matter if you've forgotten their name. You're never wrong. And she regularly said that to me too. Mr Peekaboo: 'Good day to you, Mr Peekaboo.'

My father would sometimes say to her: 'Your son's here. It's Marco.' And then she would say: 'Oh, yes.' And that was it. It was a meaningless conversation. It made no sense at all. At the time I visited her mainly for my father's sake, but as time went by I increasingly found it awkward. Because to my mind I was sitting there like a stuffed dummy. I wasn't cheering myself up, I wasn't cheering her up and I was only cheering my father up ever so slightly. So my visits gradually became less and less frequent.

My father on the other hand was there all the time. He visited her year after year, three times a day. Morning, noon and night. Regular as clockwork. Even though she didn't recognize him. He kept it up to the end, the end of September 2007. When she died. All told she had spent 22 years in nursing homes after that fateful evening in 1985. But the woman who had actually been my mother, she was long gone. And I missed her. Also as a grandma for my children, her grandchildren.

That loss rose up within me at her cremation. I wanted to say something that day, my brother Stanley and my sister Carla both preferring not to. My friends were there too, though I had said to them beforehand something like: 'Now, you don't need to come on my account. It really isn't necessary.' My thinking was that she hadn't been my mother for so long, that she hadn't really been since 1987 and that they had hardly known her.

Yet my emotions got the better of me that day when I said my few words, next to her coffin in that cheerless room in Utrecht. I know exactly how I started because I kept the speech:

'Dear mother, we've been expecting this for a long time. But now it's finally happened, it's hit hard. Harder than I expected. It's so absolute, so final…'

I had prepared a whole page, but after those first few sentences I filled up. All at once I began to sob uncontrollably. It all came from deep within me. The loss of all those years suddenly rose to the surface.

When you as a child have had to do without your mother for all those years. She had been there, but at the same time she hadn't. For more than 20 years. And also because of her own ill-fortune. That she had never again been able to enjoy her children and her grandchildren. And about how unhappy she must have been before, during her marriage to my father. What she and I had talked about when I was a teenager. It all came back to me at that moment. I stood there crying like a small child, in front of a room full of people. I looked at my children, who saw me struggling and weeping over the death of my mother. They were very sad about it themselves and my grief in turn intensified theirs. It took a while before I calmed down again and got a grip of myself. But it was a good thing too. That was what I felt. The grief was pure and heartfelt.

Afterwards I was really glad they had all been there. I hadn't expected it to evoke so much in me. I ended with the words she used to say to me when harsh words had sometimes been exchanged:

'Then she said: "There'll come a time, my lad, when you sometimes think of me. When you have children of your own." She was right about that too, my ma. Although, unfortunately, I've never been able to tell her that myself.'

WITCHES IN NIEUWEGEIN

Spring 2008

I'll be honest: since I had been national coach, stress-wise every match felt a bit like a final to me. At Milan I had been helped by Ted Troost, but I'd not been in touch with him for a while, and Erik Reep hadn't stayed with the Dutch team for long.

I've never actually been to a regular psychologist for this stress, but going to Berna in Nieuwegein now and again did help me keep it manageable. I had a little less trouble with it than in those first six months as national coach and in the end that's what it's all about. Berna sits on a broomstick and flies from roof to roof, ha-ha. But seriously, she's a kind of mother figure to me. She strokes my head as it were and speaks reassuringly to me. 'Poor thing.'

I've always been open to the alternative track. You see if it works and it works for me. Not for recharging the batteries, but more for remaining in balance and achieving some degree of understanding. I think everyone should do what's good for them. I do these kinds of things for my own benefit. And if you think that something alternative would help, then you have to do it. So that's what I did. And that's what I still do. Just as I once tried to do something about my ankle injury at the Chinese acupuncturist. You just need to see what's out there, to be open to all kinds of approaches. Without going overboard about it. I used to go to a hypnotherapist with Johan at Ajax. With Ted Troost I walked in the sea, because I thought it would help me. Even if there is only a one per cent chance that it will make me better, it's worth it.

It's interesting too, I think, because in the end it's different for everyone who is having problems with something. Everyone is on their own quest, there's never one standard approach that always works. An aspirin will work for one, an operation for another, a good talk for a third and something alternative for yet another. It's up to everyone to conclude that quest as best they can, there's no guide or manual for it. It's a matter of making yourself feel good, of feeling comfortable in your own skin. In fact, full of self-confidence, without it being too much.

It has a funny side to it as well because, in the world of coaching, if you lose you're often used as a punchbag from every side. We all accept that. You're standing on a pedestal, you get a lot of stick, but you're also well paid for it, so you need to be able to handle it.

Coaches shield themselves from this criticism. They eagerly seize all the positives, to keep the brickbats and the bouquets in balance to some extent. Some go overboard with this and keep going on about how good they are. They are simply compensating for criticism and their own insecurity. It's also odd behaviour, but it stems from the fact that they're so often the whipping boys. That's when you get reactions of this kind.

There's also a taboo in football. Showing your vulnerability. It's not tough and not strong and that's always how you want to come across. And if you do show vulnerability, it can have consequences, because it leaves you exposed. Yet if you do talk about it, it can also have a positive effect, I'm certain of that, because many people struggle with things like this.

Ultimately, in this book too, it's all about honesty. What sense is there in not being honest? Why should I put a gloss on things? I don't need to become better from it, but I won't become worse from it either.

Berna has no title. She does her thing and in the process you have a conversation. Just chatting about things. There's no hocus-pocus involved. She's a very nice, kind woman. When Johan Cruyff was having heart trouble, Berna once said to me: 'He must eat raisins. They'll be good for his heart muscle.' So I got Johan into raisins. His reaction was positive. 'Why wouldn't I do it?' he said.

RUSSIANS AND BLACK ARMBANDS

Euro 2008

As I look back on it now, nearly twelve years later, it still surprises me. How desperately sad is it that the child of one of your players is born prematurely and then dies during a European Championship? And that something sad like this should happen at a hospital less than five kilometres from the players' hotel, three days before the deciding match at that same European Championship you have all been working towards for two years?

What made it all the more distressing and painful was that a few days before, the players, almost all of them young fathers, had celebrated our unexpected victories over the reigning world champions and runners-up with their own children in their arms, in front of the delirious Dutch fans. It had been a surprise to everyone given the negative atmosphere surrounding the Dutch team. One by one they had gone round with their young children on their shoulders, in their arms or holding their hands, after Italy and France had been defeated. Celebrating in front of the world. We had also won and celebrated the third match against Romania. The mood in the team and among the fans in Switzerland after those three European Championship games really couldn't have been better. It was just a matter of waiting to see who we would meet in the quarter-final.

I was watching the Sweden v. Russia match with John on the evening of Wednesday 18 June to assess our next opponents when I received a phone call from Edwin van der Sar, my captain, at the end of the first half. He was calling from the hospital in Lausanne. Khalid Boulahrouz's wife had unexpectedly given birth to a little girl three months early. The baby had died shortly afterwards.

That week we had given the players permission to spend a day with their wives or girlfriends, after the successful group stage. Most of them were in the city, at another hotel. Khalid's wife had been rushed to hospital that afternoon, Edwin told me. As soon as Khalid had heard, he had gone to the hospital to be with his wife, but in the end their daughter sadly hadn't made it. Edwin urged me to go straight to the hospital to offer my condolences.

It was a challenging moment. You're the one with overall responsibility for the national team and you're at a major finals. You're hard at work and focused on it, but at the same time there's a human drama unfolding that's affecting one of your players. So yes, for me there was a moment of doubt. I can honestly say. Nor are there any manuals for this kind of thing. I jumped in a taxi and went to the hospital to offer my support, to wish Khalid and his wife well and just to be with them. As national coach but also as a human being. That was clearly appreciated. I found a number of other players at the hospital too, which I hadn't expected. Edwin van der Sar, Robin van Persie, Ruud van Nistelrooy and Nigel de Jong were with the Boulahrouz family. They had a good personal relationship with Khalid.

Later I was asked all kinds of questions about this. Should you have allowed the players to go to the hospital? Was it okay to expose some of the team to so much grief during a finals?

The answer is very simple: I don't know. I didn't know then and I don't know now, nearly 12 years later. At the end of 2008 the *NRC Handelsblad* newspaper gave a good account of it all, in which these questions came up. Should I have banned the players from going? They had wanted to support Khalid at the time. Was I supposed to stand in their way?

I didn't make an issue of it at the time. I too tried to support Khalid, but after about an hour at the hospital, I felt I should slowly shift focus again. That I should, in addition to my involvement in the drama, refocus on my main job in Switzerland: preparing the Dutch team for a European Championship quarter-final. When I left the hospital it was clear that Russia would be our opponents, three days later in Basel.

The next day Khalid addressed the squad after first asking for my permission. He said he had to process the loss and he was doing that. Khalid stressed that he could prepare for the next match as normal and also that everyone should act as normal, which included having a laugh.

After training I had a chat with him, face-to-face. I asked if he wouldn't prefer to be at home with his wife so they could process the grief together. He said that he particularly wanted to stay, that he had already discussed this with his wife and that she also wanted him to stay with the team. I felt he made a good case and then, in agreement with John, decided he could stay with the group, should take part in the preparation for Russia and would be in the starting line-up, at right-back.

On Friday afternoon, to our horror, Arjen Robben suddenly started limping during training. He'd come down with an injury. We had been super careful with him all these weeks. He hadn't played against Italy, he had come on for the last quarter of an hour against France and he had played an hour against Romania without incident. So we were expecting him to be able to play most of the game against

Russia – he was one of our best players, and could be decisive – but we had to scrap that idea for good on the morning of the match. His groin didn't pass a late test on Saturday morning either.

Robin van Persie was also coming back from an injury. He too had come on as a sub against France, had played the entire match against Romania, and scored, to make it 2-0 in the 87th minute, but was still short of rhythm for another whole match.

So I had a dilemma to solve. Sad to say, in the four years I was national coach I rarely had at kick-off a fit quartet of what people later came to call 'the big four': Robben, Sneijder, Van der Vaart and Van Persie. One of them was always injured. Or more than one. As now.

Now that Robben had to pull out, I tackled the issue with John: our opponents, the analysis and the line-up. The players were very mindful of what had happened to Khalid at the time. They talked about it a lot, though we didn't consider a group discussion. We let everyone deal with it in their own way. What did concern the group was whether a minute's silence should be held. The players were in favour, but the Dutch FA wasn't. In the end it was decided to wear black armbands against Russia. Most of the players were content with that, I think. Khalid certainly.

The influence of a coach is often overrated. That became painfully clear in the quarter-final that Saturday evening in Basel. There were a few things that didn't go our way. We had difficulty building up from the back. And Boulahrouz played an important part in this because the Russians kept leaving him free, so he saw a lot of the ball and the build-up was down to him.

By disrupting our build-up play, Russia ensured that our strong midfielders and forwards received few good balls. And consequently were able to create little danger. The Russian approach worked well.

As a precaution I replaced Boulahrouz with John Heitinga after Khalid had received a yellow card.

We tried to cut out Russia's best player, Andrey Arshavin, first with Boulahrouz and later with Heitinga. But that didn't work. Arshavin played the match of his life and was a constant threat. He cleverly made himself available between the lines. That was difficult for our defenders. They couldn't get hold of him. Should we keep covering him or stay in position? They were difficult choices. We had major problems with Arshavin throughout the match.

The absence of our own Arshavin, Arjen Robben, also had a major impact on the course of the match. We missed such an unpredictable dribbler of the ball who could make the difference all by himself.

In the 56th minute we fell behind. As it was a knock-out match, we had to adopt a more attacking approach, while our build-up play was going badly. We therefore made an attacking change, bringing on Ibrahim Afellay for Orlando Engelaar. And eventually, just before the final whistle, we made it 1-1. Ruud van Nistelrooy again. We had managed to grab the lifeline of extra time. The problem though was that I had already made three changes. I had also brought on Van Persie for Kuyt at half-time. I would have preferred not to, but I wanted to make us more of an attacking force in the second half.

I believe those necessary early substitutions, that push for an equalizer and the tension, maybe also compounded by the Boulahrouz situation, ultimately took their toll. Because in extra time Rafael and Ruud got cramp. You could see that on the pitch. In those extra 30 minutes, with a fresh Ruud and a fresh Rafael, we would have won. I'm certain of that.

But the strangest moment came just before the end of normal time. Wesley Sneijder was kicked by a Russian player, Dennis Kolodin, by the Russian goal line. It was 1-1 at the time. He rightly received a yellow card.

But Kolodin was already on a yellow card. This was his second yellow, and therefore red. He had to go. Then we would be going into extra time with 11 v. 10, which would have been a big advantage.

But then something very strange happened. There was a tremendous commotion. And the referee, the experienced Slovak Luboš Michel, muttered something about offside and suddenly withdrew the yellow card. Out of nowhere.

I was baffled. I briefly wondered whether we should walk onto the pitch in protest. I thought: how is this possible? It's just not on.

Because if you clobber someone, it doesn't have anything to do with the football. It's simply a yellow. Offside or not. It doesn't matter. Because it's against the rules. That's perfectly clear. And this was a nasty kick. Sneijder was sent tumbling. So offside didn't come into it. This was physical violence. And therefore his second yellow. That moment is what kept me awake the most afterwards.

UEFA later explained that the yellow card had been rescinded because the ball had already crossed the goal line when Sneijder was kicked. But the pictures show that's not how it was. It doesn't matter where the ball is. The rules are clear, a nasty kick is a yellow card. The head of UEFA's referees committee later said this was a big mistake. But that wasn't much good to me then.

THE ROLE OF THE COACH

It seems as though the role of the coach is growing in importance. Artificially so, to my mind. It's becoming hugely inflated. It used to be much more about the players. They were the ones you watched, the ones you talked about. How the players decided a match, turned it, bent it to their will. And coaches, yes, they were supposed to facilitate that. That first and foremost. Nothing else.

This came into the open again around the time of Euro 2008. Our qualifying campaign hadn't been all that great, but after the victories in the group stage, over the reigning world champions and runners-up, everything and everyone was suddenly looking and feeling very positive again. I felt all that euphoria was excessive.

I believe the coach does have a very important role to play at half-time in a match. And at hectic moments in the course of a match. Leading training, managing – I now have experience of these things. But doing exactly the right thing at those few tricky, crucial moments, the ones that can be decisive in a match – that's very specific.

The ability to do this at a particular time, you either have it or you don't. In general I don't think it was something I excelled at. Working with a good assistant is very important for this. He has to complement you, where you feel you have weaknesses. Tactically I had John alongside me.

Together you make each other strong. Just as players complement each other on the pitch. Exploiting each other's strengths and making up for each other's weaknesses.

It was something I had as a player. I knew what I had to do. I also knew exactly how I should do it. I knew exactly when. But as a coach I didn't have this instinct to anywhere near the same degree.

Ultimately therefore I would have liked a bit more of a grip as a coach. Of course, it's very satisfying when you beat the world champions convincingly 3-0 at the Euros. You win and you make a lot of people happy. But I find it hard to say what my part in all this was. Precisely because winning or losing has so much to do with chance. I wasn't the brains behind all kinds of complicated, extraordinary things at that European Championship. It was simply hard work, being consistent, handling people well, not doing anything stupid.

In retrospect I learned a lot in those four years as national coach. With a healthy dose of irony you might even say it was a well-paid work placement. But seriously, I had learned a lot and felt it was time to take the next step, to start working as the head coach of a club.

THERE YOU GO, THE KEYS TO AJAX

Spring 2008

I made my official debut as head coach of Ajax at Willem II, on 30 August 2008. It wouldn't be wrong to say it had been a roller coaster since I had first spoken to the Ajax people in December. Following a phone call in November, a month later I was at chief executive Maarten Fontein's villa, a wonderful spot on the Kager Lakes. John Jaakke, chairman of the Supervisory Board, was there too. It was a positive meeting, they were very keen. They were clearly prepared to give me all the freedom I needed to do things my way at Ajax, far more than you would normally give a head coach. We concluded matters swiftly and I signed for four years, starting after Euro 2008. And naturally Rob and John would come with me.

In the spring though the Coronel report came out, which made all kinds of criticisms of the organization. Technical director Van Geel, chief executive Fontein and Supervisory Board chairman Jaakke were then all forced to quit within a few weeks, with the inevitable uproar. So we were suddenly left on our own, with Uri Coronel, the author of the report, becoming Supervisory Board chairman, Jeroen Slob remaining as finance director and Henri van der Aat being appointed interim chief executive. He was clearly not really a football man, but we got our heads down to work together. At my request Perry did the honours as temporary technical director, until such time as Coronel acceded to our wish to appoint Danny Blind as technical manager. That finally happened in June, but until then we were more or less left to our own devices to assemble a decent squad for the new season. It was very strange because I was preparing the Dutch team for the Euros at the same time.

On 29 March I was in the Abe Lenstra Stadium watching Heerenveen v. Ajax. It was a miracle that Ajax won 4-2, because Miralem Sulejmani was toying with the entire Ajax defence. It was purely thanks to the post, the bar and Ajax keeper Maarten Stekelenburg that he only scored once. I was convinced.

Ajax had just sold Ryan Babel to Liverpool for 19 million euros and John Heitinga to Atlético Madrid for nine million. In February, when I signed a contract for four years – two years, with an option for another two years – we had been told we had around 30 million euros to spend on new players. I felt Sulejmani would be a very good replacement for Babel. He was only 19 years old, but had huge potential and later that year was voted leading talent in the Eredivisie. Everyone could see his promise. After that match against Heerenveen I told Perry: 'We must have him.'

Sulejmani was represented by Serbian agents and his previous agent had insisted on a share of the transfer fee. It was complex and the chairman of Heerenveen stood firm, but eventually the deal was done for 17 million. I wanted Sulejmani at all costs.

We also brought in forward Darío Cvitanich and defender Oleguer. Unfortunately, my duties as national coach had prevented me from taking a look at them myself. Later we were also able to sign Ismaïl Aissati from PSV Eindhoven for next to nothing and we also had strong players like Luis Suárez, Klaas Jan Huntelaar, Jan Vertonghen and Thomas Vermaelen. With these new acquisitions I had the makings of a good team.

Another surprise for us in that spring of 2008 was a Cruyff plan. He had been attached to Ajax as an unpaid adviser since the autumn of 2007 and he shone a light on the club as only he could. His appointment was a completely separate matter from the talks Ajax held with me. On one occasion he came to me with the urgent advice to dismiss all 20 youth coaches. The entire academy needed a shake-up. Everyone had to go and I was the one who should do it.

But I was still under contract with the Dutch FA and wasn't officially employed by Ajax yet. I was happy to talk about it, but Johan said: 'No, let's just do it. Everybody out. Including the good youth coaches, if necessary. Because then we won't run the risk of one or two bad ones staying in post.'

That was in February and the Euros were still on the horizon. John, Rob and I were in the midst of our preparations. It's logical to prepare for next season, but at this point we weren't the right people to dismiss all the youth coaches. That went far too far. You can't simply put them all out on the street, can you? I hadn't even met them at that point! And that's what I told Johan. So no one got sacked.

One of the things I introduced as soon as I could was performance-related pay. As Berlusconi had done at Milan. A fixed salary and bonuses are normal in football, but what you get a bonus for differs from one club to another. The rule at Ajax was that you got a little extra for every point won. Even a draw at home to Heracles generated a bonus. I thought this was nonsensical. Only after a championship would the players earn a bonus. A substantial bonus, it's true, but only if we won the title, not otherwise.

I also tried to ensure that the players were able to train in peace and quiet, away from the gaze of onlookers. That had long since been the norm in many countries, but in Holland we were comfortable with open training and felt it was of no consequence for those few people who sometimes came to watch. Closed training would mean that things could happen from time to time that wouldn't immediately find their way into the newspapers. It took a while to organize. It wasn't finally sorted out until after my departure, when training sessions were moved to the youth complex, *De Toekomst*. So in my time we were still training at the ArenA, next to the supporters' bar. Which I felt was far from ideal.

I remember playing a game during pre-season. We wanted to mimic the situation and mentality of the street. We did old-fashioned team picking where you could put together your own team. Vurnon Anita went first and chose Kenneth Vermeer, the keeper. He ignored Suárez, Huntelaar and Vertonghen. Vurnon's second choice was another friend. I couldn't understand it. If friendship is your motive, which was very clearly the case, then to my mind you're not bothered about winning. If I had learned anything from my time as a player, it was this: you have to create a climate in which winning is the only thing that matters. You don't choose your friends. You choose the best players, because you want to win.

I LAY ON MY BACK

6 May 2009

I lay on my back and stared at the ceiling, following the lines with my eyes. There was a system to it. The straight lines calmed me. I took another deep breath and exhaled very slowly. It sounded like a long-drawn-out sigh.

I had been lying there for some time. Maybe as long as an hour. In a corner of this office, against a wall with no windows, behind a conference table, with my back on the floor. It felt safe. No one could see me here. And Miel Brinkhuis, the press officer, was leaving me alone. He had enough on his plate that day.

I took another deep breath. With every sigh it was as if a little tension left my body. As if each time I was discarding one of an enormous pile of blankets over me. Now and again I could hear a shout from the training pitch below. They were carrying on without me now.

There was no need any longer. I was done with it. It seemed as if I was several pounds lighter since I had told Liesbeth that morning.

No one had come knocking on Miel's door so far, which didn't bother me in the slightest. Why shouldn't I be able to lie on the floor? I wasn't Ajax's coach any longer. Well, okay, just one more press release to go and a press conference this afternoon. Then I really was done.

Strangely enough, I was beginning to look forward to that press conference. To explaining why I wasn't suitable for this role, that I felt I'd failed, that I had done everything I could, but hadn't succeeded in getting this team to play football the way I wanted. That I clearly didn't have the flair for it and that it was therefore better for Ajax if I went.

Miel started with mitigating circumstances. No, sometimes luck was against us. Heracles at home, Groningen away. Referees. Bad luck. The squad was not especially good and there were lots of noises off on the admin side. The Coronel report, Van Geel gone, Jaakke gone and Supervisory Board members in the stands sometimes expressing criticism of my line-up at the top of their voices. Not great at all.

No, Sulejmani hadn't lived up to his promise either. 17 million. The most expensive Ajax purchase to date and maybe not immune to the pressure of a top club. We had done everything we could, John and I. Psychologists and all. It had all been to no avail.

Sometimes things were so bad that I no longer knew what to say. I remember the cup match in Volendam, in November. It was a rainy night. We lost 1-0, after extra time. It was simply spectacularly poor, well below par.

After a match we would always meet the press officer together to decide on our line for the press conference. But what should we say? It was pathetic. Ajax losing at Volendam. It really was poor.

During the press conference Frans Adelaar, the Volendam coach, was very keen to speak to the assembled journalists, but they didn't ask him a single question. I really didn't want to say anything, but was on the receiving end of a whole barrage of them. An absurd situation, if it hadn't been so painful.

As I lay there in Miel's office, while he wrote the press release to say I was resigning as head coach of Ajax with immediate effect, my thoughts wandered back to the previous week. Just one match and then it would be over. Just one game. Just one more. Of course, John started straight away, surely you can do that one. Then the season's over. Miel asked me that too. And Rik van den Boog.

But for me it was finished. Over and out. After that 4-0 against Sparta the day before yesterday, the light had gone out for me. I had stood there in front of the camera spinning a good yarn, but inside it was over. Completely dark. A black hole. How could I go on when Ajax had been trounced 4-0 by Sparta away? It wasn't on.

This really was the breaking point. This wasn't how it was supposed to be. It gnawed away at me. I lay awake all night. Another sleepless night. Whenever we lost, or if we didn't win, as Ajax were supposed to, I didn't sleep. Or hardly.

It brings you no cheer, I can tell you. Liesbeth knew how I felt after that 4-0 against Sparta. She had been full of admiration for my apparently assured performance in front of the camera. She said I deserved an Oscar for my acting; there had been no look of stress or bewilderment about me, but she knew it was gnawing away at me. That the spectre had visited me at night again. The spectre of fear.

That spectre would hold me in its grip after a defeat of this kind, especially the first night. It was terrible. The first two days after a defeat I would feel so bad. As the days went by I would pick myself up again, each night would be a little better, but only when I won again did it let me go. It would always be lurking. Over the last few months the spectre had actually grown stronger because the results were often poor. I lost more and more of my strength; I found that in everything. Lack of sleep is bad for you. You have less power to persuade people.

Winning or losing is so crucial for me. For everything. Once I had recovered, I could get through to the players again and do my work properly. So I kept getting back up and I didn't let them grind me down, but those defeats kept adding up. Every time you get a knock on a tender spot. Like a boxer who takes a blow to the kidneys. It hurts for a moment each time, but he throws himself back into the fight with everything he's got. The pain in his kidneys increases with every punch, he fights it off, but in the end it's too much. For me it was the 4-0 defeat to Sparta last week. I couldn't go on, nor did I want to.

So awaiting another match wasn't an option for me. I had no appetite for another night-time struggle with the spectre. John could wrap things up. He'd be great. No problem.

Nor did I want any money. None of this 'by mutual agreement' nonsense. No. I'd failed. All that tension that had been building up through the season and pre-season before it could now finally leave my body. And then I could lie here quite happily on this bare floor, staring at the ceiling. I couldn't hear anyone shouting now. Had training finished? I could hear Miel on the other side of the room, busy on a phone call. My name came up, but it didn't get through to me. Not at all.

I had given everything. Every day. I was the first to arrive and the last to leave. I had put everything I had into it. And that was what I would say this afternoon at the press conference: 'I've done my absolute best.' They couldn't accuse me of a lack of commitment. There would only be one conclusion: I wasn't suitable for this job. The end.

I have to say that I had previously had major doubts about whether to go on. I must also admit that I had met up with chairman Rik van den Boog twice before because I wanted to call it a day. Twice he had been able to persuade me to carry on. Twice I had gritted my teeth and carried on.

'Pancake'. Suddenly that word popped into my head; it would never sound the same to me again. We lost to Heerenveen at the ArenA that day. It was at the end of February and the third bad result in a row. But it wasn't the defeat itself that made it so painful. It was that guy who shouted 'pancake' at me from the main stand after the game. You might say: pancake, what's so bad about that? An innocent, almost light-hearted word. But in one way or another he got to me with that word.

I had held back a moment, looked up and shouted something back at him. Something and nothing really, when you look back at it. It was over in a flash. But the harm had been done. The cameras were rolling, it was on TV. The whole country could see that I had been called a pancake and that it had got to me.

At the press conference afterwards I was relaxed about it. I could do that fine, but actually no word could have hit me harder at that moment than 'pancake'. Just because it was so innocent, so ordinary. Because it's such a stupid word. And that made it extremely painful: he wasn't wrong. He was spot on. I took it personally.

And then you feel powerless. So I was angry with Ajax when I drove home. For letting the man in, in the main stand. And I was angry with the TV company for letting the cameraman film it and then broadcasting it. I know it was nonsense, but at that moment I felt so powerless, so much at the mercy of the predators. Fair game. Whether you had any understanding of football or not. Whether you had won three European Cups and three Ballons d'Or or not. It made no difference. Pancake. Nothing could affect me more at that moment. I really did feel like a pancake.

Suddenly Miel's voice came through to me loud and clear. 'Marco, the press release has gone. Shall we have a quick chat about the press conference? It's only an hour away.'

PART V

THE CRUYFF REVOLUTION,
THE SPECTRE OF FEAR AND FIFA

2009–2019

THE CRUYFF REVOLUTION

2011

AROUND THE KITCHEN TABLE

It was a Monday evening in September and starting to get dark. We were at my house, sitting around our big kitchen table that could comfortably seat eight. If you sat at the top, where Johan was sitting that evening, you could look out onto the Vondelpark.

He had walked from his apartment in Waldeck Pyrmontlaan, 300 metres away, together with Dennis Bergkamp and Wim Jonk. Frank de Boer, then head coach of Ajax, arrived five minutes later. Dennis Heijn was there too. Johan felt we should meet up as we would all soon be working together to make Ajax Ajax again.

Johan started talking before Liesbeth had even finished asking everyone what they would like to drink. He had nothing with him, no bag, no papers, nothing. He did it all from memory. He explained that he had already put three footballers in the organization in the shape of Dennis, Wim and Frank and that I would complete the set as director of football affairs, chief executive. Footballers in charge. That, in short, was his plan.

I was ready. He had approached me about this job about six months before, but it was all so casual that it felt like empty talk. 'That's not my cup of tea,' I said straight away. It didn't seem to me to be a role I was cut out for. Nor did Johan himself have any role at Ajax at the time. For me it was all rather vague, so I let it go and followed the news

274

about Ajax from a distance. I knew Johan had set the ball rolling in September 2010 with a column in *De Telegraaf*. He felt everything had to be done differently. Much had happened since then, but I'd had nothing to do with any of it.

Until the summer, when, out of the blue, I was approached by Steven ten Have, the new chairman of the Ajax Supervisory Board, who asked if we could meet for a coffee. I soon realized he was someone who knew what he was talking about. Steeped in corporate management and with a clear vision of what was needed. He made an excellent impression. Honest and dynamic.

He was very keen to have a football heavyweight at the top of 'the new Ajax'. Someone with strong Ajax DNA who also supported the Cruyff line. But this someone didn't necessarily have to be able to do everything themselves; he would have the support of a strong commercial man, someone who was comfortable communicating with the media, and an experienced member of the Supervisory Board, as at every listed company. 'I'm outlining the picture,' he said. 'It can be done this way. Think about it. There's no rush.'

The strange thing was that, following my initial scepticism, my interest was now piqued. Partly because Steven had quite clearly said I could take my own people with me. We probably spoke four or five times over the course of just a few weeks. It became increasingly serious. After a week I woke up feeling anxious about being chief executive of Ajax, but my initial doubts fortunately abated during the discussions. Things began to move. I became really interested and also came up with names for a possible management team: Dennis Heijn, a friend, was my candidate for commercial director, and Miel Brinkhuis, the press officer at the time, would be director of communications. And Perry could keep supporting me in the background.

Ten Have's line, which he discussed with the other members of the Supervisory Board, sounded good, thorough and professional. I started to see more and more advantages. I could carry on living in Amsterdam and, as chief executive, I believed, maybe a little naively, that I would be less in the spotlight than as coach. It all felt quite different from what Johan had casually asked me about a few months before.

When Ten Have wanted to formalize things, I did briefly apply the brakes. I only wanted to consider the job seriously if Johan was fully aware and also 100 per cent behind me. I knew that without his support any plan for Ajax would be doomed to failure. He was critical. In everything. It had also been him who had first approached me at that earlier stage.

I phoned Johan myself and explained exactly what had happened since we had last been in touch. He was surprised that having initially said 'no' to him, I was now seriously considering Ten Have's proposal to talk further just a few months later. I felt he wasn't hitting it off all that well with the rest of the Supervisory Board at the time. But I explained to him that I'd had to get used to the idea. That I would have professionals around me and that the fact I could put together my own management team was an important consideration for me. Only then could we possibly run the club our way.

During the call Johan eventually showed renewed enthusiasm for the idea that had originally been his own. 'I want you to meet Frank de Boer, Dennis Bergkamp and Wim Jonk first,' he said in conclusion. 'And I want to be there myself too. We can throw a few ideas around. And I also want to meet Dennis Heijn, your prospective commercial man. Then we can see what common ground we have.'

Which was why we were all sitting round my kitchen table that September evening, with Johan talking nineteen to the dozen about his plans for Ajax. The atmosphere was excellent. Footballers together, with the same idea about the future of the club. We all agreed that Ajax needed a breath of fresh air inspired by football.

They didn't even get round to a second cup of coffee. I had already shown them out when Liesbeth came down. The meeting had lasted barely an hour, but I was relieved because Johan could see it working. That was an absolute prerequisite for me.

Three days later he called in on the off chance in the early afternoon, this time alone. We talked about the future of the club and what the new management team would look like. His enthusiasm was clearly growing and he had a clear view, with me and Dennis as the new chief executive and commercial director of Ajax. He remained sceptical about the other members of the Supervisory Board, but knew our plan already had their approval, so really nothing else was standing in the way.

When Johan said he was flying to Barcelona with Danny that evening, I spontaneously offered to take them to Schiphol Airport myself. We drove in my car together to their apartment, where Danny was waiting with their hand luggage. She sat in the back and didn't say much.

Johan sat next to me and was clearly satisfied that after all these months of talking, things seemed a little more solid. And that I was on board. The plan was crystal clear. We bade each other a fond farewell at the airport and parted as friends.

The next day I phoned Ten Have to say that Johan was in agreement. He was delighted and said he would get on and prepare the contracts for me, Dennis and Miel. We would be able to sign them at his office in Utrecht in the very near future.

JOHAN'S CHANGE OF HEART

A week later, on the Thursday evening, the telephone went. Johan. He suddenly had a very different tone. He said he'd changed his mind and wanted to protect me because of my inexperience as a director. He wanted to put a kind of advisory board in above me, supposedly so as not to risk throwing me to the wolves. He wanted people like Tscheu La Ling, Maarten Fontein, Leo van Wijk and Guus Hiddink on it.

I was astonished when I heard those names. We already had a plan to help me in the job, which we had discussed in detail around the kitchen table. Not one week before he had been fully in favour of it. And now all of a sudden there was to be an advisory board to agree to important decisions, to protect me from mistakes? I had known him a long time, but this didn't sound right, it didn't sound like Johan. Where was the unanimity and decisiveness of a week before? The agreement we had during the drive to Schiphol Airport? What was going on?

It didn't feel right to me. He had suddenly had a huge change of heart. A surprising, strange change of heart. What precisely had happened in that week that meant the whole plan was being thrown out of the window? It very much appeared that Johan was under the influence of people around him, people with self-interest. People who wanted to exert influence through him. There was no other explanation.

De Telegraaf journalist Jaap de Groot had daily contact with Johan. He also worked at the Cruyff Foundation.

And Tscheu La Ling, with whom, as a footballer, Cruyff had previously not had a good relationship, was a good friend and business partner of De Groot. Why had his name suddenly emerged? Were there other people wanting to benefit from the changes at Ajax? Did they see me and the fact that I was bringing my own commercial director and director of communications with me as a threat?

That week articles written by De Groot appeared in the *Telegraaf*'s Telesport pages, explaining Johan's change of heart, and there was some straight talking that shocked me. Johan supposedly wanted to protect 'the apple of his eye'. It also contained straightforward falsehoods about a company that Perry, Dennis and I wanted to set up, but we had actually abandoned that idea because the talks with Ajax were serious. De Groot went on to say I had kept quiet about the plans and Johan wasn't happy about it. The newspaper also claimed it was a worry that I wanted to take my 'friends' Dennis and Perry with me to Ajax.

I found it completely overblown and saw right through it, knowing how things really were. But the readers of *De Telegraaf* didn't know that. They were presented with these 'facts' as 'the truth'. I found it very shoddy. I had suddenly landed in a power play that I wanted no part of.

At the same time I had a personal relationship with Johan and I didn't want any journalist or newspaper coming between us. So, the day after the article appeared, I went to speak to him in person and to clear up any misunderstandings. To look each other in the eye. I hoped we would work things out.

SHOWN THE DOOR BY DANNY

I rang the bell at his home on Waldeck Pyrmontlaan. The door buzzed open and I took the lift to the second floor. When I stepped out, Danny opened the door and let me in. 'Johan isn't here,' she said, and then promptly asked: 'Is what I've read right, that you support Ten Have's plans? You believe what that man is saying?'

I was taken aback by the question, but I gave an honest answer: 'Yes, that's right. That's what I've said. I don't think it's nonsense, no.'

'Surely not?' said Danny at once. 'That's not possible.'

I explained how I felt Ten Have's administrative know-how combined with Johan's football know-how could lead to something good at Ajax. 'That's how I see it.'

'So you still support it and you have all your wits about you?'

'Yes.'

Then Danny said: 'Well, if you're so certain, you're no longer welcome here. You'd better go.'

I hesitated for a moment. Should I make a scene? But at the same time I thought: if she's sending me away, then I won't make a fuss. So I walked out of the door, took the lift and left.

I immediately went in search of Johan. I hoped he would be at the Olympic Stadium, at the Cruyff Foundation. Luckily, I soon found him there. I said to him: 'Danny's just thrown me out. I thought that was a bit harsh. She's not normally like that.' But Johan didn't really have anything to say about it. In fact, he ignored it entirely.

'Listen, I want to tell you this in person,' I said. 'I don't think what Ten Have and the Supervisory Board are saying is wrong, but I don't think what you're saying is wrong either. To my mind the two parties aren't too far apart, they can still be brought together. That would be best. Then you can join forces and that's what's best for Ajax.'

'I can't have anything to do with it,' Johan replied quite firmly. 'If you support these people. They have no idea. They know nothing about football. You can't have a foot in both camps. You have to choose. For the footballers or not.'

I had also spent hours talking to Ten Have. And I knew that Johan was very knowledgeable about football. But running a big company was really quite different. 'What I'm hearing from both sides is reasonable,' I said. 'I think Ten Have is a very good, reasonable guy and he seems like a good administrator to me. So to my mind it's not all so black and white.'

Then Johan said: 'Then as far as I'm concerned, that's it. You can't support both sides. You have to choose. If you can't…'

'If that's how you really see it, then I'm out,' I said. 'You'll have to find somebody else. I'm not having anything to do with this.'

I walked away. For me it was perfectly clear from that moment. I wasn't angry, but I realized this wasn't going to work. I didn't feel he was prepared to listen to anything else and I wasn't prepared to brush aside reasonable, professional people, who had the good of the club at heart.

In any event, ten days after the kitchen table meeting, the entire plan for the future of Ajax, agreed to not only by Cruyff, the Supervisory Board and the head coach, but also by the technical core, had been completely and finally swept away.

The next day I phoned Steven ten Have and said I was withdrawing as prospective chief executive of Ajax. With Cruyff adopting the attitude he had, it was no longer an option for me. The contracts could be shredded. Ten Have was surprised and not a little disappointed.

In the weeks and months that followed I felt vindicated in my decision. The whole matter simply became more tedious and more embarrassing. Ten Have must have acted quickly because less than two weeks after my phone call the Supervisory Board suddenly came up with Louis van Gaal as prospective chief executive. Needless to say, Johan Cruyff was not party to this.

FAIRY TALE NEWS

A few years later I spoke critically about the 'velvet revolution'. That was in 2015. By then everyone at Ajax had quarrelled with everyone else and the academy was one big vale of tears. Only the league titles that Frank de Boer had somehow managed to win camouflaged it all. I said then that the Cruyff plan was 'one big comedy' and dubbed the whole thing Fairy Tale News. Apart from the political intrigue, the unrest and the power plays, I did not and do not think that what Johan wanted at Ajax was logical or realistic. He had undoubtedly done good work at Barcelona, but there's no comparing Barcelona with Ajax. In the football food chain Barcelona is the hunter and Ajax the prey, internationally at least. Ajax is in the middle of the chain.

By his own account he improved the Ajax academy, but at AZ Alkmaar they coach just as well as at Ajax. At Heerenveen too. At Feyenoord, at PSV Eindhoven. All good people and all good academies. The only difference is that Ajax has the appeal so it tends to pick up the better players. This makes it seem as if the Ajax academy is the best, but that's far too simplistic. More quality goes in at Ajax. If the 'good ones' train with each other, better players come out. It's as simple as that. There are no other training courses, there are no other visions. It's simply a matter of good plus good makes better. You can't just say: 'We're going to intensify the training.' That's far too short-sighted.

Frenkie de Jong is an example of someone who's very good. He comes from Tilburg, but then he went to Ajax and has therefore now done the so-called Ajax programme. Nonsense. I come from Utrecht and didn't arrive at Ajax until I was sixteen. Yes, Johan Cruyff was at Ajax from age ten, but do you think he wouldn't have become a good footballer if he had been at Feyenoord?

Barcelona, Bayern Munich, Manchester City and other big clubs of that kind are at the top of the food chain in football. They are the biggest and the richest clubs. They buy to get better and sell players because – to put it bluntly – they are 'surplus to requirements'. Ajax have to hope they get potential stars. Then they can sell players to earn money, but not to get better as a club.

At least that's how it's been until recently. What Ajax are doing now is breaking that system a bit because if you don't compete with the clubs with the bigger budgets, you'll always just be a survivor. Prey. Actually Ajax are now doing what Cruyff didn't want. He preached Ajax players, Ajax development and no expensive purchases. That approach didn't work, and two or three years ago Overmars, on behalf of Ajax, said: 'We're going to do things differently.'

Naturally, Johan launched his whole revolution to help Ajax. He had the club's interests at heart. I do believe that. But if you're reasonably intelligent, as Johan was, then you can see that the narrative he unleashed on Ajax actually belonged at a club like Barcelona.

At some point he also came up with a plan to stop giving the youth teams a regular coach any more, but to have them rotate. A different one each month. That was reversed within six months. He was trying to sell something that no one wanted to buy. That's why I said: Fairy Tale News.

Cruyff was also dependent on the people who had to implement his ideas; he didn't know everything in advance. But he certainly thought: if it doesn't work, then I'll solve it. In matters of football he was an intellectual – he saw and knew everything – but setting up an organization is a different matter altogether.

ON BAD TERMS
I honestly thought 'suit yourself'. After Danny had shown me the door and Johan had had that sudden change of heart and clearly preferred other interests over me, I was done with them. I also honestly thought that after all that had happened, it wasn't up to me to make the first move and to get in touch again myself. But after that particular autumn of 2011 Johan didn't make the first move. Nor did Danny. So I let it go.

I saw Johan twice more, at Ajax, when I took Heerenveen to play at the ArenA. But I saw him only from a distance, while I was giving an interview. That was the last time. Liesbeth and I sent something when he fell ill, but in the end his death was rather unexpected. It reduced me to silence, it really affected me.

When all's said and done, it was actually a very sad affair. I had mixed feelings: on the one hand he was my idol, my football mentor and later a dear friend, on the other he had abandoned me. And all because of that idiotic revolution and the power plays around a top club like Ajax. Such a great shame.

BACK TO HEERENVEEN

13 August 2012

I was driving along the A6, across the North East Polder. Empty plains around me, now that I had passed Lake Tjeukemeer. It was still early. I was on my way to Amsterdam the morning after my first match with Heerenveen, my new club. Yesterday afternoon we had lost to NEC. 2-0, at home as well. I was in bits about it. I wasn't driving fast, just taking it easy, but I was restless. I'd only slept a few hours in my apartment in Heerenveen. I really ought to have been taking recovery training shortly, but I'd made up my mind...

Finally, head coach again somewhere, after a three-year sabbatical, I had thought over the last few weeks. I found it comforting, the idea of working in Heerenveen.

Various offers had come my way in the intervening years, but none of them had come to anything. Too far from home. Too much stress. But out in the sticks in Heerenveen, at a manageable distance from Amsterdam, it felt different. It had to be doable. And the idea of no longer having to work under a microscope, as you do at a top club, helped too.

Pre-season had all gone smoothly. We hadn't lost any warm-up games, apart from Cologne away, but now, straight after that first league match, the tension had shot into my head again. And if I wasn't sleeping already, that wasn't normal, was it? When I got home I would call the chairman to tell him I was quitting.

I had almost forgotten about the stress. After my departure from Ajax it seemed to have completely disappeared, because I had set aside the burden and the tension of the head coach position. I had known then that I had to work on myself, on my fear of failure. I had done an NLP training course, a technique in which you consciously try to modify your fixed ways of thinking, so that you start thinking outside the box.

I had been inspired by Bouke de Boer, with whom I spoke a lot. He was one of the NLP trainers and had founded the institute. I had begun with a short course, but soon got a taste for it. And because I never do anything by halves, I threw myself into it completely and did a two-year course. All kinds of modules. I learned a lot from the communication courses in particular.

As a result I started looking differently at how I had handled players as coach of the Dutch national team and Ajax. The importance of non-verbal communication, the messages someone you're talking to is sending out and for example at what moment you choose to deliver bad news. That was all hugely helpful. I even did a course at this institute to learn how to handle my fear of failure. That was also really interesting. But could I then say that I understood why it always went wrong for me? No, not really. I was sometimes reminded of my mother. She had taken her driving test probably 20 times, but she had failed every time. That was a fear of failure too, nerves at the most untimely moment. Totally identifiable.

I really had to tell him that I was quitting in person. A phone call wouldn't do. I went off at junction 15, Emmeloord. I pulled over and let it sink in. Then I took two left turns and drove straight back onto the A6, a U-turn. Back to Heerenveen. In search of the chairman. I simply didn't want this stress again. It was certainly nothing to do with the club. They were all lovely people. The reception had been great too. It was this tension, but above all that weird feeling after a defeat. But with the knowledge that I would soon be free of it again, I already felt a little better.

The spectre of fear had paid me another visit one night in March 2011. One of the three big clubs in Portugal, Sporting Lisbon, was having presidential elections. There were three candidates and I ended up being the trump card of one of them. He wanted me as head coach of Sporting from that summer. After a few conversations it was done. He promised me I would be able to spend many millions on players if it all went through.

Surprisingly enough, the second presidential candidate had previously signed an agreement with Frank Rijkaard as prospective head coach. Frank and I were therefore in a certain sense in competition with each other. Perry had a complicated role because he was both Frank's agent and mine. He had discussed the matter with us in advance. All three of us were in agreement because it didn't harm any of our interests.

Early in the morning after the elections Perry called to say: 'I have bad news. The third candidate has won. They counted the last votes between five and six o'clock this morning…'

I had already stopped listening. I hadn't wanted to be coach there. The relief was immediate. The stress fell away from me. I was immediately a good deal happier.

I drove onto the stadium site, to my own parking spot. It looked quiet, but I wasn't feeling in the least bit calm. I was there to quit my job. After my first official match, remember. I walked into the building and asked the receptionist if she knew where Robert Veenstra was. It turned out he had just left. She didn't know where he'd gone.

In Spain too I once had it intensely, not long after the Sporting Lisbon situation. In Madrid to be precise. Perry had spent a long time there negotiating with a delegation from the Chinese football association. They were looking for a new national coach on a four-year contract. It was June 2011. Jorge Mendes, the Portuguese agent of the likes of Mourinho and Ronaldo, had made contact with us on behalf of the Chinese. Perry called me that afternoon: 'They're really serious. And the terms are good. I think it would be a good idea if you can come to Madrid yourself.' Two hours later I was on the plane.

That evening we dined and talked until about 11 o'clock. The Chinese were very serious and the feeling was good, on both sides. All the details were discussed and agreed. I could take the assistants I wanted and would be given carte blanche to do things at the association my way. Money wasn't an issue at all. The deal was sealed. Verbally. Everyone was happy and the atmosphere positive.

Early the next morning the delighted Chinese delegation boarded a plane back to Beijing. As soon as they were there, they would draw up the contracts and send them to us. A week or two later I would be presented in Beijing.

After a last drink Perry and I both went satisfied to our hotel rooms. But I couldn't sleep. It seemed as if it was only now getting through to me: four years in China. What was I getting myself into? I knew nothing about the country. I was feeling terribly anxious. It was only with great difficulty that I eventually fell asleep.

As I lay there staring at the ceiling again at 5.30, with a pain in my stomach, I could no longer stop myself and I sent Perry a long text saying I couldn't do it after all. That I didn't want to do it. That I felt anxious about the thought of four years in China. That I didn't feel it was right and fair. That they should get a coach who didn't have any doubts. And that he should call the deal off. I really didn't see any other option. Sorry.

He immediately knocked on my door and could see at once that I meant it. And he's also a realist. He wasn't happy, but immediately accepted the situation. Over. He called the Chinese as soon as they landed. They were not amused, of course, but Perry cleared up the mess for me. I felt relieved when we flew back to Amsterdam that afternoon.

I was back at the stadium and there was no sign of Robert. The players and coaches were just getting ready for recovery training and I got changed to join them. I thought: I'll see the chairman afterwards. But I didn't see Robert after training either. So I decided to go home. From the moment I sat in the car again I felt a little better. I'd enjoyed working that day, maybe it would all turn out all right. I could feel the tension gradually draining away and thought I would pack it in for the day. Time to go home.

CLEAROUT

21 July 2014

My father was dead. My brother was on his way back to Curaçao. It was Monday afternoon, three days after the cremation, and I was on my way to clear out my father's house. So now I had to go back to that room, my old room in the house on Johan Wagenaarkade. For the first time in years. Even when my father was still living there, before he went into a care home two years before, I never went in there. I went to see him, but not in my room.

I drove onto the Amsterdam Ring just past the Olympic Stadium. I was almost in the mood for this clearout. That might sound strange because there were lots of memories for me there too. The room where I would endlessly kick a ball against the wall, and where I shared a first kiss with Anne, my first girlfriend. And where my father always used to come and sit on the edge of my bed before I went to sleep. The room I left behind after my mother fell ill, when I moved in with Liesbeth at the age of 21. The words scratched on the desk top were still there: *I am the best (except for me)*. Words that had totally unwittingly acquired mythical proportions.

'We'll carry on,' my father had said to me when a doctor had said I should stop playing football because I would have a worn-out hip. I was 15, and so 'we' carried on. Very successfully. As was obvious in that room because, once I had moved out, it had become a kind of Marco museum to which my father had totally dedicated himself. With all my cups, pennants, shirts, VHS tapes and folders of records of all my matches. You name it. It was lovely for him, he could entertain journalists there, tell his story. I wasn't interested in it myself. And, after all, it was his life too.

He really loved it. I'd give him that. Just like that Marco van Basten Sports Park he was so keen to see. It could have been at my old club UVV, where there were many fond memories. In the thirty years or so since my departure that room had turned into something I wanted to get away from. A sort of gravestone for a lost footballer. A monument to 'the striker who once was'. Something of the past. I had moved on, had a family, children, different priorities. But he stayed in that period all that time. In my glory days as a player, which were his glory days too. He had never experienced such success as a player himself. From time to time I would hear he sometimes told the journalists a bit too much. That he had some regrets. That he should have paid my mother more attention when she was still 'okay'. And that he should have given my brother and sister more attention, instead of just me. That he had paid a 'high price' for it. But he never told me these things and I never read those interviews.

It was a bit busier in Utrecht itself. The Spinoza Bridge over to Oog in Al, and then right into Herderplein. In the last few years I had said certain things to him that I couldn't leave unsaid. For example, that I felt it was strange how, in a manner of speaking, he had never even glanced at my mother in thirty years, until she was taken ill. And then he was visiting her three times a day, even though she no longer recognized him. Where was the sense in that? He hardly ever saw his own grandchildren. I couldn't understand that.

Maybe it was a kind of penance, something Catholic.

But why? I got really angry about it a number of times. 'Why are you doing it?' I would say, but he would simply answer: 'That's how I feel, Marco. I have to do it.' Okay, then there was nothing more to be said.

His social circle became smaller and smaller. There was nothing left of it. And my mother noticed hardly anything. She was stuck away among people with dementia. Of course, he did try to do things in his life properly. To the best of his ability. To the best of his knowledge, I really believe that.

I have increasingly come to appreciate my mother more in the last few years. I have my sensitive and creative side from her. She was also far more sociable than my father. Just before she fell ill she had been to Canada to visit Stanley and to see his children. If she had still been here, she would certainly have had a good relationship with our children. I'm sure of that.

I remember she was keen for me to learn to play the piano. She could play really well herself. By ear. I had lessons for a while, but I would always peep out from behind the piano to see if the football had started yet.

I put the key in the lock at Johan Wagenaarkade. The reflection of Amsterdam–Rhine Canal glistened in the glass front door. In my hand I had a roll of rubbish bags. Those blue ones. I went straight through to the room. To all the knick-knacks. As I opened the door I was resolute: I would throw everything away. There was a thick layer of dust everywhere. With my hands full, everything went in the blue bags. I began to sweat and I opened a window.

I came across a pennant from a youth tournament with UVV in the south of France when I was nine. In Le Lavandou, where we played on white clay. Palm trees all around. It was incredible. We won and I was player of the tournament. Youth coach Wim Haazer arranged it all. A UVV man through and through. As winners we were invited back. A year later everyone suddenly wanted to go to the Côte d'Azur with us. It was a sort of glorified holiday where the boys happened to play a tournament. We finished 13th, ha-ha. It was a great time.

But all the rest could go. There was an unbelievable amount of junk. All the things he kept…One rubbish bag after another. Life goes on. A huge sense of relief overcame me as I hauled three bags to the front door in one go.

LIBERATION DAY

31 October 2014

You could see it in the photos. I was sitting there at AZ with a big cake in front of me, with 50 on it. I was wearing a party hat. It may have looked ridiculous, but I was really happy. That was obvious. I appreciated my colleagues' gesture. I think it's great when people treat one another this way. Like good colleagues. Warm.

But there was more behind my smile. There was relief too because I was no longer head coach. A few weeks before, with pain in my stomach, I had finally made the decision. I was now assistant to head coach John van den Brom. And from day one I was happy. There are other photos from that time. Liesbeth and I were having a party because we had both turned fifty, so together a hundred. I could see the joy, the relief. It was the same in a photo of a concert by The Toppers, with Dennis Haar, Van den Brom and a few friends.

It seemed like a good step. After the initial tension I had actually had two great seasons at Heerenveen. With the assistance of Tieme Klompe and the club management we were able to assemble a good team, but after that I wanted to work closer to home. And maybe slowly something higher up as well.

It ended up being AZ in Alkmaar. A logical step. The contracts were sorted out and I was able to choose my own assistant. Unfortunately, Tieme couldn't go with me. At Heerenveen he really had pulled me through. At the time I couldn't foresee the consequences of his absence at AZ. But it simply felt like the right thing to do, especially as the tension had in the end become more manageable for me in those two seasons at Heerenveen.

Pre-season had started well, until my father died a few weeks later. My attention was then fully focused on his cremation, the family and the 'clearout'. When I returned to AZ afterwards, unfortunately things didn't go quite so well and I wasn't feeling comfortable. But I wanted to get started on the league games, whatever it took.

The first match at Heracles we won 3-0. Things were still okay. We lost the second match 3-1 to Ajax. Okay, that can happen. But in the third match we were well beaten by Willem II, 3-0. That hit me hard. I started to have trouble with stress again and slept badly. Unfortunately, the spectre of fear was back. In the end I called Perry that same week and told him: 'I want to stop. I can't do this.'

AZ of course weren't at all happy about it, but they very sympathetically and sportingly acceded to my request to become assistant. An unusual step, but one I was very pleased with.

And the cake on my birthday, a month later, I thought was really very nice. I felt I had left them in the lurch, after all the effort they had made to appoint me and to make the job attractive to me.

What I did know then, and do know now, is that I will never be a head coach again. That chapter is closed. For good. Later I heard that Liesbeth had said: 'If he wants to do it again, I will really have to put my foot down.'

She was right. It was better for me and for those around me. They knew the routine by then. All at once, a few days after that difficult decision, I was completely on top of everything again.

As soon as it had happened, I had virtually no further trouble with it. I would put on airs again, as Liesbeth put it. I would know exactly what to say again and even tell the head coach that he should put the defeat into perspective, that he shouldn't take all the comments so seriously and that the press and the public would soon forget this defeat once the next win came along. Don't take it so much to heart, I would sometimes hear myself say.

Instead of embarrassment with the colourful decorations on my birthday, that day at AZ felt like liberation day to me. Fifty years and never head coach again. Since I'd made the decision I had once again been relaxed and I had great fun with the people around me. The strange thing was, I knew exactly what the head coach was going through and I could give him good advice. And therefore also say that he should keep calm, ha-ha.

In the end it had taken me about ten years to make the decision and no longer care about being a head coach. Of course, it helped that financial calm had been restored. And I no longer wanted to saddle Liesbeth with a stressed partner. I no longer wanted the pressure. Finished. I'd had my last night with the spectre.

FIFA (1)

'Scrap offside'

2016–2017

'I think I'm unemployed.'

As soon as I said the words, I realized how idiotic they must sound to Perry on the other end of the line. I was standing on the grass next to the massive building with the FIFA logo on it and had just had a run-in with Zvonimir Boban, my immediate boss at FIFA, who worked under FIFA President Gianni Infantino. We had parted on bad terms. I had known him a long time and, if I was being entirely honest, I had known that my remark just now would hit home, but I hadn't expected him to blow his top the way he did.

I realized I could have dented his pride when I told him he was unreliable. But for me it was actually about something else, about being taken seriously, because I had the impression that I was being sidelined here at FIFA. We hadn't been hitting it off together for months, though my job here had started full of expectation. They were so incredibly keen to have me. Everything pointed that way. But now I was no longer being invited to some of the meetings on matters that were my responsibility. It was strange to be standing there, next to the football pitch at the headquarters, and to feel so cut off from the things that really mattered. I went to my own office to collect my things. A few hours later I would in any case be on my flight to Amsterdam. I would simply be getting to the airport a little early.

I had first spoken to Gianni Infantino, Boban and Mattias Grafstrom, Gianni's right-hand man, in June 2016. They were looking for someone interested in football development. Someone interested in taking the lead, in encouraging the thinking about it, in part because it had all become very bogged down in the Blatter era.

Infantino had been elected the new FIFA president a few months before, but was having a hard time. He was trying to get rid of the negative image and was on the lookout for fresh faces. Pairing 'Marco van Basten' with FIFA was therefore an attractive idea for him.

On the very football pitch where I stood catching my breath he had organized a football match with former players a day after his appointment, in February 2016. From the PR perspective a very smart move, surrounding yourself with former footballers. Untarnished names, which made you think of football again. He wanted to send out the message that after the corruption scandal and the various international arrests in the Blatter era, FIFA was finally all about football again.

They really knew how to get to me in those initial discussions, which were all about football and the development of the sport. They had a clear passion for it. That much I already knew about Boban, having played with him briefly at Milan. I hadn't known Infantino and Grafstrom before, but they were also top people.

They wanted to create a tailor-made job for me. I would more or less be able to say what I wanted to be involved with. Three things were being rolled out at the time: the development of the laws of the game, refereeing matters and technological development in football. It felt good because the laws of the game had always interested me and in those discussions it was really all about my personal vision and fresh ideas. I felt that it wasn't just about my 'name'. I liked that.

At the time I was still assistant to Danny Blind with the Dutch national team and the discussions I had with him and Kees Jansma often jokingly ended with the words: 'Then you must go and work for FIFA.' And now FIFA was suddenly knocking at my door. It was a great opportunity, although the Dutch FA were not amused.

Three assistants left the Dutch team in a short space of time, and that in the year the team was absent from the Euros. Ruud van Nistelrooy went to PSV Eindhoven in May, his replacement, Dick Advocaat, left for Fenerbahçe after two months, and I accepted the offer from FIFA. I was present at the Dutch team's matches in September and supported Danny at the away game with Sweden, but on 1 October 2016 I started in Zurich full of energy and in good spirits.

I had an office next to Boban's, on Infantino's corridor, and attended all the important meetings about 'my' areas. During the week I lived there in my apartment, but every weekend I went home to Amsterdam. It took some getting used to. I had never had a real office job before and now I suddenly had 40 people under me and a budget of around 40 million Swiss francs. On the first day someone came to me with a query about his annual leave. I really had no idea. These were precisely the sort of things of which I had 'zero' experience, but I was supposedly going to be guided in them.

I found the meetings about the development of the laws of the game and new technologies such as the video assistant referee (VAR) very interesting. They generated lively discussions at which I always said what I thought. After the FIFA Club World Cup of 2016 in Tokyo, it was an option to carry on with VAR for the Confederations Cup and then perhaps for the World Cup. I was committed to preventing delays in this process, feeling that we should press ahead. Only the referees were not in favour. They found it complicated and threatening.

I had my first real confrontation in January 2017. I had been in post for just three months. I saw little of Infantino because he spent 260 days a year travelling the world and Boban was also having less and less to do with me. My office had now been moved to the other side of the corridor. In an interview with the German newspaper *Bild* I talked about my new job as Chief Officer for Technical Development. When it came out a week later my phone was suddenly red hot. The headline to the article read: *FIFA officer Van Basten: 'Scrap offside!'*

I immediately had Infantino and Boban on the line. They had been shocked, to put it mildly, while I had simply talked about my ideas. It really came as a bombshell, not just at FIFA itself, but worldwide. Jürgen Klopp called it a daft idea, Arsène Wenger also said something critical about it and Infantino had calls from his intimates all over the world: 'What is FIFA planning to do?' 'Is this really your idea?' Nothing but unrest and confusion.

I had explained the difference between my personal opinion and the FIFA standpoint to *Bild*, but that fell on deaf ears. I was officially FIFA's Chief Officer for Technical Development and if I put something like this out there in relation to my job, then it was virtually fact. That's how people saw it. It was naive of me. Certainly not smart.

However, I carried on in good spirits because behind the scenes I was able to work on advancing the introduction of VAR. I was a great advocate of it because it simply makes football fairer.

I was always three steps ahead and felt I was being held back in doing what I wanted. During the Confederations Cup in June 2017 I was also busy looking at Effective Playing Time. I spent many matches with my phone in my hand recording how many minutes' effective playing time there were. It usually came to around 30 minutes per half, and sometimes even less.

My ideas were based on preventing delaying tactics, time-wasting and stoppages of play. Spectators want to see movement, action and goals. Everyone gets really annoyed about time-wasting.

I still support that idea of scrapping offside. At least, I would find it interesting to see what the consequences of scrapping it would be. I think it would be to football's benefit. I really believe that. But extensive trials are needed of course. Offside or not is often a matter of the finest of margins. Really on the edge, one way or the other.

After the Confederations Cup FIFA brought in Pierluigi Collina to take over refereeing matters from me. Infantino came to tell me in person, adding: 'I want to give you the International Match Calendar in return. There's much to do there too.' When are the international tournaments? Do the players get enough rest in a season? When and how can you organize a Club World Cup without players being forced to play more matches? I found questions like these a fascinating challenge and I took them very seriously.

I remember exactly how I felt when I started at AC Milan after a hard season of football. I'd needed a minimum of four weeks to get everything out of my system, to sweat out the tension and to recharge my batteries. So I was very much in favour of four weeks' rest for footballers in the Match Calendar.

This didn't happen everywhere at the time by any means, but it was a necessity. A break like this is healthy for everyone who has anything to do with football. A little time away. Time to revive your interest. Including the fans, the press and the referees. Everyone can do with it. Just a month of nothing.

Nonetheless, it remained suspiciously quiet in my part of the corridor. Few questions were asked about the progress of my work. I was involved in the introduction of VAR for the World Cup. That was an interesting process. There were often fierce discussions about it.

That was really what I enjoyed the most. I knew they sometimes expected politically correct answers from me, but I never kept quiet.

So that day I actually went to Boban to confront him about my situation. 'What do you actually want from me?' I asked. 'You bring me nothing, ask me nothing. There are other things I could be doing. Okay. But you were so keen to have me.'

He was quiet for a moment. When the discussion then flared up with great vehemence, I called him unreliable. I know that his not keeping to agreements is something different, but I said it to provoke him. I could see in his eyes that he felt it was a stab in the back. Then he sent me away.

Oh well, I left it a while after that. I was going to celebrate Christmas in Holland and I would hear later if Boban and Infantino wanted me back in the New Year.

FIFA (2)

Coffee with Vladimir Putin

June–July 2018

Absolutely everything in the Kremlin looked really old. When we left, to go back to our cars, I had a rather unreal feeling. Who gets to go to the White House? Who gets to go to the Kremlin? It's really rather special to be invited to such an unusual place and then all of a sudden you're sitting round a table with Mr Putin.

When we first arrived we had to wait for 20 minutes in another room before being allowed into the official reception room. We had been invited because FIFA was organizing the World Cup being held in Russia that year. There were about ten of us in our delegation: four or five former footballers plus FIFA officials. Boban and Infantino were there of course. As soon as we sat down we were served coffee and small Russian pastries, and there were platters of fruit on the table. All very nice.

Putin took the floor. In Russian. An interpreter provided us with a translation through an earpiece. Initially, the press was there en masse to record the official part of the programme. I think Putin spoke for about fifteen minutes. All kinds of positives about the World Cup, mixed in with the occasional joke.

After Putin's speech Lothar Matthäus said what a wonderful country he thought Russia was. Then the press left, Putin went round the table and shook everyone's hand. He did this mainly in Russian, with an interpreter, but sometimes he spoke a few words of German or English. Everyone was very polite about what a lovely World Cup it was, but I tried to bring a bit of light relief to the otherwise rather formal, sober proceedings. I said: 'I don't know if you're still angry with me, because in 1988 we beat you in the final.' Initially, the joke fell a bit flat, but then he did manage a smile. Maybe out of politeness.

During the World Cup I stayed at the Radisson Hotel in the centre of Moscow. At the matches they were keen for me to sit among the official guests in the FIFA VIP seats, but I didn't take up those tickets. I preferred to watch from the press gallery. You weren't constantly accosted there and could follow the match reasonably well. But most of all I liked to watch in the peace and quiet of my hotel.

I did go to a few matches at the Luzhniki Stadium. I had to put in an appearance at the opening match. And later on at Iceland v. Argentina and the Russia v. Croatia quarter-final. We had a chat group where we discussed match situations and VAR incidents that occurred during the tournament.

Things went wrong after the Switzerland v. Brazil match. When Switzerland scored their equalizer from a corner, with a header by Steven Zuber, I made a comment in our chat group. Seen from a particular camera angle the replay clearly showed that Zuber had given the Brazilian defender Miranda a nudge in the back, which left him on his own and free to head in from close range. It looked like an infringement and the goal really shouldn't have been allowed to stand.

It was precisely for incidents of this kind that we had come up with VAR, but it wasn't consulted, while that nudge was clear to see for everyone watching TV worldwide. I didn't think it was right. The Brazilians were furious. The game ended 1-1, which meant they lost two points.

It was common knowledge that referees were having a lot of trouble with VAR. I felt it was more than a pity therefore that VAR didn't intervene at that point. Even afterwards they wouldn't admit it was a mistake.

So I made my view clear in our chat group. It wasn't doing FIFA any good, the whole world could see it clearly on the replay. But my observations weren't appreciated. Nothing was done about it.

I bumped into a Brazilian journalist at the Radisson the next day, who asked me about it. I started by saying: 'I'm not talking about it.' I deferred to the referees. But he kept pressing. 'What do you think about it yourself?' Eventually I said: 'It wasn't great, VAR should have looked at it.'

It was online within half an hour and I had Boban on the phone within an hour. What was I doing? 'You no longer have anything to do with refereeing matters, so you're not the spokesman, leave it to others.'

Of course, I perfectly well understand that I was employed by FIFA and that my words therefore carried extra weight, but the incident during the Brazil v. Switzerland match really wasn't on, I felt. Of all teams it was Switzerland that gained an 'irregular' advantage in the game because VAR hadn't intervened. Even worse because FIFA is based in Switzerland and the FIFA president, lording it in the grandstand at this game, was himself Swiss. I was therefore extremely concerned about the referee's decision immediately afterwards and could feel the storm brewing. I worried about any recriminations heading the way of FIFA, Infantino and Switzerland on account of this incident, but my concern was evidently not welcomed by my colleagues.

The following January, after some exchanges by text, I went to Boban to offer him my apologies for my remark about his unreliability. He accepted and was grateful for my apology. He had been rather offended by it. The air between us was therefore fortunately cleared. But my activities didn't change much thereafter.

When all's said and done you can say that during the 2018 World Cup I was slowly working my way towards the exit door at FIFA. I worked on a report about 'VAR at the World Cup', but I was curious to know if anyone would actually ask for it after the summer. I had really felt a bit of a Don Quixote for some time in Zurich. I finally left FIFA in October 2018.

CRUYFF IN TURIN

2 September 2019

I was in Turin at Gianluca Vialli and Massimo Mauro's annual golf tournament, always held in September. I had first gone sixteen years before. It's for a good cause and also very well organized.

You play in teams with a pro, a well-known footballer and an amateur, or someone who has bought in. The cause is ALS, the muscle disease from which Fernando Ricksen recently died. Former fellow player Stefano Borgonovo also died from it as far back as 2013.

Johan Cruyff always liked coming here. He often drove with his wife Danny and a few friends from Barcelona to Turin and made a real occasion of it. Circumstances had prevented me from going for the past seven years, but I always used to see him there before. Now Danny was alone. She played golf herself, but she didn't take part.

We saw each other on the morning of the tournament in the clubhouse at the golf course and greeted each other briefly. Very cool, fleeting and matter-of-fact. In the evening there was a dinner. At the end I noticed she was standing right behind me. She turned to me and said: 'We can't say goodbye like this. Such a cold hand and so distant. That's no good. Johan wouldn't have wanted it like that.' She took my hands. 'Johan had two apples of his eye, you and Pep. So please let's just be normal with each other.'

I was moved by what she said. A tear came to my eye. Something changed there. Then we hugged, gave each other a kiss on the cheek and exchanged some pleasantries.

The next morning we met again at breakfast. It was so much warmer now. She asked whether I was happy in Amsterdam. I said we very much enjoyed living there, having the children nearby. I asked if she still had the apartment, round the corner from me. She wanted to sell it because she was hardly ever there and it made her think of Johan too much. I said I still clearly remembered the time she showed me the door. That I had thought: suit yourself. She said she could well understand, but she thought that was better than creeps who just followed Johan around.

She told me about the new apartment she had bought in Barcelona and how, strangely enough, when she had stripped the paper off the walls, a few old newspapers had emerged with photos and articles about Johan. She found that pretty remarkable and it moved her. It was an extra reason for her to go and live in that apartment. Just before we went our separate ways she told me Johan would be looking down from above and would be happy to see us being normal with each other.

PART VI

NOTES IN THE ATTIC

2019

PRINCE OF ORANGE

2019

We usually fly, but when we took the car to Austria last winter, I put together a playlist of music as entertainment along the way. It included some Dutch-language songs. One was by Lange Frans about Holland. And about the European Championship, Johan Cruyff and Abe Lenstra. And it occurred to me that it was really rather strange that I don't get a mention, because if there's been anyone apart from Cruyff who has written football history in Holland, then it's me. I won a European Championship with the Dutch team and had an important part in it. It's really daft, I thought. I have to be the Prince of Orange, to be idolized, in a manner of speaking.

Of course, I realized that Euro '88 was a wonderful experience and that Ruud was really the face of the Dutch team. In football terms I did maybe play a big part, but let's not make it any bigger than it was. I'm in two minds about it. On the one hand I can say: 'I'm the best.' And on the other: 'I had a really fantastic role, be grateful for that.'

That modesty also comes from me always being critical of my own game. It could always be better. I'm very good at putting the successes into perspective. I can also look at them critically. To see at a detailed level what could have been even better. But as a footballer you want to win trophies and be the best. And I succeeded. That's what it was all about for me originally. I was no Johan Cruyff, but emotionally I came close to his level.

If you look at it another way, I was unlucky with my injury. Even in the years when I did play football my ankle was never a hundred per cent. Can you imagine what I could have achieved with a decent ankle…I think I could have won three more European Cup finals. We wouldn't have lost the one to Marseille in 1993 if I'd been fit and I'm absolutely sure we wouldn't have lost the one against Ajax in 1995, ha-ha. And I could maybe have won a few more. Then I could have ended up with Cristiano Ronaldo-like stats. But no, that's not how things turned out.

I've also always been caught in two minds about public recognition. If I saw a banner with 'And on the eighth day God created Marco' on it, then I would be inclined to make a joke of it, saying that they shouldn't exaggerate so much. I don't like that self-congratulation. Just be ordinary. Just look at what I haven't won. Or at what I still could have won.

At the same time I get irritated if I'm not mentioned at all, or forgotten. If people make out that it was all entirely run of the mill. Then I'm inclined to raise my hand and say: 'Hey, I'm still here. I did something good too.'

In that regard I have an unusual personality. After the ankle episode I mainly looked at what I hadn't achieved, but more recently I've begun to appreciate more what I was able to achieve.

Great players, such as Romário and Ronaldo, win trophies between the ages of 19 and 22. And so I belong among them. It's just that I was never able to finish what I had started. But in the end I increasingly realize that the glass is half full when, for example, I think about that Frenchman on the beach in Juan Les Pins. Luckily, I'm able to do that more and more often now.

As a coach it's been a completely different story. In retrospect I don't think I was all that bad as a coach, but it did cause me far too much anxiety because I'm so demanding of myself. There's a bit of a kink in my story because of that time as a coach. Especially when for the first time things didn't go so well. The blessed San Marco became an ordinary mortal again. Actually, that's fine as well, experiencing the painful side too. I was disowned, reviled then. It's a valuable lesson. And it's how I can now laugh about my children creating a WhatsApp group just after that 'pancake' incident which they named 'The mini pancakes'.

I also sometimes think about how I would like to be remembered later on. Johan for example was something of a missionary. I'm not. I have a different personality. But maybe it's also because I wasn't able to achieve that status, as I had to stop when I was just 28, and was unable to put my stamp on anything for 20 years, as Johan was able to do. As were Messi, Ronaldo, but also Pelé and Maradona.

Johan always wanted to talk about football and influence others in how they thought about it. Maybe I would have had that too if I'd carried on playing for another ten years. If I'd had a different life, without all the ankle problems. Then I would have played football with far more pleasure, it would all have been a little easier and lighter and I would maybe have also felt a bit more gratitude for what I had achieved. Now I've had to work through a lot of anger and frustration. It's not been handed to me on a plate, I've had to fight for it. I was only able to play football unfettered for a short part of my career, that's the sad thing. I got my ankle injury when I was just 22. Before that I played at a high level for three years; afterwards I was always taped up.

I was no hero as a child, nor a very tough boy. Everything that I experienced around me at a personal level was quite intense. I come from a family in which there was little warmth, although I did have the warmth of my mother. But even she could be bad-tempered. My brother and sister were much older than me and I had little to do with them. And my father was mainly at work, making ends meet. He was also very focused on football and my career in particular. Not much on the personal side. So I soon discovered a love of the ball. The football pitch felt like a safe place. Where I could be myself, where I could be free. On the pitch I usually felt fine – it was where I felt at home. Where I could excel.

I think this achievement-oriented side of me has a link with my feeling of self-worth. I think my fervour is sometimes unhealthy. If I lose, I think: what on earth am I doing? Why am I here? But if I win, everything's all right. Then I think: *yesssss!*

I don't know if the way I grew up had any part to play in this. Growing up in a family in which I really had to do everything by myself. In the end I got going with the ball myself. It was me who wanted to be the best, become a pro, get rich. That really came from me.

This week Adriano Galliani, the former AC Milan CEO, sent me a clip of Berlusconi, who said in a TV interview that the European Cup win in Barcelona in 1989 was one of the best days of his life. I was thrilled to hear that. Can you imagine, a man like Berlusconi, successful businessman, billionaire, prime minister of Italy, saying that winning the European Cup had been one of the best days of his life. How special, how great is football's impact in Italy!

I am, despite everything, really very pleased with the successes I achieved. I had a lovely time at Milan, the San Siro felt like my home. They are all very positive things. But sometimes you don't realize that until afterwards because as it's happening you just carry on. Someone clips you, you take a tumble, you escape from something and you pick yourself up again. Over and over again.

And now that I'm sitting with this book in front of me, I'm really only now looking and asking myself: 'What actually happened to me? And why did it actually happen?' Now, for the first time, I'm actually reflecting seriously on things from my past and reacting to things. This is reflected in the way all kinds of emotions come to the surface. It's a marvellous process. As a result you become more sure of certain things because they become clearer.

For me my bookcase was figuratively well stocked, but everything was mixed up. However, through all the weeks and months of talking about my life, I tidied it all up, I discussed it, drew conclusions, gained insights. So now I've tidied the bookcase, not just in order, but also in value. You get a clearer picture of the highs and lows of the past fifty years. It's less cluttered and you can see everything in the right light. The nice things and the downsides.

Now, for example, I'm better able to enjoy a tape of my best goals in Serie A. When I was in the middle of it all, that was far less so. You're always on the move. When you're 20, you know you have a journey in front of you. And those first 20 years have to prepare you for the journey. You do everything to prepare well: you do your packing properly, you have to learn the route, and so on.

Then you're on your way, and having to react appropriately to each new situation; you have to survive, make good decisions, do the right things and fight to stay fit and healthy. You're constantly doing something. There's no time to rest. Now I'm at the stage of looking back and putting a value on things. And I'm learning from that too. Things gain a certain perspective. That's a plus.

I'm glad I met Liesbeth and that we're still happy together after all these years. There aren't very many people who can say that after more than thirty years. That's really fortunate for me. Maybe it's also more precisely because I didn't have the best example at home in my younger days and I mainly saw how it shouldn't be.

But you do have to be lucky in this regard and I am with her. I'm really happy that we have a lovely family, with my daughters Rebecca and Angela and my son Alexander. And next year I'm going to be a grandad too. Such an abundance of riches.

Ultimately, it's a challenge for people who go into football to come out unscathed. Success usually has a downside, in fact it always does. It's often by no means as wonderful as it seems from the outside. You have to do a great deal yourself, make many sacrifices, have the discipline not to do things. And everyone wants a bit of you, if you're successful. If things don't go so well, you're usually on your own.

But to come out of love unscathed, especially with a football career like mine, you must have a special, strong partner, work hard and enjoy good fortune.

The same is true of friendship. I don't think there are many people, apart from Liesbeth and my children, who know me better than my few close friends. I've been hanging around with three of them all my life. We still regularly go and eat together and then we talk about everything. I like that tradition.

In the end I went through a lot of woe with my ankle. And later had problems as a coach too. But I would perhaps have become a very tiresome individual if I had just kept winning all my life and remained the best. If I had never got that injury.

At the time there was something arrogant about me. That would perhaps have just got worse. Maybe I would have had to cool it a bit. If you don't know what being unhappy is, then you don't know what being happy is either.

ANKLE (9)

Notes in the attic

July 2019

Up in the attic, on the exercise bike, I can let my thoughts run free. No one disturbs me up here. It's a ritual I've been following at least three times a week for nearly 25 years. Really ever since the Ilizarov apparatus meant I could no longer stand. The exercise bike is an almost prehistoric white model I got from Technogym in 1994. A big, unwieldy piece of kit, with a really wide saddle, as if you're sitting on an old moped. I don't necessarily need the latest version. It makes no difference to me. As long as the thing works, that's fine. I'm not someone who's quick to get rid of something when it suits me. I know its every little sound and movement.

It's actually been the silent witness to my life since 1994. It has travelled with me all that time. In the summer of 1996 to Monaco, in 1998 to Badhoevedorp and in 2010 to Amsterdam. It's always been in the attic. And it's been here, at the Vondelpark, for nearly ten years now. It may not have much life left in it, but it's been a faithful companion.

If you've played sport at the top level for years and you suddenly stop because you can no longer walk properly, then you have to do something else. For your fitness, but also to burn off energy. I've always needed to do that, otherwise I get grouchy. I still do. If I don't play squash or work out for a long time, Liesbeth notices it straight away. With golf it's different. I can lose myself in that. Liesbeth knows I have to exercise, preferably obsessively and competitively.

All these years I've always kept a record of what I did on the bike. Entire notepads full of records, all neatly laid out. The date, the minutes, the resistance, the heart rate, the distance. I wrote everything down. In Badhoevedorp I wrote it in pen on the roof beams. I remember a potential buyer of that house asking me what they meant during the guided tour, all those neat rows of data on the roof beams.

These records gave me peace of mind. As if it were real only if it had been written down. Here in Amsterdam I have whole notepads full of my exercise bike records for the last few years. Not that I ever look at them, but nevertheless. I suppose you could call them the logbooks of self-discipline, proof of my never-say-die attitude.

But that's not all. I used to do this before the ankle as well. Actually, I've been doing it all my life, keeping records. Writing things down. As an adolescent I used to record all my matches in ring binders, or those colourful A5 loose-leaf folders. Every week I would carefully record the date, the match, the line-up, the result and how many goals I'd scored. And sometimes a few comments. I kept doing that for years, even when I had long been a professional footballer. Certainly for four or five years.

These folders or notebooks, whatever you want to call them, lay in my old room on Johan Wagenaarkade all those years. In the room my father later set up as a sort of Marco museum. We used them in the programme about my career with Hugo Borst in 1997. Afterwards they went back to Utrecht.

After my father died I took the notebooks from the room with me. They're here in a box in the attic.

Every match is recorded in my youthful handwriting. One page per match. The date, the line-up, the result, sometimes even the formation in which we played, the substitutions, and how often I scored.

On 15 November 1983 it says: 'On 1 November 1983 I was diagnosed with glandular fever.' And then a list of missed matches. And by Ireland v. Holland in Dublin, 12 October 1983 it says: 'First half: 4-4-2; 2-0 down; Second half: 4-3-3; won 3-2!' And then very drily: 'scored 1'. And sometimes there would be my autograph at the bottom. I was practising it even then. Ha-ha.

But there was always the result and the number of goals I scored. No match overlooked. It's quite special that I kept a record of everything as a young footballer. I was 18 then. Perhaps I had copied it from my father, who wrote a bit of a report on the team he coached in his notebook every Sunday evening. And every Sunday I used to look over his shoulder.

It came to me, as I was sitting on my exercise bike, that there should be another of these folders. A folder of notes from that rubbish year when I could no longer walk because of the pain, after that Ilizarov apparatus. It took me ten minutes to find it, in the third box. A dark red folder of the same size. With my initials on it. The notes from twenty-five years ago. When I no longer knew what I was going to do. I opened it up.

Badhoevedorp, 8 April 1995

Today I lay on the physiotherapist's couch and he asked me:
'Do you actually think you have learned anything if someone
were to grab hold of your ankle and cure it with one magic spell?'
Yes, I said at once. But as I said it, I also heard something in me
that said I should write it down [...] because otherwise I would
probably quickly forget it and move on to the order of the day.
That's why I've put pen to paper today. It seems as if I have a 'jam',
with my ankle. I've been working on my ankle's recovery for the
past two and a half years, but nothing has led to improvement or
recovery. In fact, it's now far worse than a year ago.

I have undergone the following therapeutic procedures:
1) haptonomy T. Troost
2) orthopaedics R. Marti

	[ankle]	*operation*	*Dec 86*
	[ankle]	*„*	*Dec 87*
	[ankle]	*„*	*Dec 92*
Martens	*[knee]*	*„*	*Sept 89*
	[ankle]	*„*	*June 93*
	[Ilizarov!]	*„*	*June 94*

3) acupuncture T. Zhang + Milan AC
4) physiotherapy R. van Dantzig, Milan AC, Jos Wiewel
5) 'aura' practitioner Bert van Driel
6) Yomanda medium (Liesbeth and Toon)
7) podologist Milan AC (Zucchini)
            Schrijver (Utrecht)
8) hypnotherapist F. Gast
9) pranotherapy Roberto (Italy)

I may have missed out one or two, but okay, it's more to get an idea.
I've also had a number of injections [Marti-Monti] in my ankle.
And I've also followed courses of treatment. [...] Also many letters
with all sorts of advice in the medical, alternative and paranormal
spheres. None of this has led to anything. Today I limp when I
stand up, limp if I walk a lot (stroll), to say nothing of sport or other
intensive activity. So I'm now working on my 'mind'. This is all very
indefinable. Many thoughts are going through my head. So many
and so fast that I'm thinking: I'll write them down too.

I can recall the feeling from that time only too well. I was at absolute
rock bottom. I'd been in pain for so long and could no longer walk

properly. I had to try to keep myself as fit as possible for someone in poor physical shape who three years before had had the world at his feet. And who now had to get through each day without too much pain with a minimal number of things he could do, because he was physically constrained. What I did do was some cycling. On the exercise bike, but outdoors sometimes too.

We regularly travelled to Holland for medical matters, even though we lived in Italy, and later Monaco. Because I couldn't walk without crutches, I would sometimes cycle round Badhoevedorp, from our home. A breath of fresh air. I wasn't happy at the time, but it gave me a break. And it got rid of some energy.

Once when I returned from my ride, our daughter Angela came outside. She must have been four or five years old. She greeted me. Daddy's back. And as I clambered off the bike, she came up to me and, so that I wouldn't feel any pain, gave me the crutches as fast as she could. It was a moment I'll never forget because I remember what I thought: this isn't the way it should be. The children looking after me. It was an intense feeling. This really wasn't how it should be. Absolutely rock bottom. Because I should be there for my children. It was a lovely thing for her to do, but for me it was a moment when I said to myself: 'Yes. Enough of this misery.'

I was so restless then. I couldn't burn off any energy. I couldn't play with my children. I would often just watch a bit of TV. I did get something out of writing though.

I know that even now. Although I no longer have a clue what it was all about.

There's no such thing as coincidence. Things happen to you. I have to go back to the moment it happened. Groningen, Dec. 1986. During the Groningen v. Ajax match I went into a sliding tackle and wham, my ankle said: Okay, that's enough. I was so keen to prove myself (my brother was sitting in the stands, on a visit from Canada) and that's why something like this happened. From that day on the moaning and groaning about my ankle has never really stopped. Now, looking back, I think: I've never looked at it like this. But I do understand that I was very impatient, that I had trouble with my own huge ambition that was at the expense of myself. I didn't listen. I must and would be fit. I must and would play football.

I went to see Prof. Marti at the AMC with Cruyff. Cruyff wanted to know if he could select/use me. Marti said that it couldn't do any harm. I might now think that Marti is an idiot or Cruyff or Martens or Troost or whoever, but:

1) it won't make me any the wiser
2) I let myself be used in all my ignorance.

I was living in a materialistic world with tangible thoughts and tangible solutions.

I nevertheless believe that I acted in good faith. I just didn't gain any understanding of the situation (in so far as I have now).

That's quite a punchy analysis for someone of 30. And quite firm too. They were certainly harsh words. I was looking, so it seems, mainly to blame myself. Maybe that also came from the conversations I had that spring with the man from Oibibio, Bert van Riel.

I had tried all the physical and medical solutions and alternative methods too. And nothing had helped. In fact, things had just got worse. So then I went searching into the psychological side of things. Ronald Jan Heijn, the founder of Oibibio, is my friend Dennis's brother. And Bert van Riel was the man who inspired Ronald Jan.

Bert had a practice in Rijswijk and I went there a few times for consultations. Ted sometimes went with me.

The consultations really went into some depth because I was keen to know if there was something in my mindset that could be changed. All with a view to healing my ankle. I kept searching. I can still remember the atmosphere of the consultations. I was quite inquisitive. Just as I tackled NLP later on, I threw myself into it completely. It's because I like to do things properly. I wanted to understand their way of thinking. And I hoped to get something out of it. If the purely physical didn't work, then maybe the psychological or spiritual would help. Who knows if I would get something out of it. I was at my wits' end.

> *Breathing exercises into your stomach against stress*
> <u>*You must from memory.*</u>
> *Lie on back – Hands on stomach – Breathe deeply – Then feet up*
> *I cannot currently burn off my energy as I used to for years (football). Above all, I used to be able to get rid of my anger by giving free rein to my aggression in football/training. I cannot do that now.*
> *Consequence -> restless in bed -> not sleeping well -> in your head -> friction -> hot -> not sleeping.*
> *I often connected my emotion/anger to my mind, which is why I could be very cold, cool, clinical and above all relentless when I was angry.*
> *I must sit behind the steering wheel myself to control my life and I mustn't let myself be driven by the outside world. I must not be as strict, stubborn, stiff, rigid or obstinate as my father, but actually be flexible. Mental flexibility is physical flexibility. Your body is a reflection of your mind. The body never lies (Ted Troost book). My aim was financial independence and now I realize that I must look to mental independence.*

I recognize that last one. I always wanted to be financially independent. Even as a child. Simply through how I grew up. And somewhere I came to an understanding of myself, with these notes. I had become stuck in my pursuit of wealth and fame, with my ankle as an obstacle. I was searching for more here. For the story behind it. But I could mainly see the reflection of a busy mind, one that was trying to understand everything in this misery.

The strange thing is that you get the idea that you have an ankle injury because you're not mentally flexible enough. That seems nonsensical, but you almost believe it when you're in that condition. 'You're holding your leg stiff,' was one such expression from that time.

> *I think I'm having trouble with my ego. My ego is very big and strong. I've really worked very hard at it over the last few years. My ego weighs heavily on my mind. It (my ego) wants to understand everything. Understanding everything is something you do because you're afraid of not understanding things. Not understanding means no control. And it's also fear of the unknown, fear of disappointments. My thoughts are going faster than my pen.*
>
> *My ego is accustomed to fighting, but right now I must fight in a different way. My struggle is not to struggle, but my ego doesn't agree. It strikes at weak moments; tired, pain, lonely. Then it strikes and takes me with it to my mind. And then I have negative thoughts: injured for two and a half years, mental mush, it must be solvable, I must grin and bear it, etc…*
>
> *I must come up with the peace and quiet to heal myself.*

Those were the nights. With so much pain. When I was sleeping in the playroom. Sleeping badly month after month. That was such an unbelievably rubbish time. With things just going through my head.

325

I see the words of Bert van Riel in this. I talked to him a lot about my ego. He tried to make me aware of my deeper driving forces and sought the cause of the fact that I had 'a jam' in them. That I could no longer stand on my legs. This is certainly painful. I kept searching, analysing, trying.

In the end it was failed surgeries that messed up my ankle, but I obviously took no satisfaction from that. I kept seeking solutions. I'm reading here words of a man, a boy, a footballer, who is prepared to do anything to get better again. Even looking very, very deep into his own soul with a spiritual guru. However you look at it, I'm not a quitter by any means and I don't just lay the blame at others' feet.

So I carried on playing football. Ever better and ever higher. My ego was fed and I let it feed. I've always had a lot of trouble with injuries during my career. (Left ankle, left knee, right ankle.) But these three serious, long-term injuries that were difficult to diagnose in particular. Only now do I think, as I write this down, that I know how all this has come about => ego and flexibility. Now that I'm 30, this will be a difficult task, because my ego has grown very big.

I think I've done all this myself, that I have no need to thank anyone or anything for everything I've achieved. The consequence is pride (comes before a fall). I've recently come to realize that God exists and we must be grateful for everything He has given us and will give us. I think I've become ever more ungrateful in my life. I think I've believed less and less in God in my life and I think/thought I should just thank myself more and more (I was becoming a heathen).

God probably came knocking every day but I took no notice (in my megalomania). I had such trouble with my ego, which just so wanted to achieve, that I didn't let anything or anyone get in my way.

The boss above is the conductor of the piece. The musician puts his own expression into the music. Only the music had already been written. So here's the difference between living and being lived (in the sense that everything is already determined).

God has given me a body in good condition. Return it in good condition too. It's too wonderfully beautiful to wear it out or break it down.

I'm rather surprised I brought God into it. I was brought up a Catholic of course, but religion is really totally unimportant for me. But if you're unbelievably deep in trouble, something of religious awareness apparently rises to the surface again. You look for answers. Ways of learning to live with something. Being able to accept it. That everything is fixed in advance. I sometimes believe that too. But I don't just point to God. I point to myself too.

My rational thinking is so strong and chastising of my emotion/ feeling. I must reach my emotion through my mind. My mind rules (still!) over my feeling. The God element and the upbringing by my father make Marco van Basten. Fear of failure is resolute action or, if there is a moment of thought, doubt. Fear of failure comes from your superior. The superior is your father.

If I were to describe my father in a few words, they would be: strong – stubborn. If I look at myself, then I look pitifully very like him. All in all this is not what I want. I would like to be a little more flexible. A better person. More generally developed. I mustn't blame my father for this, because he too is only cast in the same mould as his parents. I must count myself lucky that I am acquiring the strength to recognize this kind of thing and to do something about it.

*My father is traumatically dominant. He passes his dominance
to his surroundings. He gives you the feeling: I like it like this. Me
too. He ensures that everyone is a satellite around him. I was one too
and in reality the biggest.*

*I had ground to make up in that family. I had to prove who
I was. But I actually had far greater need of a good conversation.
That never came. So the factor of not being understood, the need for
confirmation and perfectionism has arisen from this.*

The strange thing is that in the period of my injury my father was actually mostly absent because he had his hands full with my mother. It was even more so because the fact that I could no longer play football spoiled his only outing. The only thing he still actually liked doing was flying to Milan every two weeks to watch my match. I would arrange plane tickets and match tickets for him for all the home games. Liesbeth would pick him up from the airport and I would take him back to Linate after the match. He could be just as critical as when I was small, but it didn't affect me any more. Otherwise, apart from the football, we had little to talk about. He showed little interest in our children. He spent the whole week with my mother, visiting her in the different nursing homes she lived in. His small world became smaller and smaller. Completely, when I was no longer playing football. Then the trips to Milan were a thing of the past.

But when I was still small, he was very dominant. I think that I became even more of a perfectionist because of that. But the drive to succeed as a footballer mainly came from myself. I still believe that.

I see my father as a strong, big, determined man.

*But also as a chain smoking, stubborn, rigid man showing little
emotion. Had a poor marriage, in my view.*

My father was always doing something with football. He coached all the time and was usually out on weekday evenings.

On Saturday he watched my team and on Sunday he had a league game with his club. If he was at home in the evening, then he often sat there reading about football.

My mother didn't like this of course. She liked shopping, socializing, chatting and doing nice things (day trips). These interests didn't really go together.

I saw, at least I felt, little/no warmth between my father and mother. They would often row at home too. My mother was full of pent-up emotion that spilled out from time to time.

My father on the other hand always tried to keep the peace and quiet (Catholic upbringing, old-fashioned, stiff (not flexible) and quiet + peace for the children, I think).

My mother was unable to speak her mind because she got no response from my father. He always tried to remain calm, until he actually blew his top and then there was no holding him back.

My father is traumatically dominant. My mother walked into that trap. My mother wasn't able to cope with it. So she put her body under a lot of strain, too much frustration -> heart/brain problem.

On Herderplein my mother once took an overdose of pills, I remember.

I was still small. It was a weekday evening when my father and I went to eat on Neude Square in the centre of Utrecht. We never went out to eat so it stuck in my mind. Nor was it an ordinary restaurant. It was the type of place where you can eat if you can't cook at home. A soup kitchen, it was called.

I think I must have been ten. We were still living on Herderplein. My brother and sister weren't there. I was alone with my father, but he didn't say much. Something had happened to my mother, but he didn't talk about it. Something to do with pills. She'd been admitted to hospital, the ambulance had come. But I didn't know exactly what was going on. You don't really understand these things as a child. So you put it out of your mind. I think this happened to my mother a few times.

Later, when we lived on Wagenaarkade, and my brother and sister had left home, during my adolescence, I would often talk to her. I'd finished my homework, my father was still out at some football club, and then we would sit together in front of the TV. We talked a lot together then. About everything, except football. About other things in life. About what being in love is and how you must do things when you're married later on. I never spoke about that sort of thing with my father. I also asked her about her marriage to my father. But she no longer saw the point of it. She was really unhappy. The book was closed, she often said. And in the end, a few years later, she was suddenly gone. Then she had lost her memory, except for that bit of her childhood. She simply wanted to forget, erase, the present, I think.

My mother didn't go through all this ankle misery. But she was right. I did think about her a lot in the years after her brain haemorrhage. In fact, just last week I had a row with Rebecca and I couldn't help but think of her. You can trace the line from my mother, through me to Rebecca. Fierce and emotional. Passionate. We're not easy to tie down. And not just like that. Never let ourselves be caught.

I'm sure my mother would have been a lot of good to me in those dark times with my ankle. I'm sure she would have had a good relationship with my children. She would have done her best for them. She thought things like that were important. She went to Canada, before she fell ill, to visit Stanley and his children. I'm almost sure that she would have continued playing an important part in my life if she had remained well.

1 Aug. 1995

In the morning I walk with a heavy limp for around two hours.
I must do stretching exercises to improve it slightly. I'm now walking
with a good limp (still in a lot of pain). Once I've had sufficient
exercise (still in a lot of pain), then, after about an hour and a half,
I can manage ordinary walking pace without any pain.

Running is a drama
Tennis is a drama
Football is a drama
Golf with a buggy is a drama
Fear that it won't get better
Aggression that it won't get better
Unbelievable aggression that it won't get better
Depression that it won't get better
I'm getting overstressed with the pain
I've taken too many painkillers -> I don't want any more
They're making me nervous.
Screws in my ankle.
Can't I sometimes stand it?
I feel very bad, miserable, aggressive.
I've had a lot of pain for a year now.
Before I couldn't play football, now I can't even live.
Can't there even once just be an improvement after an operation on
my right ankle?
Damn it.
What on earth must I do? What can I do?

The last page but one: *Good heavens. The despair. Damn it.* That was
really the darkest time. On the very last page it says:

Tuesday 6 Feb. 1996

Yesterday I called Dr Van Dijk to make an appointment (around mid-Feb.) to finally have the ankle fused. Last week Wednesday (31 Jan. '96) I went to see Bert van Riel. He confirmed to me what I thought last time: the fusing of the top tarsal joint.

I snapped the folder shut and put it back in the box, on the top shelf. I walked down the stairs and realized how very happy I was that I could no longer feel any pain.

EPILOGUE

Never a letter from God

Now I realize what a strange journey it's been. As I now, at the age of fifty-five, calmly look back at those ankle problems, other things are coming to the fore. The contrast between the highs and the lows was enormous. Before and after 21 December 1992. The difference was so extreme. From the highest peak in life, being celebrated by the world, down into a deep valley, where you end up in the mudflows full of muck. I had really ended up in a sewer.

It was that particular period of three years that I found difficult to bear. When I really had a big problem, but didn't know what I should do. And what I did was try to get out of the rotten situation, to find solutions. All the time trying to understand. What must I do? Who do I need? It was a huge quest.

And I didn't succeed. Yes, I did eventually succeed in living normally again. Without any pain, but with a sacrifice. And that sacrifice was huge. It was the matter of someone's life. Of course it wasn't that I had died. It was a case of me dying as a footballer.

Nor was I concerned then with whose fault it was, or who should take the credit for it. My only concern was getting fit. Only now am I actually thinking about the question: 'Who is all this down to?'

I went through all sorts of emotions. Disbelief. I had never ever thought it would happen to me, that I would have to stop playing football. Because I was totally unconcerned about it and I was also too good. I was on a completely different level. It wouldn't happen to me.

If you compare it with the loss of a great love, then that would be an understatement. Football was much more than that for me. From the age of four I lived with a football. Always with a ball. In the street, at school, at the football club, wherever. Always.

And then it stops. And you feel really bad. The total disbelief that something like this could happen to me. But when it happened, when it was over, it wasn't a love that I lost. I had lost my whole life. I lost my life. My life was football.

In the end you rise to the surface again. The bombing has stopped and the war is over. And then you look around you. What's left? What do you still have? Can I still build something? Then came the realization: I was really the one to get the blame. I mean, I had lost an ankle.

Football was no longer possible. That was the cast-iron reality. But that didn't actually affect me so terribly much at that point. I was glad finally to be free of the pain. Only afterwards did the realization dawn that I now really had to try to make something of my life. Perhaps I went about it far too egotistically. I wanted to do it all by myself.

It's a great shame that from the age of twenty-eight I was unable to show people anything more and unable to let people enjoy what I did any more. Because there were many people who enjoyed what I did. Including me. It was great to do.

The question of why I got injured is one to which I won't get an answer. Because God has never told me why. I've never received a letter from him.

Why this happened to me, I don't know that either. I'm glad though that now I'm happy, because I *am* happy. And the why question is also difficult because you don't get an answer.

Maybe I would have become really tiresome and insufferable if I had won everything and been proved right about everything.

I don't know that either, but I could have been. I mean, you look for answers. You look for meaning.

I shared my successes with millions of people but in my misery I was often alone. I didn't find that a problem though because that's not something I should think of sharing with everyone else. Hmm, that would be even worse.

It was great to give, it was great to share success with the fans and it was a wonderful experience. The moments when you're idolized and the feeling that gives, that's so incredibly good. At times there were such hugely wonderful moments. If I scored early in a match and the stadium was in ecstasy. Or we were already 2-0 or 3-0 up and still had half an hour to go. And you know the win is in the bag. That's really enjoyable. We won a lot and we made people really happy.

But it was also unbelievably demanding and intense. It wasn't often relaxed. And looking back, that's something else positive about life now. Only now that I'm looking back and holding everything up to scrutiny, do I see that. That it was always hurried then, always demanding, never calm. And however lovely things were then, I'm happy with how they are now.

The question that keeps cropping up for me these days, now that we are working on this book, is whether things have balanced out in the end. Whether the toll that I paid cancels out what I received. Whether it was all worth it. The stakes were high. The sacrifice, my ankle, was great. And was that sacrifice worth it?

It's an interesting question. And then again maybe it isn't. Because did I have a choice? It happened as it did and if I had left it, hadn't become a footballer, without the highs and lows, what would my life have looked like? And when I think about it, then in all the occupations that I can think of, I would never have known as much joy as in my life as I did as a footballer.

It may sound mad with all the misery I had with my ankle, but I'm sure I made the right decision in the end. That the sacrifice was worth it. That I alternated very many wonderful and intense years with many short dark periods. I'm happy with that. Now, afterwards. With that deal, that balance.

Also of course because I can now function normally as a person again. My ankle is a limitation, but more recently I've been able to live normally again. That's worth a huge amount. When I look back I ask myself why it happened as it did. And what my own role was. I was always someone who took the shortest route from A to B. The best and the fastest route. I didn't let anything or anyone stop me. I always succeeded. Throwing caution to the winds. Straight through. And this time something bigger blocked my path. A wall. And I broke down that wall, as I was accustomed to clearing obstacles out of my way. Relentlessly. But breaking down that wall proved not to be so sensible.

With my ankle I didn't therefore find the short cut or detour around that wall. To my mind my ankle should simply have been clean and healthy as soon as possible. This – due to circumstances, due to others and due to myself – proved impossible. And so there was no longer any chance of football. But I adapted, after a number of years of misery, in such a way that I have found my happiness in other things. I took up tennis and golf and for a few years now I've been a fanatical squash player. And I looked to see if I could approach football in some other way, as a coach.

Maybe the fact that I was someone who always went to great lengths to achieve my goal was what brought me my ankle problems. Of course, it was failed surgery that messed it all up, but maybe I should have dealt with it differently, by telling myself: 'That trouble with your ankle, that pain, put up with it. Don't go and get it cleaned out again.' Then maybe I wouldn't have done it.

Then perhaps I would have been able to carry on at that level and with that pain for another few years. But you really want surgery to make it better, and then you're always taking a risk. So I had personal experience of the perils of cutting into a body and, in retrospect, I shouldn't have let it happen so much. A body is so complex. And maybe it would all have been far better without all the doctors. Better to listen to your body is a cliché, and difficult for me because I was so keen.

That maybe is my own part in this story, of which I say: I should have done it differently. It sounds quite ridiculous, but I should have been far more wilful. When I'm already so wilful. It's a pity I didn't make that choice. I don't regret it though because I did it all knowing the risks. But afterwards I can say it's a pity I didn't from day one say: 'As long as I'm in pain, I won't play' because then I would certainly have been able to play longer without all the fuss.

But somehow I know I would do the same again next time. With my personality, the person I am, there's a good chance I would make the same mistake again.